Revolutionary Russia

A HISTORY IN DOCUMENTS

ВЫШИБЕМ

КУЛАКОВ
ИЗ КОЛХОЗОВ

Цена 20 коп.   ГОСУДАРСТВЕННОЕ ИЗДАТЕЛЬСТВО
МОСКВА 1930 ЛЕНИНГРАД

Revolutionary Russia

A HISTORY IN DOCUMENTS

Robert Weinberg
Laurie Bernstein

New York   Oxford
OXFORD UNIVERSITY PRESS
2011

General Editors

Sarah Deutsch
Professor of History
Duke University

Carol K. Karlsen
Professor of History
University of Michigan

Robert G. Moeller
Professor of History
University of California, Irvine

Jeffrey N. Wasserstrom
Professor of History
University of California, Irvine

Cover: Vladimir Lenin addressing the military, c. 1900.

Frontispiece: A 1930 Soviet poster in which a peasant wants to "Kick the *kulaks* off the collective farm."

Title page: Moscow workers march to a meeting about collectivization in 1929.

Oxford University Press, Inc., publishes works that further
Oxford University's objective of excellence
in research, scholarship, and education.

Oxford New York
Auckland   Cape Town   Dar es Salaam   Hong Kong   Karachi
Kuala Lumpur   Madrid   Melbourne   Mexico City   Nairobi
New Delhi   Shanghai   Taipei   Toronto

With offices in
Argentina   Austria   Brazil   Chile   Czech Republic   France   Greece
Guatemala   Hungary   Italy   Japan   Poland   Portugal   Singapore
South Korea   Switzerland   Thailand   Turkey   Ukraine   Vietnam

Copyright © 2011 by Robert Weinberg and Laurie Bernstein

Published by Oxford University Press, Inc.
198 Madison Avenue, New York, New York 10016
http://www.oup.com

Oxford is a registered trademark of Oxford University Press

Library of Congress Cataloging-in-Publication Data
Weinberg, Robert.
  Revolutionary Russia : a history in documents / Robert Weinberg, Laurie Bernstein.
    p. cm.
  Includes bibliographical references and index.
  ISBN 978-0-19-533794-5 (pbk. : alk. paper) — ISBN 978-0-19-512225-1 (hard-
cover : alk. paper) 1. Soviet Union—History—1917–1936—Sources. 2. Russia—
History—Nicholas II, 1894–1917—Sources. 3. Social change—Soviet Union—History—Sources. 4. Social change—Russia—History—20th century—Sources. 5.
Soviet Union—Social conditions—1917–1945—Sources. 6. Russia—Social conditions—1801–1917—Sources. 7. Communism—Soviet Union—History—Sources.
8. Political culture—Soviet Union—History—Sources. 9. Soviet Union—Politics
and government—1917–1936—Sources. 10. Russia—Politics and government—
1894–1917—Sources. I. Bernstein, Laurie. II. Title.
  DK266.A3W45 2010
  947.084′1—dc22
                                                                    2009038666

Contents

What is a Document?

To the historian, a document is, quite simply, any sort of historical evidence. It is a primary source, the raw material of history. A document may be more than the expected government paperwork, such as a treaty or passport. It is also a letter, diary, will, grocery list, newspaper article, recipe, memoir, oral history, school yearbook, map, chart, architectural plan, poster, musical score, play script, novel, political cartoon, painting, photograph—even an object.

Using primary sources allows us not just to read *about* history, but to read history itself. It allows us to immerse ourselves in the look and feel of an era gone by, to understand its people and their language, whether verbal or visual. And it allows us to take an active, hands-on role in (re)constructing history.

Using primary sources requires us to use our powers of detection to ferret out the relevant facts and to draw conclusions from them; just as Agatha Christie uses the scores in a bridge game to determine the identity of a murderer, the historian uses facts from a variety of sources—some, perhaps, seemingly inconsequential—to build a historical case.

The poet W. H. Auden wrote that history was the study of questions. Primary sources force us to ask questions—and then, by answering them, to construct a narrative or an argument that makes sense to us. Moreover, as we draw on the many sources from "the dust-bin of history," we can endow that narrative with character, personality, and texture—all the elements that make history so endlessly intriguing.

Cartoon

This political cartoon addresses the issue of church and state. It illustrates the Supreme Court's role in balancing the demands of the 1st Amendment of the Constitution and the desires of the religious population.

Illustration

Illustrations from children's books, such as this alphabet from the *New England Primer*, tell us how children were educated, and also what the religious and moral values of the time were.

Treaty

A government document such as this 1805 treaty can reveal not only the details of government policy, but information about the people who signed it. Here, the Indians' names were written in English transliteration by U.S. officials; the Indians added pictographs to the right of their names.

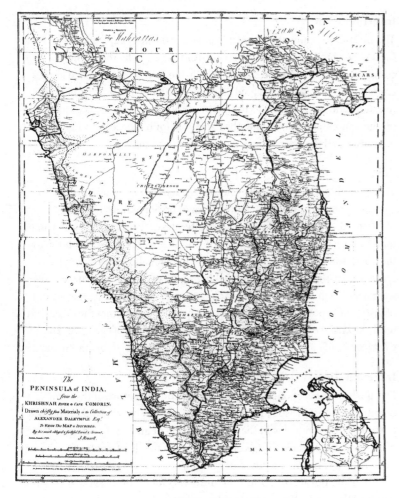

Map

A 1788 British map of India shows the region prior to British colonization, an indication of the kingdoms and provinces whose ethnic divisions would resurface later in India's history.

Object

In this fifteenth-century ewer, both the physical materials of brass and silver and the iconic depiction of heaven as a forest display the refinement of the owner, an Egyptian sultan's wife. Objects, along with manuscripts and printed materials, provide evidence about the past.

How to Read a Document

Students of history base their knowledge of the past on what they read in history books. But from where do the authors of history books derive *their* information? How do they put their stories together? In most cases, historians work with documents, also known as "primary sources," they collect from the period in question. Then, much as a detective builds a case, they use those documents to build their story. As you can see from this book, documents come in many forms, including diaries, photographs, newspaper articles, minutes from meetings, essays, art, artifacts, fiction, and any other sources that contain clues to the historical past.

Just as detectives must unravel each clue that comes their way, so must historians. They must learn everything possible about their source so they can discover its particular value, asking questions like: Is the source trustworthy? Is the story believable? Who is its author? Is there some reason that the author would want to present things in a certain way? What's left out? In other words, documents are not transparent to historians; they need to read with care, drawing conclusions based on common sense and on other knowledge and information they have learned. They need to gain insight into the historical context in which the document was produced. Moreover, historians may differ in how they interpret the same sources.

Subject

This photograph of soldiers looting a monastery church in the 1920s reveals the Bolshevik attitude and policy toward religion. Supporters of the revolution's attack on religion would have viewed the actions of the soldiers in a positive light. The government presumably was not embarrassed by the soldiers' actions; indeed, it may have hoped that the photograph would inspire others to follow suit. While many of the soldiers appear to be barely out of their teens, adult men, probably the soldiers' superior officers, stand off to the side in the background. The young man in the front carefully watches his step, while the joyful, almost playful attitude of the other soldiers is evident in their smiles and bemused looks. Were they responding to a humorous comment made by one of the soldiers in the group? On the other hand, the photograph may have unwittingly helped the enemies of the revolution: the sight of soldiers plundering a place of worship would have intensified their hatred of the Bolsheviks as "godless communists." Were churchgoers and members of the congregation watching the desecration of the church? Did anyone try to prevent the looting? Why not? Contrary to the intent of the government, opponents of the revolution may have used the photograph to publicize what they believed to be the repressive measures of the government.

Interpretation

The Bolsheviks' campaign against Russian Orthodoxy explains why the soldiers removed religious objects from the church. The economic conditions of the 1920s shed light on why the soldiers also carried away chunks of stone, along with gold and silver artifacts. The government used the stone and other materials from looted churches for other construction projects and melted down the silver and gold found in icons (religious paintings) and the church building for use as currency.

Text

This account of the work of the *Cheka* (Extraordinary Commission to Combat Counter-Revolution and Sabotage) on September 17, 1918, illustrates the operation of justice soon after the outbreak of civil war, when martial law had been decreed by the Bolshevik government. In addition to the 16 persons listed by name, another 41 individuals were arraigned and sentenced by the *Cheka* that day, making a total of 57 persons whose cases were handled in one day. There is no mention of a jury, and the meting out of justice in a summary fashion raises the question of whether the defendants received what we understand as fair trials based on rules of evidence. The *Cheka* made life-and-death decisions for a large number of persons in one day.

Interpretation

Did the harshness of one's sentence depend on the nature of the crime committed or on the social class of the accused? What role did one's links to the tsarist regime play in the determination of guilt and sentence? Why did defendants Brazhko and Kondratiuk avoid the death sentence, whereas defendant Gepner, not accused of murder, was sentenced to death by shooting? It appears that common murderers found more sympathy at the hands of the *Cheka* than former police officers.

The session took place in the presence of seven members of the Extraordinary Commission (Cheka) and two members of the Central Collegium of the Russian Communist Party.

The following were arraigned:

1. Antonevich, S., former (army) officer, an active participant in a counter-revolutionary plot to overthrow Soviet rule. *Decision*: He is to be shot.
2. Gepner, Vladimir, former chief of police of Smolensk. *Decision*: He is to be shot.
3. Korshonboim, former assistant inspector of Smolensk Prison. He flogged political prisoners while holding the position of prison inspector. *Decision*: He is to be turned over to the People's Court and his case is transferred to the Department of Justice.
4. Revknev, I., arrested for serving in the Polish Corps. *Decision*: He is to be released from arrest in view of the fact that he was only a private in the Polish Corps.
5. Sorokin, V., former general and head of the secret police. *Decision*: He is to be shot.
6. Mikhailov, M., a criminal, . . . charged with participation in murders and robberies. *Decision*: He is to be shot.
7. Romanov, Zakhar, former police guard, . . . notorious for cruelty to peasants. *Decision*: He is to be shot.
8. Kondratiuk, G., charged with drunkenness and murder. *Decision*: He is to be transferred to the People's Court.
9. Brazhko, charged with drunkenness and murder. *Decision*: Three months in jail.
10. Toptunov, Leiba, charged with giving a bribe. *Decision*: He is to be released from arrest and to receive his money back.
11. Goncharov, E., Piroga, A., Kozlov, and Egorov, members of the militia, charged with violation of official duties. *Decision*: They are to be released.
12. Dorman, M., former general, involved in the organization of a counter-revolutionary plot against the Soviet government. *Decision*: He is to be shot.
13. Dorman, Vladimir, son of General Dorman. . . . *Decision*: Being only fifteen years old, he is to be released.

[An additional 41 names follow, of whom 25 are sentenced to be shot.]

Chairman of the Extraordinary Commission of the Western Region

Introduction

The revolutions of 1917 upended not only the lives of the Russian Empire's 180 million inhabitants, but the entire world. Coming as they did in the middle of the First World War, the revolutions had devastating consequences for the Allied powers and, in quick succession, dethroned the 304-year-old Romanov dynasty and led to the establishment of the world's first socialist state. The Bolshevik Revolution of October 1917 in particular, with its call for freedom, equality, and social justice, inspired millions of men and women in Europe, the Americas, Asia, and Africa to follow in its footsteps. The self-proclaimed socialist revolution stood as a beacon for those who sought an alternative to the poverty and oppression associated with imperialism, urbanization, and industrialization. Many others, however, believed that the Soviet leaders who replaced Tsar Nicholas II were simply power-mongers who cynically used despicable means to justify their ends, and thereby resembled the Nazis in Germany who fostered totalitarian rule and used violence to achieve "National Socialism." In both countries the state ruthlessly deprived millions of people not only of their liberty but also their lives. In the United States fear of communism led to periods of political witch hunting—1919–1921 and the years of the Cold War—when the government engaged in campaigns to arrest, imprison, and deport persons who were or were suspected of being members of the Communist Party.

This book views the October Revolution and the rise of the Soviet Union from neither of these two extremes. Not only was the Soviet period one of immense tragedies, some a result of deliberate political machinations but others with less discernible blame, but it was also an era of tremendous potential and achievements. The documents in this collection, spanning from the end of World War I until the eve of the Second World War, are therefore designed to convey not only the confusion, anguish, and shattered dreams of those two decades, but also the promise, excitement, and accomplishments. The revolutionaries who took charge of Russia in 1917 were self-consciously engaging in a novel historical experiment. They did not expect immediate results, and so the long time frame offers an opportunity to examine the revolutionaries' intentions and policies over a period of two decades and through several phases of revolution.

Beginning with the collapse of the tsarist government in 1917 and closing with the consolidation of the socialist regime by the end of the 1930s, the documents cast a wide net so that readers can understand this period as involving more than a change in the nature of Russia's government. Readers can explore how Soviet citizens experienced and reacted to the wholesale effort to transform virtually all facets of life. The revolutionaries who took charge of Russia in 1917 set out to create an entirely new "Soviet person" free of the prejudices and egotism believed to stem from capitalist society and economic inequality. Sources from the period between the wars afford readers the opportunity to examine the revolutionaries' intentions and policies through several phases of revolution: the consolidation of Soviet power; the challenge of civil war; the rise of Joseph Stalin; the advent of forced industrialization; the consolidation of rural Russia into collective farms; the Stalinist Terror.

Historians have identified at least four issues that need to be reckoned with in any treatment of the Russian Revolutions: the role of ideology; the clash between ideals and reality; the legacy of political culture; and the role of the individual. The revolutionaries who seized power in 1917 believed they were fulfilling the prediction of Karl Marx that socialism was an inevitable stage of historical development. Socialist revolution by industrial workers, contended Marx, would end capitalist exploitation and usher in an age of equality and freedom based on the abolition of private property. Using Marx as their bible, the Bolsheviks interpreted the world as driven by a relentless class struggle between capitalists and proletarians. At the same time, they worked to speed this process up, subscribing to their leader Vladimir

In 1919 and 1920 U.S. Attorney General A. Mitchell Palmer organized a series of raids that led to the arrest of thousands of people who were accused of supporting a communist takeover of the government. The government deported several hundred people and, in many instances, violated the civil rights of those arrested.

Lenin's notions about the need in Russia for an elite revolutionary party to lead the proletariat along the road to revolution.

Yet even though the Bolsheviks remained wedded to their beliefs, not all of their decisions were ideologically driven. The hard reality of life in early 20th-century Russia interfered with the implementation of their vision and provoked the adoption of policies that took Russia far afield from the goals of social justice and equality. Most importantly, peasants made up the overwhelming majority of the populace and Russia's economy was not yet fully capitalist or industrial, two preconditions Marx set forth in his analysis of the end of the bourgeois order and the advent of socialism. Similarly, the terms of the revolutionary settlement in October 1917 strengthened traditional peasant society and agriculture, making it even less likely that Russia after 1917 would achieve the stage of social and economic development in which Marxian socialism would be possible. Furthermore, several years of civil war and invasion by Western powers attempting to overthrow the Bolsheviks followed Russia's withdrawal from the Great War, creating countless refugees and eviscerating Russia's industrial sector. Famine and epidemic diseases in the early 1920s resulted in the deaths of millions more, adding to the devastating numbers of those dead from the wars and revolutions. Indeed, the fledgling socialist regime faced such overwhelming challenges in its initial years that its very survival was at stake. Hence, it should not surprise us to learn that circumstances rather than ideology shaped many of the Bolsheviks' policies.

The legacy of Russia's pre-Revolutionary political culture also played no small role in shaping political developments after 1917. Tsarist authoritarianism and the lack of individual freedom meant that Russia had a weak democratic tradition. The prospects that Russia's pressing social, economic, and political problems could be resolved peacefully through the workings of liberal values and democratic institutions were, according to many historians, bleak. As a result, society easily fell victim after 1917 when the Communist Party made clear its determination not to share power with other political parties.

Finally, the overarching roles played by the first two leaders of the regime, Lenin and Joseph Stalin, loom large in any treatment of the revolutionary Russia. The historian who ignores or even underestimates the impact of Lenin and Stalin risks writing shoddy history. Yet we should temper an emphasis on the impact of Lenin and Stalin with the awareness that as political actors they too were creatures of circumstance, much as the regime they helped to construct had its options constrained by the realities of governing an agrarian society on the verge of modernity. In other words, the ability of political leaders to shape the social, economic, and political landscape was limited, though there is no denying their tremendous impact as individuals. The documents presented here thus highlight the dynamic interplay among ideology, circumstance, and people.

The effort to build socialism in Russia affected the lives of ordinary people, most notably peasants and workers, but also intellectuals and artists. Different social groups understood the aims and goals of the revolution and reacted to the policies of the Bolshevik state in different ways, fashioning lives that reflected their particular understanding of the revolution's goals. Society's diverse visions of the revolution frequently came into conflict with the needs and objectives of the Soviet Union's leadership. The documents presented here do not focus, for the most part, on high politics, foreign affairs, or national minorities, but provide a view of the revolution from within, from the perspective of ordinary persons caught up in the experiment to establish the world's first socialist society. Readers are urged to leave at the door their preconceived notions, beliefs, and judgments in order to understand how revolutionary and ordinary citizen alike experienced the momentous events of the Russian Revolution. Doing so increases the likelihood that they will finish reading this book with a firmer grasp of both the promises of the revolution and reasons for its ultimate failure.

The Russian revolution inspired Chinese communists, particularly their leader Mao Zedong, whose political education was shaped by the figures on the banner: Stalin, Lenin, Engels, and Marx.

The overthrow of the Russian tsar, or emperor, in 1917 and the establishment of the Soviet Union as the first socialist state shaped social and political developments for the remainder of the 20th century. Historians have the benefit of hindsight and know that the Russian experiment in socialism did not fulfill many of the goals and aspirations of the revolution; indeed, it came to a grinding halt in December 1991 with the dissolution of the Soviet Union. But knowing what happened nearly three quarters of a century after 1917 should not interfere with efforts to explore the revolution on its own terms.

After all, Russians who experienced the years of revolutionary up-heaval did not know how the story would turn out.

Note on Dates

Until Feb. 1, 1918, the Russians followed the old Julian calendar, which was 13 days behind the Gregorian calendar used by other countries in the 20th century. In this book all dates before Feb. 1, 1918 are given in the old style. Hence, the February Revolution occurred from Feb. 24 through Feb. 28, 1917, according to the calendar then in use, but from March 8 through March 12, 1917, in the new style. Similarly, the Bolshevik seizure of power happened on Oct. 25, 1917, according to the Julian calendar, but on Nov. 7, 1917, according to the Western-style calendar.

Note on Terminology

In 1922 the Russian Empire formally became the Union of Soviet Socialist Republics (U.S.S.R. or Soviet Union), a federation comprising Russia, Ukraine, Belarus, Georgia, Armenia, Azerbaijan, Moldova, and several Central Asian territories. In terms of geography, the Soviet Union looked remarkably similar to that of the tsarist empire (though the Baltic countries of Lithuania, Latvia, and Estonia were now independent states). The term "Soviet" refers to the political institutions of this new state and stands in contrast to "Russian," which refers to a particular Slavic people who are distinct from the many non-Slavic nationalities who lived within the tsarist empire and the Soviet Union. There was no Soviet nationality or group of people; rather, "Soviet" refers to the institutions, culture, officials, and citizens of the Soviet Union.

Note on Sources and Interpretation

For many decades historians had to contend with what were frequently one-sided, distorted, and incomplete sources that interfered with the writing of well-balanced accounts of Soviet history. Most information tended to derive from official publications such as journals and newspapers, speeches by the Communist Party elite, and reports of party congresses and conferences. Yet such sources, while providing essential knowledge of events and developments in the Soviet Union, suffered from the biases imparted by the doctrinaire views of a leadership determined to present Soviet communism and society in a heroic light. The press and publishing industry were under strict state supervision and mostly served as mouthpieces for government propaganda. Materials that challenged positive portrayals of the communist regime were excised from the public record, and writings by prominent communists who had fallen into disfavor were relegated to closed stacks of libraries to which very few historians had access.

This state of affairs shaped the nature of historical scholarship. Historians outside the Soviet Union focused their research on topics for which sources were available, namely politics on the highest levels of government and the roles that ideology and prominent personalities played in the formulation and implementation of policies. Consequently, the interpretations offered by historians tended to emphasize how the communist regime acted to mold Soviet society according to ideological imperatives and the actions of communist leaders, particularly Stalin. Scholars tended to write history from the top down—that is, from the perspective of the national leadership—with little attention to how Soviet citizens not only responded to events but also influenced the Kremlin. All too frequently scholars offered a one-dimensional analysis of Soviet history, representing a regime intent on transforming an essentially passive society helpless at the hands of a coercive state. In so doing, historians paid insufficient attention to the dynamic interaction between the government and the citizenry that exists in all societies. Despite these shortcomings, many historians managed to write excellent books that provided profound insights into the Soviet Union and made the study of Soviet history a well-respected academic discipline.

At the other extreme were sources by émigrés who, by definition, were opposed if not antagonistic to the Soviet polity. They provided key information in the form of memoirs and responses to interviews, describing what it was like to live in the Soviet Union. But like official communist publications, these memoirs also suffered from biases, though in these instances they were rooted in fervid anticommunism and the conviction that the Soviet Union was a totalitarian system intent on dominating the world. During the Cold War, these kinds of attitudes were often reflected in Western interpretations of Soviet society and history.

The picture expanded in the wake of a series of academic exchanges between the Soviet Union and the United States, Canada, and Western Europe that began in the late 1950s. Lengthy research visits made it possible for foreign historians to spend time working in the libraries and, at times, archives of the Soviet Union. These exchanges, many of which lasted for a full academic year, enabled scholars from the West to establish close relationships with Soviet citizens and to collaborate with colleagues at universities and institutes, thereby broadening outsiders' acquaintance with Soviet society and history. Access to published and unpublished materials unavailable outside the Soviet Union allowed historians to study topics in greater detail than had been the case previously. In addition, historians could focus on entirely new themes, given the expanding opportunities for research in the Soviet Union. By the late 1960s and early 1970s the burgeoning field of social history prompted historians to investigate Soviet history from the perspective of society—that is, from the bottom up, which was difficult when access to materials was limited.

It was not until after 1991, however, when the communist regime lost power and the Soviet Union broke apart into some 15 independent and sovereign states that foreign historians finally could tap the riches of many Soviet libraries and archives. Politically sensitive topics such as the purges of the 1930s and the collectivization of agriculture could now be studied in greater depth with the availability of new documentation. Even more mundane subjects could be re-examined. Foreign scholars were finally able to conduct research in the archives of the Communist Party, a development that underscored the fundamental changes in the ability of foreign historians to work in post-communist Russia. Entirely new fields of exploration opened up as recorded Party debates, documents labeled "top secret," diaries, and correspondence long hidden from public view saw the light of day, perhaps for the first time since they were written decades ago. Finally, document collections, published both in Russian and English and free of the ideological imprimatur of the government, have appeared since 1991, broadening our horizons and enhancing our understanding of the history of the Soviet Union.

The result is that we now know much more about the history of 20th-century Russia than we did 20 years ago. Our knowledge of the first two decades of communist rule, the subject of this volume, is much more detailed, nuanced, and balanced. Greater access to libraries and archives has brought to light events that had been absent from the historical record because of censorship. In many instances new sources have led to new interpretations of key Soviet events and developments, while in other cases new documentation has confirmed what we have known or suspected. The new information has challenged historians to rethink their perspectives and interpretations.

CHAPTER 1

Prelude to Revolution

Villagers pose for a news photographer in the 1890s. In spring dirt roads became impassable as snow melted, turning them into a morass of mud. Peasant *izby* (huts) were made out of wood and had thatched roofs that were very susceptible to fire.

Russia in 1900 was a multinational empire that encompassed some one sixth of the globe's landmass. Comprising nearly 200 national and ethnic groups who spoke about 125 languages and dialects, the Russian Empire stretched from Europe to the Pacific Ocean and covered 11 time zones. It was situated at the crossroads of Europe and Asia and included peoples with diverse cultures and traditions. The government, located in St. Petersburg, relied on an overburdened and inefficient bureaucracy to rule the diverse, multicultural population. Russians made up some 44 percent of the empire's population, while other Slavic groups such as Ukrainians, Poles, and Belarusians living within the borders of the Russian Empire made up nearly 30 percent. Non-Slavs such as Turkish-speaking Muslims in Central Asia, Jews, Finns, Georgians, Armenians, and Baltic peoples made up the bulk of the remaining inhabitants.

By the turn of the 20th century, Russia was a land of contrasts and contradictions, with the veneer of the modern world slapped on top of a traditional society. Russia had its feet in two worlds, the traditional world of the peasantry and the modern world of the westernized elite. These two worlds coexisted, and their values, culture, and way of life drastically differed from each other. The vast majority of inhabitants were peasants who eked out meager, subsistence livings and were mired in a grinding poverty made all the more desperate because of overpopulation, land shortages, and primitive tools and agricultural techniques.

Despite the persistence of an agrarian society and economy, Russia experienced pronounced urban and industrial growth during the second half of the 19th century. Responding to the hopelessness of village life, many peasants streamed out of the countryside in search of employment as workers in factories and workshops, laborers, servants, waiters, and clerks in retail stores. Toward the end of the century the government embarked on a concerted campaign to promote industrial growth in order to maintain Russia's standing as a world power. The tsarist regime solicited foreign investment, fostered the development of manufacturing, and took to exporting grain in order to pay for the technology needed for industrialization. By 1900 Russia had become a major industrial power.

On the eve of World War I Russia remained a deeply fragmented country, with unresolved conflicts that challenged the legitimacy of the autocracy. The country had begun the transition to a modern society, but industrialization and urbanization sowed the seeds of social and political instability. Moreover, the weight of rural Russia held back the effort to bring the country into the 20th century, and the accumulated impact of peasant and worker grievances underscored the reality of the two Russias and the seemingly unbridgeable chasm that separated the "haves" from the "have nots." Even privileged Russia, including many nobles, had grown disenchanted with the autocracy at the same time that they recognized the resentment of peasants and workers.

It is the consensus of most historians of Russia that the autocracy's chances for survival were slim by the time World War I broke out in the summer of 1914. A host of social and political characteristics made it unlikely that Russia could evolve peacefully into a modern society with a government similar to England or the United States. Tsarist Russia's political culture was rooted in authoritarianism that stifled individual freedom and initiative. Unlike other societies in Western Europe, Russia lacked a meaningful democratic tradition, and no social group was able to challenge the autocracy effectively. A strong, independently minded middle class, crucial in the forging of democracy in Western Europe, was in short supply in tsarist Russia. In addition, the imperial bureaucracy was hesitant to share power with other groups in society and jealously guarded the powers of the autocrat.

A Land of Contrasts

Until the middle of the 19th century, virtually all peasants in Russia were serfs, which meant that they were legally bound to live and labor on land owned by private landowners (gentry), the state, and the royal family. While the serf emancipation of 1861 granted peasants their personal freedom, it saddled peasants with onerous financial obligations and did not give them control of the land. Consequently, most peasants remained impoverished and believed that they had been denied genuine

Peasants confer at a village meeting, presided over by the male elders. The men are wearing *valenki* (felt boots), common footwear among peasants.

freedom. By 1897 there were some 100 million peasants (84 percent of the total population), and they occupied the lowest rungs on the social ladder. In the late 1870s Gleb Uspenskii, a journalist living in rural Russia, wrote about the living and working conditions of peasants in an essay entitled "From a Village Diary." Uspenskii engaged peasants he encountered in conversation about their lives and drew conclusions regarding the causes of their dire economic circumstances.

While strolling about the country place where I spent the summer of 1878 I could see an old peasant walking toward me. He was carrying a little girl, about one-and-a-half years old. Another about twelve, was walking beside him. . . . They resembled beggars, . . . in their outward appearance. Even for country folk they were poorly dressed. The man's trousers were ragged and torn, exposing his bare body beneath, and he was barefoot. The little girl was so thin and jaundiced that she seemed ill. Her blond hair was disheveled and hung in uneven dirty strands, with little cakes of dirt visible between them. The other girl's appearance also bespoke poverty and ineradicable untidiness. . . .

I . . . begged his pardon, and said:

"The little girls are so thin, . . ."

"That they are, my friend, and how else when there's no food for them?"

"How is it they have no food?"

"There isn't any, that's all. We had a cow, but the Lord took her from us—she died—So, no milk."

"Then what do you feed this little one?" I asked.

"What do we feed her? Same things we eat—kvas, bread—"

"To such a little child?!"

"And just what would you do?—God willing, this fall the heifer will be grown, and we'll sell her. And for the summer I have to be watchman for the master—Adding in what I make from that, God willing we'll buy a cow before winter. But in the meantime, we have to endure—can't be helped!—. . . ."

The first thing one notices from observing the contemporary rural order is the almost complete absence of moral bonds among members of the village commune. During serfdom, the village people were united by the awareness of common misfortunes, for all were bound to obey every whim of the landlord. The master had a right to interfere with a family's affairs, and arbitrarily direct a man's private life: . . . The continual possibility of such arbitrariness bound the commune through the same belittling of human dignity. . . . Nowadays no one interferes with the family life except the government, which conscripts soldiers. Nowadays everyone answers for himself, and runs his own affairs as he knows best. But the bond of the "moral yoke," that unity fostered by common resentments, has not been replaced by any positive appreciation of the necessity for general prosperity, and for a better life for all. In place of the old arbitrary rule has come neither knowledge, nor development, nor even a kind word between neighbors. Nothing has destroyed the old habit of trembling before authority, seeing oneself as a perpetual laborer, or the habit of making daily bread the goal of one's entire existence on earth. These habits hold the peasant in their power to this day.

Arbitrary authority is much less of a factor in the peasant family life now than during the days of serfdom. And yet little value is

Kvas

Kvas is a drink made from fermented bread.

placed on another's existence, and no sympathy or concern for another's private interests. . . .

Each such household then is like an isolated island, where a stubborn struggle with life goes on from day to day, with a patience and frantic labor which is scarcely comprehensible to its inhabitants. The weight of those cares is so great that it seems impossible to exist in the face of them. It is this burden of cares which forces the peasant family to struggle so, and thus produces a deep fatalism in their way of thinking:

"It is God's will that thousands and millions of people struggle just as we do." This is how each peasant household explains its lot to itself, as the family rises at cock's crow to begin another day's work. . . .

At the other end of the social order were the nobles, who were society's elite in terms of privilege, power, and wealth. A miniscule percentage of the population, the nobles dominated political, military, and bureaucratic institutions and retained a preeminent position in the countryside as major landowners and local power brokers. Not all nobles were enormously wealthy and powerful, yet a deep cultural and economic chasm existed between them and the peasants. Beginning with the reign of Peter the Great in the early 18th century, Russia's nobles were exposed to Western European ideas, culture, and ways of life, and received an upbringing and education similar to those enjoyed by their counterparts in Europe. The westernized noble elite differed from the peasants not only in terms of the clothing they wore but also the languages spoken at home. It was not unusual for noble parents to speak French with their children, while reserving the use of Russian for conversations with peasants, servants, and other social underlings. Indeed, the last tsar of Russia, Nicholas II, and his wife Alexandra corresponded with each other in English, French, Danish, and Russian. The Russian writer Leo Tolstoy captures the extravagance and luxury of the Russian nobility in this scene from *Anna Karenina*, where Prince Oblonsky selects oysters rather than the traditional Russian meal of buckwheat groats and cabbage soup preferred by his companion Levin, another nobleman. The use of French is also a sign of the social and cultural divisions.

"This way, your excellency; come this way, and your excellency will not be disturbed," said a specially obsequious old Tatar, whose monstrous hips made the tails of his coat stick out behind. "Will you come this way, your excellency?" said he to Levin, as a sign of respect for Stepan Arkadyevitch, whose guest he was. In a twinkling he had spread a fresh cloth on the round table, which, already covered, stood under the bronze chandelier; then, bringing two velvet chairs, he stood waiting for Stepan Arkadyevitch's orders, holding in one hand his napkin, and his order-card in the other.

This January 1900 dinner menu, written in French, underscored the deep social and cultural chasm that existed between Russia's upper classes and the rest of society. Russia's educated and wealthy elite prided themselves on knowing French and keeping abreast of cultural and intellectual trends in Europe.

"If your excellency would like to have a private room, one will be at your service in a few moment. . . . Prince Galuitsin and a lady. We have just received fresh oysters."

"Ah, oysters!"

Stepan Arkadyevitch reflected. "Supposing we change our plan, Levin," said he, with his finger on the bill of fare. His face showed serious hesitation.

"But are the oysters good? Pay attention!"

"They are from Flensburg, your excellency; there are none from Ostend."

"Flensberg oysters are well enough, but are they fresh?"

"They came yesterday."

"Very good! What do you say?—to begin with oysters, and then to make a complete change in our menu? What say you?"

"It's all the same to me. I'd like best of all some shchi (cabbage soup) and kasha (buckwheat groats), but you can't get them here."

"*Kasha à la russe*, if you would like to order it," said the Tatar, bending over toward Levin as a nurse bends toward a child.

"No. Jesting aside, whatever you wish is good. I have been skating and should like something to eat. Don't imagine," he added, as he saw an expression of disappointment on Oblonsky's face, "that I do not appreciate your selection. I can eat a good dinner with pleasure."

"It should be more than that! You should say that it is one of the pleasures of life," said Stepan Arkadyevitch. "In this case, little brother of mine, give us two, or . . . No, that's not enough, three dozen oysters, vegetable soup. . . ."

"*Printanière*," suggested the Tatar.

But Stepan Arkadyevitch did not allow him the pleasure of enumerating the dishes in French. . . .

At the apex of the social and political order was Tsar Nicholas II, the emperor and head of the Romanov dynasty that had been ruling Russia since the early 17th century. Russia was an autocracy where formal power and authority rested in the person of the tsar and where, in principle, no formal checks on the tsar's exercise of unlimited power existed. The tsar's rule was viewed as ordained by God. In reality, the tsar relied on the services of the nobility who filled the ranks of the imperial bureaucracy and served as his close political advisers. In exchange for serving the autocracy, the tsar guaranteed nobles their social, political, and economic well-being. Until the beginning of the 20th century the tsar and his ministers did not seriously entertain the thought of sharing power with society and vigorously defended the prerogatives of autocratic rule. Konstantin Pobedonostsev

Nevskii Prospekt, the main thoroughfare of St. Petersburg, in 1914. Lined with luxury retail shops, apartment buildings, and palaces, Nevskii Prospekt marked the city's place as a Europeanized center of culture, commerce, and society, a world strikingly different from the one of the overwhelming majority of the Russian Empire's inhabitants.

taught law at Moscow University and also tutored the last two emperors, Alexander III and his son Nicholas II. In 1898 he published a book defending the principles of autocracy and rejecting efforts to undermine the power of the tsar. His *Reflections of a Russian Statesman* is a resounding condemnation of political reform. For Pobedonostsev, parliamentary democracy is a sham that promotes the self-interest and power of elected representatives, who do not express the will of the people.

What is this freedom by which so many minds are agitated, which inspires so many insensate actions, so many wild speeches, which leads the people so often to misfortune? In the democratic sense of the word, freedom is the right of political power, or, to express it otherwise, the right to participate in the government of the State. This universal aspiration for a share in government has no constant limitations, and seeks no definite issue, but incessantly extends. . . . For ever extending its base, the new Democracy now aspires to universal suffrage—a fatal error, and one of the most remarkable in the history of mankind. By this means, the political power so passionately demanded by Democracy would be shattered into a number of infinitesimal bits, of which each citizen acquires a single one. What will he do with it, then? How will he employ it? In the result it has undoubtedly been shown that in the attainment of this aim Democracy violates its sacred formula of "Freedom indissolubly joined with Equality." It is shown that this apparently equal distribution of "freedom" among all involves the total destruction of equality. Each vote, representing an inconsiderable fragment of power, by itself signifies nothing; . . . By themselves individuals are ineffective, but he who controls a number of these fragmentary forces is master of all power and directs all decisions and dispositions. . . . In a Democracy, the real rulers are the dexterous manipulators of votes, with their placemen, the mechanics who so skillfully operate the hidden springs which move the puppets in the area of democratic elections. Men of this kind are ever ready with loud speeches lauding equality; in reality, they rule the people as any despot or military dictator might rule it. . . .

The history of mankind bears witness that the most necessary and fruitful reforms—the most durable measures—emanated from the supreme will of statesmen, or from a minority enlightened by lofty ideas and deep knowledge, and that, on the contrary, the extension of the representative principle is accompanied by the abasement of political ideas and the vulgarization of opinions in the mass of the electors. . . .

The manipulation of votes in the game of Democracy is of the commonest occurrence in most European states, and its falsehood, it would seem, has been exposed to all; yet few dare openly to rebel against it. . . .

Among the falsest of political principles is the principle of the sovereignty of the people, the principle that all power issues from the people, and is based upon the national will—a principle which has unhappily become more firmly established since the time of the French Revolution. Thence proceeds the theory of Parliamentarism, which, up to the present day, has . . . unhappily infatuated certain foolish Russians. It continues to maintain its hold on many minds with the obstinacy of a narrow fanaticism, although every day its falsehood is exposed more clearly to the world.

The government's effort to transform the Russian economy created unexpected social and political tensions by giving rise to new social groups, namely factory workers, industrialists, and urban professionals. Industrial workers, virtually all of whom were peasants seeking better lives outside their native villages, encountered horrendous living conditions in urban Russia, which reinforced their resentment of the social and economic disparities between their lives and those of Russia's upper classes. Russian workers toiled in unsafe enterprises and could not defend their

interests because strikes and labor organizations were illegal. The government enacted legislation concerning female and child labor and the length of the workday, but enforcement was lax. The government's commitment to rapid industrial growth conflicted with efforts to safeguard the safety and welfare of workers. In the 1880s the ministry of finance established a factory inspectorate to investigate factory conditions and report violations of labor legislation. In the late 1880s several inspectors reported their findings on the working and living conditions of workers employed in a variety of enterprises.

Sanitary conditions in the workers' settlement . . . are highly conducive to the contraction and spread of disease. The market place and streets are full of filth. The air is rotten with the stench from factory smoke, coal and lime dust, and the filth in gutters and organic wastes on streets and squares. The interiors of most workers' living quarters are just as unhygienic. . . . The majority of workers live in so-called "cabins" built in the outskirts of the settlement, along the river Kalmius. These cabins are simply low, ugly mud huts. The roofs are made of earth and rubbish. Some of them are so close to the ground that at first sight they are nearly unnoticeable. The walls are covered with wood planks or overlaid with stones which easily let in dampness. The floors are made of earth. These huts are entered by going deep down into the ground along earthen stairs. . . .

Oil wells line the coast of Baku on the Caspian Sea in 1890. Russia was the world's largest producer of oil and the fourth largest industrial power at the turn of the 20th century, a sign of the imperial government's policy of promoting industrial growth's success.

Working conditions in factories and mines also promote disease and illness. . . . There are frequent cave-ins, which make the inadequate ventilation even worse. The air becomes so thick in the underground passages that the lamps go out—or as the miners say, "the sun stops shining." Can you imagine how hard it is to breathe this air! . . .

The very worst, most unhealthy conditions I saw were in tobacco factories. . . . The shops where tobacco is chopped and dried are so filled with caustic dust and nicotine fumes that each time I entered one of these rooms I had spasms in my throat and my eyes watered. If I stayed there very long I even became dizzy, though I am a smoker myself. Yet even women sometimes work in this atmosphere, as I myself can testify. Children work in these tobacco factories as wrappers, baggers (making the little paper tobacco bags), and packers. There were even children under twelve working there. . . .

In factory No. 135 the workers are still treated as serfs. Wages are paid out only twice a year, even then not in full but only enough to pay the workers' taxes (other necessities are supplied by the factory store). Furthermore, this money is not given to the workers directly but is sent by mail to their village elders and village clerks. Thus the workers are without money the year around. Besides, they are also paying severe fines to the factory, and these sums will be subtracted from their wages and the final year-end accounting.

Men and boys make wooden models and molds for machines in a factory at the turn of the 20th century. Child labor was a common feature of Russia's early industrialization, as it was elsewhere in Europe and the United States.

A woefully inadequate health-care system and the absence of basic sanitation meant that the cramped, overcrowded slums of Russia's capital city, St. Petersburg, were breeding grounds for disease. In 1911 Prime Minister Petr Stolypin announced efforts to build a sewer system in the city.

Nobody will be able to deny that the government should take special measures to deal with a city where the number of deaths exceeds the number of births, where one third of the deaths are caused by infectious diseases, where typhoid claims more victims than in any West European city, where smallpox is still rife, where recurrent typhus, a disease long eradicated in the West, is still occasionally seen, and which is a favorable breeding ground for both cholera and plague bacteria. . . .

It is the capital's poor who most need this sewerage scheme. I have seen them in the city's hospitals, resignedly submitting to death, poisoned because they have no access to clean water. I am well aware of the 100,000 deaths from cholera over the last year; I feel hurt and ashamed when my country is singled out as the source of all types of infections and diseases. . . .

Beginning in the 1890s Russian revolutionaries, inspired by the ideas of Karl Marx, began to organize workers in factories and workshops. Not surprisingly, the cultural and social chasms between the student radicals, who were educated and hailed from families with money, and workers affected the ability of these two groups to establish trust. Semen Kanatchikov was a teenager from a small village when his father sent him to work in a factory in Moscow in the mid-1890s. The radical ideas of the revolutionaries attracted Kanatchikov, who eventually joined the revolutionary movement. But at first he, like many of his fellow workers, was self-conscious when he met radical students, who he believed viewed him as an exotic specimen in a zoo.

I was received cordially. Several guests had apparently been invited to join us: about three male students, some kind of gentleman dressed in civilian clothes, and a female student with close-cropped hair.

They looked me over as if I was some kind of fossil. They asked me if I read Marx, . . . if I thought that workers would struggle for a constitution, and so on. Although I did not feel very comfortable in this company, I couldn't figure out how to escape with dispatch. The hostess, a young student who had recently become a mother, tried to start a general discussion, but without any success.

To make matters worse, I committed a serious blunder at the table. When thin little pancakes were served on a platter, no one wanted to be the first to take them. The hostess proposed that, as a new guest, I be the one to begin, but I too refused, since this was an entirely new dish for me and I had no idea how to handle it. The hostess insisted. Then, collecting my courage, I took a fork—which I wielded very ineptly—and poked it into the pile of pancakes right down to the bottom of the platter. But then, since I had made no effort to shake the pancakes off the fork, nothing remained on the platter; instead, I managed to put the entire pile on my plate, leaving the astonished guests without any pancakes. However, the kind hostess quickly came to the rescue by bringing a second pile of pancakes from the kitchen. I was extremely embarrassed. The other guests pretended not to have noticed. By now my mood was definitely ruined. After drinking a glass of tea out of politeness, I made haste to depart.

Revolutionary Politics

Despite censorship and the efforts of the secret police, the tsarist regime was unable to stem the spread of liberal and radical ideas and halt the emergence of parties that demanded political reform. In 1898 a group of Marxist (also known as Social Democratic) revolutionaries formed the Russian Social Democratic Workers Party, which was committed to the establishment of a socialist society in Russia without a state, social classes, and private property. But two factions soon emerged, the Mensheviks

Marxism Defined
Karl Marx believed that the working class (industrial proletariat) would rise up and overthrow its oppressors, the owners of property and factories (the bourgeoisie), and usher in an age of social, political, and economic equality. He argued that there would be two stages of revolution: the first phase, called socialism, would sweep away capitalism and serve as the prelude to the next phase, known as communism. Under socialism the proletariat would replace the bourgeoisie as holders of political power, deprive the bourgeoisie of their property, take control of the economy, and establish the foundations of a classless, collectivist society. Under communism the state and its institutions would "wither away" and social classes would cease to exist. Communism would mean an end to poverty and exploitation because all members of society would share equally in the wealth of communist society.

[F]rom each according to his ability, to each according to his need.

—Karl Marx, *Critique of the Gotha Program*, 1875

and Bolsheviks, reflecting a disagreement over the organization of the party. Mensheviks preferred a mass political party open to all workers who subscribed to the principles of Marxism, but the Bolsheviks insisted on a small, conspiratorial party comprising professional revolutionaries under the strict control of the leadership. Vladimir Lenin formulated the tenets of Bolshevism in his 1902 essay "What Is to Be Done?"

The history of all countries shows that the working class, exclusively by its own effort, is able to develop only trade union consciousness, i.e., the conviction that it is necessary to combine in unions, fight the employers, and strive to compel the government to pass necessary labor legislation, etc. The theory of socialism, however, grew out of the philosophic, historical, and economic theories that were elaborated by the educated representatives of the propertied classes, the intellectuals. By their social status, the founders of modern scientific socialism, Marx and Engels, themselves belonged to the bourgeois intelligentsia. In the very same way, in Russia, the theoretical doctrine of Social Democracy arose altogether independently of the spontaneous growth of the working class movement; it arose as a natural and inevitable outcome of the development of thought among the revolutionary socialist intelligentsia. . . .

It is only natural to expect that for a Social Democrat, whose conception of the political struggle coincides with the conception of the "economic struggle against the employers and the government," the "organization of revolutionaries" will more or less coincide with the "organization of workers." This, in fact, is what actually happens; so that when we talk of organization, we literally speak in different tongues. . . . I had in mind an organization of revolutionaries as an essential factor in "bringing about" the political revolution.

. . . . The political struggle of Social Democracy is far more extensive and complex than the economic struggle of the workers against the employers and the government. Similarly (indeed for that reason), the organization of a revolutionary Social Democratic Party must inevitably be of *a kind different* from the organizations of the workers designed for this struggle. The workers' organization must in the first place be a trade union organization; secondly, it must be as broad as possible; and thirdly, it must be as public as conditions will allow (here, and further on, of course, I refer only to absolutist Russia). On the other hand, the organizations of revolutionaries must consist first and foremost of people who make revolutionary activity their profession (for which reason I speak of the organization of *revolutionaries*, meaning revolutionary Social Democrats). In view of this common characteristic of the members of such an organization, *all distinctions as between workers and intellectuals*, and not to speak of distinctions of trade and profession, in both categories, *must be effaced.* Such an organization must perforce not be very extensive and must be as secret as possible.

I assert: (1) that no movement can endure without a stable organization of leaders maintaining continuity; (2) that the broader the popular mass drawn spontaneously into the struggle, which forms the basis of the movement and participates in it, the more urgent the need for such an organization, and the more solid this organization must be (for it is much easier for demagogues to side-track the more backward sections of the masses); (3) that such an organization must consist chiefly of persons engaged in revolutionary activity; (4) that in an autocratic state, the more we *confine* the membership of such an organization to people who are professionally engaged in revolutionary activity and who have been professionally trained in the art of combating the political police, the more difficult will it be to catch the organization, and (5) the *greater* will be the number of people from the working class and from the other classes who will be able to join the movement and perform active work in it. . . .

The active and widespread participation of the masses will not suffer; on the contrary, it will benefit by the fact that a "dozen" experienced revolutionaries, professionally trained no less than the police, will centralize all the secret aspects of the work—the drawing up of leaflets, the working out of approximate plans; and the appointing of bodies of leaders for each urban district, for each factory district, and for each educational institution, etc. (I know that exception will be taken to my "undemocratic" views, but I shall reply below fully to this anything but intelligent objection.) Centralization of the more secret functions in an organization of revolutionaries will not diminish, but rather increase the extent and enhance the quality of the activity of a large number of other organizations, that are intended for a broad public and are therefore as loose and as non-secret as possible, such as workers' trade unions; workers' self-education circles and circles for reading illegal literature; and socialist, as well as democratic, circles among *all* other sections of the population. . . . We must have such circles, trade unions, and organizations everywhere in *as large a number as possible* and with the widest variety of functions; but it would be absurd and harmful *to confound* them with the organization of *revolutionaries*, to efface the border-line between them, to make still more hazy the all too faint recognition of

Born in 1870, Vladimir Ulianov adopted the name Lenin when he joined the revolutionary movement in the 1890s. After his first arrest at a demonstration while he was a university student, Lenin purportedly told the police that he was rebelling because Russia was "tottering, you only have to push it for it to fall over."

the fact that in order to "serve" the mass movement we must have people who will devote themselves exclusively to Social Democratic activities, and that such people must *train* themselves patiently and steadfastly to be professional revolutionaries.

Yes, this recognition is incredibly dim. Our worst sin with regard to organization consists in the fact that *by our primitiveness we have lowered the prestige of revolutionaries in Russia.* A person who is flabby and shaky on questions of theory, who has a narrow outlook, who pleads the spontaneity of the masses as an excuse for his own sluggishness, who resembles a trade union secretary more than a spokesman of the people, who is unable to conceive of a broad and bold plan that would command the respect even of opponents, and who is inexperienced and clumsy in his own professional art—the art of combating the political police—such a man is not a revolutionary but a wretched amateur!

Let no active worker take offense at these frank remarks, for as far as insufficient training is concerned, I apply them first and foremost to myself. I used to work in a study circle that set itself very broad, all-embracing tasks; and all of us, members of that circle, suffered painfully and acutely from the realization that we were acting as amateurs at a moment in history when we might have been able to say, paraphrasing a well-known statement: "Give us an organization of revolutionaries, and we shall overturn Russia!"

Entrepreneurs, lawyers, doctors, other professionals, and even nobles pressured the government for liberal political reforms that would give voice to the educated members of Russian society. In particular, they demanded that the tsar grant a constitution and establish a popularly elected legislature to share power with the tsar. Conservative forces also organized. The program of the Union of Russian People, issued in late 1905, rejected any diminution of the autocrat's power and affirmed the role of religion, monarchy, and Russianness as the underlying principles of politics, society, and culture. It also singled out Jews for continued discrimination.

The UNION OF THE RUSSIAN PEOPLE aims to unite all true Russians, loyal to their sworn oath in the name of Faith, TSAR and Fatherland. . . .

1. Orthodoxy
   The UNION recognizes the Orthodox faith, held by the indigenous Russian population, as the FOUNDATION OF RUSSIAN LIFE, . . .

2. Autocracy

   The AUTOCRACY of the Russian TSARS . . . has remained unchanged . . . and should always remain so for the good and enlightenment of Russia.

   The autocratic sovereign is THE SUPREME TRUTH, LAW AND STRENGTH. . . .

3. Nationality

   THE UNION OF THE RUSSIAN PEOPLE believes that the Russian nation as the consolidator of the Russian land and the founder of the Russian state is the SOVEREIGN NATION; other nationalities, with the exception of the Jews, have equal rights. . . .

5. The Jewish Question

   The Jews have, over many years, declared their uncompromising hatred for Russia and all things Russian, their incredible detestation for humanity, their complete alienation from other nationalities and their unique Jewish outlook. . . .

   As is well known, and as the Jews themselves have announced . . . the general revolutionary movement in Russia . . . is almost exclusively the work of Jews and is conducted with the help of Jewish money. . . .

The Revolution of 1905

In 1905 a revolution broke out in which peasants, workers, professionals, and national minorities seeking their independence from Russia challenged the autocracy, giving voice to a host of social, political, and economic demands. The revolution began on January 9, "Bloody Sunday," when troops opened fire on a procession of striking Petersburg workers seeking to present a petition of their demands to Nicholas II. The ruthless killing of hundreds of peaceful demonstrators triggered strikes and mobilized people across the social spectrum. Father Gapon, a priest who led the demonstration on January 9, helped write the workers' petition, which reflected their desire for a life of dignity and freedom from need.

Sovereign!

We, workers and inhabitants of the city of St. Petersburg, members of various sosloviia, our wives, children, and helpless old parents, have come to you, Sovereign, to seek justice and protection. We are impoverished and oppressed, we are burdened with work, and insulted. We are treated not like humans [but] like slaves who must

Sosloviia

Sosloviia refers to the legal social categories to which all Russians belonged.

Nearly 1,000 people were killed or wounded when the army opened fire on peaceful demonstrators in St. Petersburg on Jan. 9, 1905, known as Bloody Sunday. The shootings sparked mass civil unrest throughout Russia and signaled the start of the Revolution of 1905.

suffer a bitter fate and keep silent. And we have suffered, but we only get pushed deeper and deeper into a gulf of misery, ignorance, and lack of rights. Despotism and arbitrariness are suffocating us, we are gasping for breath. Sovereign, we have no strength left. We have reached the limit of our patience. We have come to that terrible moment when it is better to die than to continue unbearable sufferings.

And so we left our work and declared to our employers that we will not return to work until they meet our demands. We do not ask much; we only want that without which life is hard labor and eternal suffering. Our first request was that our employers discuss our needs together with us. But they refused to do this; they denied us the right to speak about our needs, on the grounds that the law does not provide us with such a right. Also unlawful were our other requests: to reduce the working day to eight hours; for them to set wages together with us and by agreement with us; to examine our disputes with lower-level factory administrators; to increase the wages of unskilled workers and women to one ruble per day; to abolish overtime work; to provide medical care attentively and without insult; to build shops so that it is possible to work there and not face death from the awful drafts, rain and snow.

Our employers and the factory administrators considered all this to be illegal: every one of our requests was a crime, and our desire to improve our condition was slanderous insolence.

Sovereign, there are thousands of us here; outwardly we are human beings, but in reality neither we nor the Russian narod as a whole are provided with any human rights, even the right to speak, to think, to assemble, to discuss our needs, or to take measure to improve our conditions. They have enslaved us and they did so under the protection of your officials, with their aid and with their cooperation. They imprison and send into exile any one of us who has the courage to speak on behalf of the interests of the working class and of the people. They punish us for a good heart and a responsive spirit as if for a crime. To pity a downtrodden and tormented person with no rights is to commit a grave crime. The entire working people and the peasants are subjected to the proizvol of a bureaucratic administration composed of embezzlers of public funds and thieves who not only have no concern at all for the interests of the Russian people but who harm those interests. The bureaucratic administration has reduced the country to complete destitution, drawn it into a shameful war, and brings Russia ever further towards ruin. . . . The people is deprived of any possibility of expressing its wishes and demands, or of participating in the establishment of taxes and in their expenditure. Workers are deprived of the possibility of organizing into unions to defend their interests. Sovereign! Does all this accord with the law of God, by Whose grace you reign? And is it possible to live under such laws? Would it not be better if we, the toiling people of all Russia, died? Let the capitalists—exploiters of the working class—and the bureaucrats—embezzlers of public funds and the pillagers of the Russian people—live and enjoy themselves.

Sovereign, this is what we face and this is the reason that we have gathered before the walls of your palace. Here we seek our last salvation. Do not refuse to come to the aid of your people; lead it out of the grave of poverty, ignorance, and lack of rights; grant it the opportunity to determine its own destiny, and deliver it from them the unbearable yoke of the bureaucrats. Tear down the wall that separates you from your people and let it rule the country together with you. You have been placed [on the throne] for the happiness of the people; the bureaucrats, however, snatch this happiness out of our hands, and

Narod
Narod is the Russian word for people.

Proizvol
Proizvol means arbitrariness.

it never reaches us; we get only grief and humiliation. Sovereign, examine our requests attentively and without any anger; they incline not to evil, but to the good, both for us and for you. Ours is not the voice of insolence but of the realization that we must get out of a situation that is unbearable for everyone. Russia is too big, her needs are too diverse and many, for her to be ruled only by bureaucrats. We need popular representation; it is necessary for the people to help itself and to administer itself. After all, only the people knows its real needs. Do not fend off its help, accept it, and order immediately, at once, that representatives of the Russian land from all classes, all estates of the realm be summoned, including representatives from the workers. Let the capitalist be there, and the worker, and the bureaucrat, and the priest, and the doctor and the teacher—let everyone, whoever they are, elect their representatives. Let everyone be free and equal in his voting rights, and to that end order that elections to the Constituent Assembly be conducted under universal, secret and equal suffrage.

This is our main request, everything is based on it; it is the main and only poultice for our painful wounds, without which those wounds must freely bleed and bring us to a quick death.

But no single measure can heal all our wounds. Other measures are necessary, and we, representing all of Russia's toiling class, frankly and openly speak to you, Sovereign, as to a father, about them.

The following are necessary: . . .

Constituent Assembly

A constituent assembly is a popularly elected body that drafts a constitution.

2. Immediate proclamation of the freedom and inviolability of the person, of freedom of speech and of the press, of freedom of assembly, and of freedom of conscience in matters of religion. . . .

III. Measures against the oppression of labor by capital

1. Abolition of the office of factory inspector.
2. Establishment in factories and plants of permanent commissions elected by the workers, which jointly with the administration are to investigate all complaints coming from individual workers. A worker cannot be fired except by a resolution of this commission.
3. Freedom for producer-consumer cooperatives and workers' trade unions—at once.
4. An eight-hour working day and regulation of overtime work.
5. Freedom for labor to struggle with capital—at once.

6. Wage regulation—at once.
7. Guaranteed participation of representatives of the working classes in drafting a law on state insurance for workers—at once.

These, sovereign, are our main needs, about which we have come to you; only when they are satisfied will the liberation of our Motherland from slavery and destitution be possible, only then can she flourish, only then can workers organize to defend their interests from insolent exploitation by capitalists and by the bureaucratic administration that plunders and suffocates the people. Give the order, swear to meet these needs, and you will make Russia both happy and glorious, and your name will be fixed in our hearts and the hearts of our posterity for all time—but if you do not give the order, if you do not respond to our prayer, then we shall die here, on this square, in front of your palace. We have nowhere else to go and no reason to. There are only two roads for us, one to freedom and happiness, the other to the grave. Let our lives be sacrificed for suffering Russia. We do not regret that sacrifice, we embrace it eagerly.

Georgii Gapon, priest

1905 witnessed an explosion of peasant activism and unrest aimed at wresting control of the land from the landlords and thereby realizing the peasant dream of "genuine emancipation." Many peasants limited their activities to issuing manifestos and drawing up petitions. This petition from a village of slightly more than 100 inhabitants illustrates their desperation.

The land should be available to the plowers; each peasant should receive an adequate amount of land from the village, and the government must provide material aid for its cultivation. . . .

Do not think that our needs can be satisfied by half measures. We have become so demoralized, so in need of land, and ruined under our wardship that the measures we ask can bring us help only after several years. Therefore, it must be clear to you that we are driven to extremes by large-scale conditions of misery and by a dismal life. Either you give us all we have asked for or you can shoot us all and live on, obtaining all your wants, whims and luxuries. But to us life is actually a hundred times more burdensome than death, and therefore we dare to face it. We are interested in the question of how you would go about killing us. Our children and our brothers are under your orders (in the army) but they promised that they

Polish, Russian, and Jewish Marxist revolutionaries holding wreaths and banners honor the victims of anti-Jewish violence at a ceremony in October 1905. Angry mobs vandalized stores and homes of Jews and beat and murdered Jewish men, women, and children in response to the popular belief that Jews were responsible for the revolutionary opposition to the autocracy and for social and economic problems.

would not kill us, for they understand that having killed us, they, having returned (from service) into our position, would be subject to suffering like ours and would risk being killed by their brothers and children in turn.

Other peasants took matters into their own hands by seizing land and grain and looting the manor houses of landlords. In some instances, they attacked their landlords as well. While disturbances were for the most part spontaneous, it appears that peasants in some cases acted in an organized, planned manner and even coordinated attacks with peasants from nearby villages. This report by police officials to the ministry of interior describes events in several small villages.

On the night of February 6, peasants of the villages of S. . . and Kh. . . of Dmitriev District . . . undertook mass pillaging on the estate of the merchant Popov, who had bad relations with the peasants. In the course of these events, armed resistance was rendered by the police officials. On the night of February 15 the estate of the merchant Chernichin was destroyed and since then the movement spread with astonishing swiftness and proceeded according to an obviously pre-arranged plan. It works as follows:—in each village, come evening, the peasants harness their horses and await the signal given them by looters who set fire to piles of straw. Then the whole village, yelling, screaming and firing guns, hurls itself upon the nearest estate. At the same time as the attack upon Chernichin's estate took place, arson was committed on the properties of Baron Meyendorf. . . . On February 18 the peasants fell upon the farm of proprietress Meyer, seizing grain and valuable possessions. . . .

This gave the . . . peasants the opportunity to raid still more estates on February 22 and to move into Khinel, where the fields and the brandy distillery of Tereshchenko are located. At a given signal a huge mob, aided by local peasants, began to batter and burn the distillery. All the buildings of the plant were destroyed and the grain and spirits robbed.

Strikes by workers all over urban Russia were endemic in 1905. But in October a general strike paralyzed the country and compelled Nicholas II to grant civil and political freedoms and authorize elections to a legislature, the State Duma. Known as the October Manifesto, the proclamation marked what many hoped would be the political liberalization of Russia and end of the autocracy.

Manifesto on the Improvement of State Order
Manifesto of October 17, 1905

Unrest and disturbances in the capitals and many other areas of the Empire fill Our heart with great and heavy grief. The well-being of the Russian Sovereign is inseparable from the well-being of the people, and the people's sorrow is His sorrow. The disturbances that have occurred may give rise to grave tension among the people and may threaten the integrity and unity of Our State.

The great vow of service We took as Tsar compels Us to use all Our wisdom and authority to bring about the speedy end to the unrest that endangers Our State. We have ordered the responsible authorities to take measures to put an end to direct outbreaks of disorder, lawlessness, and violence, and to protect people who only seek to go about their duties in peace. In order to carry out successfully the measures designed to restore peace to the life of the State, We believe that it is necessary to coordinate activities on the highest level of Government.

Workers demonstrate in the streets of Moscow in 1905. The banners proclaim "Down with the Autocracy" and "Proletarians of All Countries, Unite!"

We have ordered the Government to take measures to implement Our unshakable will:

1. To grant the population the basic foundations of civil freedom based on the principles of genuine inviolability of the person, freedom of conscience, speech, assembly, and association.

2. Without postponing the scheduled elections to the State Duma, to admit to participation in the Duma, insofar as is possible in the short time remaining before its scheduled convocation, of all those classes of the population that are now deprived of the franchise, and to leave the further development of a general statute on universal suffrage to the future legislative order.

3. To establish as an unbreakable rule that no law shall take effect without the approval of the State Duma and that the elected representatives of the people should be guaranteed the opportunity to participate in the supervision of the legality of the actions taken by officials appointed by Us.

We call upon loyal sons of Russia to remember their duties to their country, to assist in ending this current unprecedented unrest, and together with Us to make every effort to restore peace and tranquility to Our native land.

Not all workers were satisfied by the promise of civil liberties and political freedom, and many continued to press the government for additional reforms. In December 1905 workers in Moscow attempted to overturn tsarist authority through an armed insurrection. Workers set up barricades and engaged soldiers in battles that lasted more than a week. The October general strike culminated in the emergence of the St. Petersburg Soviet of Workers, a grassroots organization with representatives directly elected by workers and other lower-class residents of the city. In the "Resolution of the Executive Committee of the St. Petersburg Soviet of Workers' Deputies on Measures for Counteracting the Lock-Out," adopted on Nov. 14, 1905, the Soviet sought to render assistance to unemployed workers and to displace tsarist authority in the city.

Soviet
Soviet means council in Russian.

Citizens, over a hundred thousand workers have been thrown onto the streets in St. Petersburg and other cities.

The autocratic government has declared war on the revolutionary proletariat. The reactionary bourgeoisie is joining hands with the autocracy, intending to starve the workers into submission and disrupt the struggle for freedom.

The Soviet of Workers' Deputies declares that this unparalleled mass dismissal of workers is an act of provocation on the part of the government. The government wants to provoke the proletariat of St. Petersburg to isolated outbreaks; the government wants to take advantage of the fact that the workers of other cities have not yet rallied closely enough to the St. Petersburg workers, and to defeat them all piecemeal.

The Soviet of Workers' Deputies declares that the cause of liberty is in danger. But the workers will not fall into the trap laid by the government. The workers will not accept battle in the unfavorable conditions in which the government wants to impose battle on them. We must and shall exert every effort to unite the whole struggle—the struggle that is being waged both by the proletariat of all Russia and by the revolutionary peasantry, both by the Army and by the Navy, which are already heroically rising for freedom.

In view of the foregoing, the Soviet of Workers' Deputies resolves:

1. All factories that have been shut down must immediately be reopened and all dismissed comrades reinstated. All

sections of the people that cherish freedom in reality, and not in words only, are invited to support this demand.

2. In support of this demand, the Soviet of Workers' Deputies considers it necessary to appeal to the solidarity of the entire Russian proletariat, and, if the demand is rejected, to call upon the latter to resort to a general political strike and other forms of resolute struggle.

3. In preparation for this action, the Soviet of Workers' Deputies has instructed the Executive Committee to enter into immediate communication with the workers of other cities, with the railwaymen's, post and telegraph employees', peasant and other unions, as well as with the Army and Navy, by sending delegates and by other means.

4. As soon as this preliminary work is completed, the Executive Committee is to call a special meeting of the Soviet of Workers' Deputies to take a final decision with regard to a strike.

5. The St. Petersburg proletariat has asked all the workers and all sections of society and the people to support the dismissed workers with all the means at their disposal— material, moral and political.

On the Eve of War and Revolution

Between 1906 and 1914 Nicholas II and his ministers undermined the concessions to democratic principles granted in 1905. As autocrat, he did not believe in sharing power with his subjects and was not bound by the laws establishing the State Duma. In 1907 the tsar changed the electoral laws in order to ensure a more docile and pliable legislature. In July of the previous year he had dissolved the First Duma because he opposed legislation under consideration by liberals and leftists, who made up some three fifths of the deputies. The deputies then met in the Finnish city of Vyborg and issued what is known as the Vyborg Manifesto.

To the people, from the people's representatives.

Citizens throughout Russia! The decree of 8 July dissolved the State Duma. When you elected us as your representatives, you entrusted us with the task of securing land and freedom. Fulfilling your charge and our duty, we drafted laws to assure the people's freedom and demanded the removal of irresponsible ministers who suppressed freedom with impunity, in violation of the law. But above all we wished to promulgate a law concerning the allotment of land to the working peasantry . . . by the compulsory expropriation of privately owned lands. The government declared such a law inadmissible and replied to the Duma's insistent reaffirmation of its resolution concerning compulsory expropriation by dismissing the people's representatives. . . .

Citizens, stand firmly for the trampled rights of the people's representatives, stand firmly for the State Duma. Russia must not remain a single day without popular representatives. We have the means of achieving this: the government has no right either to collect taxes from the people or to mobilize men for military service without the consent of the people's representatives. Now, therefore, when the government has dismissed the State Duma, you have the right not to give it either soldiers or money. . . . And so, until the convocation of the people's representatives, do not give a single kopek to the Treasury or a single soldier to the army. Be firm in your refusal. Defend your rights together. No force can prevail before the united and unbending will of the people. Citizens, in this forced and unavoidable struggle your elected representatives will be with you.

Not unexpectedly, workers and peasants remained disenchanted with the regime. But even moderate politicians from gentry, commercial, and manufacturing circles that had hoped the government and Duma could work together had grown alienated from the regime by 1914. In 1913 Alexander Guchkov, a leader of a Duma faction, delivered a speech in which he underscored the distrust and suspicion he and others had for Nicholas II and his ministers, and made ominous predictions about Russia's future.

What is to be the issue of the grave crisis through which we are now passing? What does the encroachment of reaction bring with it? Whither is the government policy, or lack of policy, carrying us?

Towards an inevitable and grave catastrophe? In this general forecast all are agreed; people of the most sharply opposed political views, of the most varied social groups, all agree with a rare unanimity. Even representatives of the government, of that government which is the chief offender against the Russian people, are prepared to agree to this forecast, and their official and obligatory optimism ill conceals their inward alarm.

When will the catastrophe take effect? What forms will it assume? Who can foretell? Some scan the horizon with joyful anticipation, others with dread. But greatly do those err who calculate that on the ruins of the demolished system will arise that order which corresponds to their particular political and social views. In those forces that seem likely to come to the top in the approaching struggle, I do not see stable elements that would guarantee any kind of permanent political order. Are we not rather in danger of being plunged into a period of protracted, chronic anarchy which will lead to the dissolution of the Empire? . . .

Will our voice be heard? Will our cry of warning reach the heights where the fate of Russia is decided? Shall we succeed in communicating our own alarm to the government? Shall we awaken it from the lethargy that envelops it? We should be glad to think so. In any case, this is our last opportunity of securing a peaceful issue from the crisis. Let those in power make no mistake about the temper of the people; let them not take outward indications of prosperity as a pretext for lulling themselves into security. Never were those revolutionary organizations which aim at a violent upheaval so broken and impotent as they are now, and never were the Russian public and the Russian people so profoundly revolutionized by the actions of the government, for day by day faith in the government is steadily waning, and with it is waning faith in the possibility of a peaceful issue from this crisis. . . .

The catastrophe Guchkov predicted took the form of World War I. Russia's involvement in war exposed its lack of preparation for modern warfare and revealed that its social and political system was poorly equipped to endure the pressures of war. The human cost of the war was enormous, and the army's poor showing demoralized the citizenry and fueled opposition to the regime. By the beginning of 1917 the tsarist regime had lost all credibility because of incompetent generals and poor civilian leadership. In 1915 Tsar Nicholas II wrote to the commander of the armed forces, Grand Duke Nicholas, that he was taking command of daily military operations, a move that backfired because the tsar was unfit for the post. It also accelerated a loss of faith in Nicholas II since the populace now associated the failings of the military with the person of the tsar.

Tsar Nicholas II to Grand Duke Nikolai
5 September 1915

At the beginning of the war I was unavoidably prevented from following the inclination of my soul to put myself at the head of the army. That was why I entrusted you with the Commandership-in-Chief of all the land and sea forces.

Grigorii Rasputin, a Siberian priest, gained the confidence of Tsar Nicholas II and Tsarina Alexandra.

Under the eyes of the whole of Russia your Imperial Highness has given proof during the war of steadfast bravery which caused a feeling of profound confidence, and called forth the sincere good wishes of all who followed your operations through the inevitable vicissitudes of fortune of war.

My duty to my country, which has been entrusted to me by God, impels me to-day, when the enemy has penetrated into the interior of the Empire, to take the supreme command of the active forces and to share with my army the fatigues of war, and to safeguard with it Russian soil from the attempts of the enemy.

The ways of Providence are inscrutable, but my duty and my desire determine me in my resolution for the good of the State.

The invasion of the enemy on the Western front necessitates the greatest possible concentration of the civil and military authorities, as well as the unification of the command in the field, and has turned our attention from the southern front.

At this moment I recognize the necessity of your assistance and counsels on our southern front, and I appoint you Viceroy of the Caucasus and Commander-in-Chief of the valiant Caucasian Army.

I express to your Imperial Highness my profound gratitude and that of the country for your labours during the war.

The royal family believed Rasputin could stop the bleeding of Alexei, heir to the throne, who suffered from hemophilia. Rasputin's influence over Tsarina Alexandra enabled him to acquire behind-the-scenes power, particularly when Tsar Nicholas II left Petrograd to command the troops during World War I. Rasputin's scandalous behavior, rumored to include orgies, led to his downfall. In December 1916 several prominent nobles drowned Rasputin after first poisoning and shooting him.

CHAPTER 2

1917: The Year of Revolution

Lenin addresses a crowd of workers and soldiers in Moscow in 1920. The soldiers were headed to join forces fighting the army of newly independent Poland, which had seized control of territory also claimed by the Bolsheviks.

The end of the autocracy occurred on International Women's Day in February 1917. The hardships of the war and persistent food shortages prompted women to protest deteriorating living standards and the rising cost of living. When soldiers in Petrograd refused orders to disperse the crowds of men, women, and children spontaneously demonstrating in the streets of the capital, the tsar's closest advisers suggested that he give up the throne. One week after the demonstrations had begun, Nicholas II abdicated, thereby ending three centuries of rule by the Romanov dynasty. Known as the February Revolution, the collapse of the autocracy created a power vacuum, and two organizations emerged to fill it. A "Provisional Government" composed of Russia's leading liberal politicians set itself up as a temporary, caretaker government until a democratically elected constituent assembly could establish a permanent regime that would determine the nature of Russia's new government. The Petrograd Soviet of Workers' and Soldiers' Deputies emerged as a rival political organization, giving rise to a situation known as "Dual Power." The word "soviet" means council in Russia. Soviets emerged all over urban and rural Russia in the wake of the tsar's abdication, represented the interests of workers, soldiers, and peasants, and claimed to be the fundamental institution of the revolutionary order.

While the Provisional Government held formal political power and was seen as representing the interests of Russia's middle and upper classes, it was the Petrograd Soviet, along with other soviets that sprouted up throughout the Russian Empire, that enjoyed popular support and commanded the loyalty of workers and soldiers. Relations

In their eyes, what has occurred is not a political but a social revolution, which in their opinion they have won and we have lost.

—An army officer stating how the soldiers under his command at the front understood the events of 1917

between the two competing centers of power quickly grew strained and underscored the social and political tensions that marked Russian society in the heady days after the tsar's abdication. Indeed, the fate of the Provisional Government was tied to its inability to resolve the pressing demands of workers, peasants, soldiers, and national minorities. Although the collapse of the autocracy initiated a democratic overhaul of Russia's political institutions, the Provisional Government was overwhelmed by a vast social upheaval that pitted Russia's lower classes against the upper classes. It shelved all serious discussion of granting peasants more land, ending the war, democratizing the military, extending workers the power to control factories, and allowing national minorities to determine whether they wanted to become independent of Russia.

Workers, peasants, soldiers, and national minorities grew increasingly frustrated with the Provisional Government's unwillingness to address their concerns and, as 1917 wore on, many of them grew weary of the "dual power" arrangement and began demanding that the soviets seize control of the reins of government. Soldiers tended to welcome the overthrow of the tsar because they hoped that the new regime would wage a more effective military campaign against Russia's enemies. However, the inability of the Provisional Government to succeed where Tsar Nicholas had failed contributed to disillusionment among the troops and gave rise to discontent, desertion, and mutiny by the summer months. Soldiers also refused to obey orders to go to the front, preferring to remain in the rear rather than risk their lives in the trenches. Soldiers grew so weary of the war that they began to fraternize with German and Austrian troops and demanded an immediate end to the hostilities. In addition, they began to desert and make the way back to their native villages in order to seize land from landlords.

However, the leadership of the Petrograd Soviet refrained from challenging the Provisional Government, preferring instead to ally with it. In late spring socialists from the Petrograd Soviet began to assume positions in the Provisional Government in order to endow it with popular support, and by July socialists enjoyed a majority in the Provisional Government.

The political tide shifted in favor of the Bolsheviks by the early fall of 1917 because they were the only group that correctly read the political mood of Russia's workers, soldiers, peasants, and national minorities. Under the leadership of Vladimir Lenin, the Bolsheviks willingly tied their fortunes to the demands of the people, who were growing more and more radical as the year progressed. Their slogan "Bread, Peace, and Land" summed up the appeal of the Bolsheviks, who understood what workers, peasants, and soldiers wanted. Lenin recognized that the Provisional Government's grip on power was tenuous at best and therefore agitated for "All Power to the Soviets" as a way to move Russia one step closer to the establishment of a socialist government. In addition, the Bolsheviks won popular support by spearheading the effort to quash an attempt in late summer by General Lavr Kornilov, commander-in-chief of the army, to seize power and destroy the Petrograd Soviet. By the fall the Bolsheviks had grown in numbers and political influence, and on October 25 the Bolsheviks seized the reins of power and installed themselves as the world's first socialist government. In the words of the prominent Bolshevik leader Leon Trotsky, Russia's rival socialist parties had been swept into the "dustbin of history."

The assumption of power by the Bolsheviks marked a turning point not only for Russia but also for the world. The establishment of the first socialist government was a momentous occasion that helped shape political developments for the remainder of the 20th century. The Bolsheviks were intent on building a society rooted in the principles of Marxism and free of class oppression and exploitation, a society where private property did not exist, workers and peasants controlled the factories and land, and social, political, and economic equality was the order of the day. Achieving the Bolshevik future implied that all remnants of the old Russia, from the gentry and industrialists to members of the royal family, had to be stripped of their wealth and power and replaced by the masters of the new Russia, the working class. Precisely how this vision of the future Russia would be realized was unknown, and the Bolsheviks had to meet this challenge. They turned their attention to building a socialist society, but as the Bolsheviks soon learned, the costs were enormous and the consequences tragic for the Russian people.

The Radicalization of Society

When the February Revolution broke out, the Bolsheviks did not enjoy much popularity among workers and had little influence in the Petrograd Soviet, which was dominated by Mensheviks and Socialist Revolutionaries. Their acknowledged leader, Vladimir Lenin, was living in exile in Europe, where he had been for the previous decade, and party affairs inside Russia were in the hands of Joseph Stalin, Lev Kamenev, and Grigorii Zinoviev. Bolsheviks in Russia accepted the arrangement of "Dual Power" and were shocked by what they considered Lenin's extremist pronouncement (known as the "April Theses" after they appeared in the party's newspaper *Pravda*), issued upon his return to Russia in April 1917, that the time was ripe for the transfer of power to the Petrograd Soviet. Lenin also outlined his vision of what a socialist Russia might look like, though he was careful to note that he was not calling for the establishment of a socialist order, but the first steps on the road to socialism. He condemned the Provisional Government as capitalist in nature and therefore automatically suspect by the proletariat.

Women march on Nevskii Prospekt in April 1917 with signs demanding "extra food rations for families of soldiers, defenders of freedom and the people's peace" and "food for children."

1. In our attitude towards the war, which also under the new government ... unquestionably remains on Russia's part a predatory imperialist war owing to the capitalist nature of that government, not the slightest concession to "revolutionary defencism" is permissible.

2. The specific feature of the present situation in Russia is that it represents a *transition* from the first stage of the revolution—which, owing to the insufficient class consciousness and organization of the proletariat, placed the power in the hands of the bourgeoisie—*to the second* stage, which must place power in the hands of the proletariat and the poorest strata of the peasantry. ...

3. No support for the Provisional Government; the utter falsity of all its promises should be explained, particularly those relating to the renunciation of annexations. Exposure

in place of the impermissible illusion-breeding "demand" that *this* government, a government of capitalists, should *cease* to be an imperialist government. . . .

4. It must be explained to the masses that the Soviets of Workers' Deputies are the *only possible* form of the revolutionary government and that, therefore, our task is, as long as *this* government yields to the influence of the bourgeoisie, to present a patient, systematic, and persistent *explanation* of the errors of their tactics, an explanation especially adapted to the practical needs of the masses.

   As long as we are in the minority we carry on the work of criticizing and exposing errors and at the same time we preach the necessity of transferring the entire power of the state to the Soviets of Workers' Deputies, so that the masses may by experience overcome their mistakes.

5. Not a parliamentary republic—to return to a parliamentary republic from the Soviet of Workers' Deputies would be a retrograde step—but a republic of Soviets of Workers', Agricultural Laborers' and Peasants' Deputies throughout the country, from top to bottom. Abolition of the police, the army, the bureaucracy. . . .

6. In the agrarian program, the emphasis must be shifted to the Soviets of Agricultural Laborers' Deputies.

   Confiscation of all landed estates

   Nationalization of *all* lands in the country, the disposal of the land to be put in the charge of the local Soviets of Agricultural Laborers' and Peasants' Deputies. . . .

7. The immediate amalgamation of all banks in the country into a single national bank, and the institution of control over it by the Soviets of Workers' Deputies.

8. It is not our *immediate* task to "introduce" Socialism, but only to bring social production and distribution of products at once under the *control* of the Soviets of Workers' Deputies. . . .

Immediately after the fall of the autocracy, the Soviet issued Order No. 1, a directive authorizing all army units to elect committees and send deputies to the Soviet. Order No. 1 struck a blow at military discipline, since the Soviet instructed soldiers to obey officers only if their orders did not conflict with the policies of the Soviet. For soldiers and revolutionaries alike, the February Revolution had ushered in an era of grassroots, participatory democracy where the common people now enjoyed some control over their lives and possessed the right to challenge the prerogatives and decisions of their superiors, be they military commanders or factory managers. Order No. 1 illustrated the turning upside-down of traditional chains of command and authority, a signal of the rising tide of revolution.

Tsarist officials changed the name of St. Petersburg, the capital of Russia founded in 1703, to Petrograd soon after hostilities between Russia and Germany began in August 1914. They feared that the city's original name sounded too German and decided to rechristen the city with a more Russian-sounding name. Petrograd literally translates into "Peter's City." In 1924 it was renamed Leningrad, in honor of the Bolshevik leader Vladimir Lenin. An old joke from the Soviet period satirizes this process of renaming.

A man applying for a passport to travel abroad was asked by an official: "Where were you born?" He answered, "Petrograd." "Where do you live?" "Leningrad." "Where do you want to die?" "St. Petersburg."

To the garrison of the Petrograd Military District, to all soldiers of the guard, army, artillery and fleet for immediate and exact execution, and to all the workers of Petrograd for their information.

The Soviet of Workers' and Soldiers' Deputies has decreed:

(1) Committees are to be elected immediately in all companies, battalions, regiments, parks, batteries, squadrons, and individual units of the different forms of military directorates, and in all naval vessels, from the elected representatives of the rank and file of the above-mentioned units.

(2) All troop units which have not yet elected their representatives to the Soviet of Workers' Deputies are to elect one representative per company. Such representatives are to appear, with written confirmation, at the State Duma building at 10 A.M. on 2 March.

(3) In all political actions, troop units are subordinate to the Soviet of Workers' and Soldiers' Deputies, and to the committees thereof.

(4) The orders of the Military commission of the State Duma are to be obeyed, *with the exception of those instances in which they contradict the orders and decrees* of the Soviet of Workers' and Soldiers' Deputies.

(5) All types of arms, such as rifles, machine guns, armoured cars, and others, must be put at the disposal of company and battalion committees, and under their control, and are not, in any case, to be issued to officers, even upon demand.

(6) On duty and in the performance of service responsibilities, soldiers must observe the strictest military discipline, but when off duty, in their political, civil and private lives, soldiers shall enjoy fully and completely the same rights as all citizens.

In particular, standing at attention and compulsory saluting when off duty are abolished.

(7) In the same way, addressing officers by honorary titles ("Your Excellency," "Your honour," etc.) is abolished and is replaced.

Addressing soldiers rudely by anyone of higher rank, and in particular, addressing soldiers by *ty* is prohibited, and any breach of this provision, as well as any misunderstandings between officers and soldiers, are to be reported by the latter to the company committees.

This order is to be read to all companies, battalions, regiments, ships' crews, batteries and other combatant and non-combatant units.
Petrograd Soviet of Workers' and Soldiers' Deputies

In early July a two-day demonstration by militant workers and soldiers in Petrograd tried to force the Petrograd Soviet to seize power and end the war. Led by Alexander Kerensky, who had become prime minister in late spring, the Provisional Government refused to implement land reform, remained committed to the war, and supported the efforts of General Kornilov to restore military discipline, all of which undermined the Provisional Government in the eyes of the populace. Most Bolshevik leaders were wary of the protests, believing that support for soviet power was still inadequate throughout Russia. But the Party reluctantly threw its support behind the demonstrators when it became clear that the people of the capital were going ahead with the protests despite the wishes of the Soviet and Bolsheviks. In one incident, an irate demonstrator yelled at Victor Chernov, a leading Socialist Revolutionary and current minister of agriculture who was trying to disperse the protesters, "Take power, you son-of-a-bitch, when it's given to you." In his memoirs a member of the Petrograd Soviet describes the demonstration. His characterization of one worker as a *sans-culotte* indicates that Russians believed they were experiencing their own "French Revolution."

I went back to the meeting. There was nothing new there. Suddenly like an arrow the news sped through the meeting: the men from the Putilov Factory had come, 30,000 of them, bearing themselves extremely aggressively; . . . The hall was full of excitement, hubbub and frenzied yelling. Just then a crowd of about forty workers, many of them armed, burst in tempestuously. The deputies leaped from their seats. Some failed to show adequate courage and self-control.

One of the workers, a classic *sans-culotte*, in a cap and short blue shirt without a belt, with rifle in hand, leaped up on to the speakers' platform. He was quivering with excitement and rage, stridently shouting out incoherent words and shaking his rifle:

"Comrades! How long must we workers put up with treachery? You're all here debating and making deals with the bourgeoisie and the landlords . . . You're busy betraying the working class. Well, just understand that the working class won't put up with it. There are

Unlike English, Russian has both polite and familiar forms of "you." The second-person plural, *vy*, is a polite form of address, while the second person singular, *ty*, is a familiar form of address. The use of these forms of address in pre- and post-revolutionary Russia indicated social hierarchy as well, with social superiors using *ty* toward those of lower social ranking, who showed their respect by responding with *vy*. By banning the use of *ty* by officers when addressing their troops, the Soviet was insisting that officers treat their soldiers with respect and was elevating the peasant conscripts into social equals with their upper-class commanders.

Sans-culottes
Sans-culottes (without knee-breeches) were radical Parisian workers during the French Revolution whose clothes distinguished them from the well-to-do.

During the spring of 1917 two socialist parties, the Socialist Revolutionaries and Mensheviks, dominated the Petrograd Soviet of Workers' and Soldiers' Deputies.

30,000 of us all told from Putilov. We're going to have our way. All power to the Soviets! We have a firm grip on our rifles! . . ."

. . . But to this day I can still see that *sans-culotte* on the platform . . . , shaking his rifle in self-oblivion in the faces of the hostile "leaders of the democracy," trying in torment to express the will, the longings, and the fury of the authentic proletarian lower depths, who sensed treachery but were powerless to fight against it. This was one of the finest scenes of the revolution. . . .

Russia was a multinational empire with nearly 200 ethnic, national, and religious minorities. Many of these minorities bristled under the oppressive policies of the autocracy, which limited their cultural and national aspirations. After the abdication of Nicholas II, the Provisional Government faced the challenging task of responding to the demands of the national minorities. Even though the Provisional Government recognized that non-Russian minorities possessed the right of self-determination, its members feared the breakup of the Russian empire. The inaction of the Provisional Government spurred national minorities in Finland, Central Asia, the Caucasus, and Ukraine to take matters into their own hands and assert their right to establish autonomous and even independent states. By the summer months of 1917, as the authority of the Provisional Government dissolved, the national minorities grew more assertive in their demands for control over their political destinies. In Ukraine, for example, Ukrainian nationalists formed the *Rada* ("council" in Ukrainian) soon after the February uprising and began acting as the government of Ukraine in defiance of the Provisional Government. In a manifesto issued in June 1917 the *Rada* outlined the goals of the Ukrainian people.

Without separating from Russia, and without breaking away from the Russian State, let the Ukrainian people on its own territory have the right to dispose of its life, and let a proper Government be established in the Ukraine by the election of a Ukrainian national Assembly . . . on the basis of universal, equal, direct, and secret suffrage. Only such an assembly has the right to issue laws which are to establish permanent order in the Ukraine, while those laws which affect the entire Russian State must be issued by an All-Russian Parliament. No one knows better than ourselves what we want, and what are the best laws for us. No one better than our own peasants knows how to manage our own land.

For that reason we wish . . . that the constitution and public order in our Ukrainian territories should be entirely in our own hands, that is, in the hands of a Ukrainian Diet. . . . We thought at first that the Central Russian Government would lend us a hand in this work, and that we, the Ukrainian Central *Rada*, would be able, in cooperation with it, to organize our country; but the Provisional Russian Government has rejected our demands and has refused the stretched-out hand of the Ukrainian people. We have sent out delegates to Petrograd to submit to the Russian Provisional Government our demands, the principal of which are as follows:

That the Russian Government should publicly, by a special Act, proclaim that it is not opposed to the national will of the Ukraine and to the right of our people to autonomy. . . .

That a definite portion of the taxes collected from our people into the State Exchequer should be handed over to us, the representatives of the Ukrainian people, for cultural and national needs.

All these demands have been rejected by the Central Russian Government, which did not want to say whether it recognized our people's right to autonomy and to dispose of its own life. It has

The mob dragged out from the guardhouse three generals and one colonel, kicked them off the bridge into the water, and killed them. These men had been arrested . . . on the charge of being implicated in the Kornilov affair. After these men had been murdered, the mob went after other officers in the regiments. These, too, were thrown into the water and then killed.

—Newspaper of the Soviet of Workers' and Soldiers' Deputies, September 15, 1917 evaded a direct reply by referring us to the future All-Russian Constituent Assembly. . . .

It is for this reason that we are issuing this Universal Act to our people, proclaiming that henceforth we alone shall regulate our life. . . .

The Central *Rada* hopes that the non-Ukrainian peoples living on our land will also concern themselves with the maintenance of law and order in our country, and will, in this grave hour of general political anarchy, cooperate cheerfully with us to organize the autonomy of the Ukraine.

Young women use hoes to tend their crops in early 20th-century Ukraine.

Uezd

Uezd is the Russian word for "county."

Peasants, who made up four fifths of the population, adopted a wait-and-see attitude with regard to the Provisional Government and the issue of land reform. They believed the February Revolution would satisfy their yearning for more land, even if it meant the forcible confiscation of land from the gentry (landowners). The Provisional Government insisted that the resolution of this pressing problem had to wait until the meeting of the Constituent Assembly and postponed serious discussion of the matter. Notwithstanding its sympathetic hearing of peasant grievances, the Provisional Government was wary of violating the property rights of landowners. The Provisional Government therefore found itself in the delicate position of trying to balance two conflicting claims, and its failure to implement any land reform provoked the peasants, who began to take matters into their own hands by late summer. Not only did peasants seize land and destroy rent records, but they frequently set fire to the houses of the landowners and destroyed symbols of privilege and culture such as books, artwork, and furniture. These telegraph dispatches from fall 1917 paint a grim picture of events in the countryside.

TAMBOV, September 27.—Accurate information about the disorders in Kozlov *uezd* has not been received up to the present time. It is definitely known that one estate has been pillaged and twenty-five have been burned. . . .

SARATOV, October 10.—The agrarian disturbances in Serdobsky *uezd* embrace a large district. Peasants are stealing cattle, dividing the land and forests, and carrying off the grain. . . .

KISHINEV, October 10.—Peasants of Megura village, Beletsky *uezd*, influenced by propaganda, began to divide among themselves the land and pastures of the neighboring estates of Borchel and Slobodzei. . . .

VORONEZH, October 20.—In Zadonsky *uezd* . . . The estates of Chertkov and other landowners have been partially destroyed by the peasants. More than 60,000 puds of wheat and other grain have been burned. Valuable old furniture has been destroyed. . . .

SPAASK, October 27.—A wave of destruction swept over the whole *uezd*. Felling and stealing of trees is going on. The estate of Shreder has been pillaged and set on fire. The estate of Grabe has been destroyed, including his valuable library.

The Petrograd Soviet frequently published accounts of events in the countryside in its newspaper *Izvestiia* (News) that highlighted the destructive nature of the rural revolution.

VILLAGE OF TELIAZH, ORLOV GUBERNIIA (August 1917)

Each year the peasants rented their land from the landholder. This year they went to him as usual and he asked the usual rent. The peasants refused to pay it, and without much bargaining went home. There they called a meeting and decided to take up the land without paying. They put the plows and harrows on their carts and started for the field. When they arrived, they got into an argument as to the division of the land because it was not all the same quality. When they had quarreled for a time, one of the party proposed that they proceed to the landholder's warehouse, where some good alcohol was kept. They broke into the place, where they found fifty barrels. They drank and drank, but could not drink it all. They became so drunk that they did not know what they were doing and carelessly set the place on fire. Four burned to death; the ninety others escaped. A few days later they returned to the field and once more quarreled. It ended in a fight in which thirteen were left dead, fifteen were carried off badly injured, and, of these, four died.

Soon after that a quarrel started over the rich peasants. In the village there were eighteen farmers who had from twenty-five to thirty *desiatins* of land. They had a reserve of grain of various kinds. About thirty of the villagers seized this reserve. Another village meeting was called. A few of the more intelligent peasants came out strongly against this act of robbery. It ended in another fight in which three were killed and five badly wounded. One of these peasants, whose son was killed, shook his fist and shouted, "I will make you pay for my son."

In their demand for land peasants acted out of economic self-interest. Yet they justified their actions with reference to religious and moral values.

Pud
A *pud* is approximately 36 pounds.

Guberniia
Guberniia is the Russian word for "province."

Desiatin
A *desiatin* is equal to 2.7 acres.

This letter, written by a peasant who hoped newspapers would publish it, offers insight into the peasant world-view.

The land we share is our mother; she feeds us; she gives us shelter; she makes us happy and lovingly warms us; from the moment of our birth until we take our final rest in eternal sleep on her maternal breast, she is constantly cherishing us with her tender embraces. And now, despite this, land is put on the market for appraisal and so-called sale. But selling land created by the Heavenly Creator is a barbaric absurdity. The principal error here lies in the crude and monstrous assertion that the land, which God gave to all people so that they could feed themselves, could be anyone's property. This is just as much an act of violence as slavery. Land is the *common and equal legacy of all people* and so cannot be the object of private ownership by individual persons. . . . The bodies of men and women, and even more so their souls, should not be bought or sold, and the same goes for land, water, and air, because these things are the essential conditions for the support of people's bodies and souls. Ownership of land, as property, is one of the most unnatural of crimes. The repulsiveness of this crime goes unnoticed by us, the poor, only because in our immoral world this crime is deemed a right according to human laws. *Remember and do not forget* that you do not have *any right whatsoever* to the land, that you are a servant of that principle which gave you life, and so you have only obligations to fulfill the teaching of Christ. The land belongs to almighty God, as His creation, and to all the sons of man, as His heirs in equal part, just as we give it to our heirs in equal part for working on it, or to those who would work it with their own hands. It is the property not of any one generation but of all past, present, and future generations who work it and who will work it, each with their own hands, in order to feed themselves, and not according to the whim of the so-called private owners of the land. These people descend, for the sake of satisfying their own animal needs, to the level of cattle, while those people by whose labor an abundance of wealth is created struggle in poverty. Each person, upon being born into the world, does not bring any property with him into the world, and also no one being born is designated to own private land.

Many peasants continued to support the Provisional Government into the late summer, notwithstanding its failure to end the war and implement land reform. But as this "declaration" from peasants in one village suggests, their patience as "citizens" was running out.

We, the citizens of the village of Stenshino ... gathered for an assembly on 21 August of this year and discussed the difficult situation in our homeland and arrived at the conclusion that we, all the citizens, are bound to make every effort to support all the undertakings of the Provisional Government leading up to and including the Constituent Assembly. We declare: that we shall give all our grain to the front and the needy population, but we definitely remember that the land is for all the people and that a final long-awaited resolution of the land questions must be made by national decision, the decision of the Constituent Assembly.

Until it is conclusively decided and while the confusion over land mounts, impatience over our landlessness mounts, too. We insist before the Provisional Government that it not slow down but immediately issue the already completed Draft Provisional Land Law.

Only by this measure, we think, can the Provisional Government make sure that the peasantry works calmly until the Constituent Assembly.

The refusal of soldiers to obey their officers led to growing disarray and hurt the ability of the army to fight the German and Austrian troops. It also ensured that Russian counter-offensives had little chance of succeeding, as this army intelligence report from October 1917 makes clear.

Northern front—The situation in the army has not changed and may be described as a complete lack of confidence in the officers and the higher commanding personnel. The belief is growing among the soldiers that they cannot be punished for what they do.... The influence of Bolshevik ideas is spreading very rapidly. To this must be added a general weariness, an irritability, and a desire for peace at any price.

Any attempt on the part of the officers to regulate the life of the army ... is looked upon by the soldiers as counter-revolution.... The soldiers seem to believe that the arrest of Kornilov made void all the orders which he issued reinstating discipline. The army committees are in most cases helpless to guide

Orthodox priests bless members of the Women's Battalion of Death in Red Square before female soldiers leave for the front in early 1915. The Provisional Government established this all-female fighting force, which saw combat in the months after the collapse of the tsarist regime. Some 2,000 women joined the battalion, and many defended the Provisional Government housed in the Winter Palace during the Bolshevik insurrection in October 1917.

the mob and are often compelled to follow it so as not to lose completely the confidence of the masses. . . .

Western front—. . . . Because of general war weariness, bad nourishment, mistrust of officers, etc., there has developed an intense defeatist agitation accompanied by refusals to carry out orders, threats to the commanding personnel, and attempts to fraternize with Germans. Everywhere one hears voices calling for immediate peace, because, they say, no one will stay in the trenches during the winter. . . . There is a deep-rooted conviction among the rank and file that fraternization with the enemy is a sure way of attaining peace. . . .

Among the phenomena indicative of tendencies in the life in the rear of the Western front are the recent disturbances at the replacement depot in Gomel. On October 1 over eight thousand soldiers who were to be transferred to the front demanded to be sent home instead. . . . Incited by agitators they stormed the armory, took some fifteen hundred suits of winter equipment, . . .

Southwestern front—. . . . Defeatist agitation is increasing and the disintegration of the army is in full swing. The Bolshevik wave is growing steadily, owing to the general disintegration in the rear, the absence of strong power, and the lack of supplies and equipment. The dominant theme of conversation is peace at any price and under any condition. Every order, no matter what its source, is met with hostility. The dark soldier masses have become completely confused and lost in the midst of innumerable party slogans and programs, so that now they mistrust everyone and everything. . . .

. . . The soldiers are engaging in armed invasions of the surrounding country estates, plundering provisions . . . of which there is a scarcity in the army. Not a thing can be done to counteract this restlessness . . . as there is no force which could be relied upon in any attempt to enforce order. . . . The position of the commanding personnel is very difficult. There have been instances of officers committing suicide. . . .

The Bolshevik Rise to Power

Concern over Russia's future and growing social and political unrest was not a monopoly of upper-class Russians who feared the spread of Bolshevik appeal and influence. Even some advocates of the working class whose political sympathies leaned toward Bolshevism criticized certain aspects of the revolution. One such critic was Maxim Gorky, one of Rus-

sia's most influential writers and political ob**[...]**
revolution. Despite his reputation as being a "voice **[...]**
was alarmed at the direction popular unrest had taken **[...]**
1917. For Gorky the Bolsheviks were encouraging the wo**[...]**
diers to engage in wanton acts of violence and destruction. He **[...]**
against confusing freedom with anarchy, and he worried that the re**[...]**
of pent-up hostility and anger allowed the basest human sentiment**[...]**
and values to surface rather than the elevation of Russian society to a
higher moral plane where all people were liberated from oppression and
exploitation. The Bolsheviks may have gained from these developments,
but Gorky doubted whether Russian society as a whole would reap any
benefits.

Gorky wrote this editorial when he was editor of the socialist newspaper *New Life* in 1917. He believed that the Bolshevik seizure of power
was premature. Russia's cultural backwardness would give rise to more
bloodletting and destroy the human aspects of the socialist revolution.

Rumors are more and more persistently being spread that some "action by the Bolsheviks" will take place on October 20; . . . This means,
again, trucks tightly packed with people holding rifles and revolvers
in hands trembling with fear—and these rifles will fire at the windows of stores, at people, at anything! They will fire only because
those armed with them want to kill their fear. All the dark instincts
of the crowd irritated by the disintegration of life and by the lies and
filth of politics will flare up and fume, poisoning us with anger, hate,
and revenge; people will kill one another, unable to suppress their
own animal stupidity.

An unorganized crowd, hardly understanding what it wants,
will crawl out into the street, and, using this crowd as a cover, adventurers, thieves, and professional murderers will begin to "create the
history of the Russian revolution."

In a word, there will be repeated that bloody and senseless
slaughter which we have already witnessed and which has undermined the moral meaning of the revolution in the whole country
and has shaken its cultural significance.

It is very likely that this time events will assume an even more
bloody and destructive character and will deal an even more serious
blow to the revolution. . . .

The Central Committee of the Bolsheviks is obliged to refute the
rumors about the action of the 20th. It must do this if it is really a strong
and freely acting political body capable of guiding the masses, and not
a weak-willed toy of the moods of the wild crowd, not an instrument in
the hands of utterly shameless adventurers or crazed fanatics.

...ervers at the time of the

...of the people," Gorky

...by the summer of

...kers and sol-

...cautioned

...lease

The Bolshevik Rise to Power

51

...o inspired his audience and
...en though he had become a
...d not join the Bolsheviks until
...role in organizing the seizure of
...for the assumption of power by
...Provisional Government to safe-
...edom of the Russian people. This
...rotsky to the general public given
...f the Provisional Government illus-
...n support for their actions.

Trotsky immediately began to in-
flame the atmosphere—with his
skill and brilliance. I remember
how he at length and with extraordinary force sketched the picture,
difficult in its simplicity, of hardship
in the trenches. Before me flashed
thoughts of the inevitable incom-
patibility of the parts in this oratorical whole. But Trotsky knew what
he was doing. The essential thing
was the frame of mind. The political conclusions had been known for
a long time. You could make a mess
of them—provided only you did it
with sufficient striking effect.

Leon Trotsky and Lenin wanted the Bolshevik seizure of power to correspond with the opening of the Second Congress of Soviets, scheduled to meet in late October. Hopes that the Bolsheviks would seriously welcome the establishment of a coalition government of all socialist parties foundered when Lenin wound up at the head of an all-Bolshevik government.

Trotsky did it . . . with sufficient effect. The Soviet power was not only called on to abolish the hardship of the trenches. It would give land and would heal the internal ruination. Once more the remedies against starvation were repeated: a soldier, a sailor, and a working woman, who would requisition bread from the wealthy and send it free to the city and to the front. . . . But Trotsky went even further. . . .

> "The Soviet Power will hand over everything that there is in the country to the poor and to the men in the trenches. You, bour-geois, have two coats—give one to the soldier, who is cold in the trenches. You have warm boots? Stay at home. Your boots are needed by the worker. . . ."

These were very fine and righteous thoughts. They could not help arousing the enthusiasm of the crowd, which had been trained by the Tsarist whip. . . .

Around me was a spirit close to ecstasy. It seemed that the crowd would, at once, without any urging or leadership, sing some sort of religious hymn. . . . Trotsky formulated some sort of short general resolution, or proclaimed some sort of general formula, like, "we will stand for the cause of the workers and peasants to our last drop of blood."

Who is in favor? The crowd of thousands, as one man, raised their hands. I saw the raised hands and the burning eyes of men, women, youngsters, workers, soldiers, muzhiks, and—of typically lower middle-class persons. Were they in a soulful passion? Did they see, through the raised curtain, a corner of some sort of "Holy Land" toward which they were striving? Or were they imbued with a consciousness of the *political moment*, under the influence of the political agitation of the socialist? Do not ask! Accept it as it was. . . .

Trotsky continued to speak. The uncounted throng continued to hold their hands high. Trotsky rang forth the words:

> "Let this your voting be your oath—with all your strength, at any cost to support the Soviet, which is taking upon itself the great burden of carrying to a conclusion the victory of the revolution and to give land, bread, and peace!"

The countless crowd held high their hands. They agreed. They pledged themselves. . . . Again, just take it as it was: I with an unusually heavy feeling looked on this truly magnificent picture.

Trotsky finished. Some other person came out on the platform. But there was no reason to wait and watch any longer.

In all Petrograd approximately the same thing was happening. Everywhere there were the final inspections and the final oaths. Thousands, tens of thousands, hundreds of thousands of people. . . . This, in reality, was already an insurrection. The affair had already begun.

Lenin delivered this speech to the Congress of Soviets one day after the overthrow of the Provisional Government on October 25, 1917. In it he stressed that the Bolsheviks had acted in the name of the soviets, which now constituted the foundation of the new government. He also called for the end of the war and emphasized that the establishment of soviet power in Russia was a prelude to international proletarian revolution and the overthrown of capitalism throughout the world.

Comrades, the workmen's and peasants' revolution, the need of which the Bolsheviks have emphasized many times, has come to pass.

Muzhiks
Russian word meaning peasants.

Russia is betraying and selling out, and the Russian people wreak havoc and raise hell and are absolutely indifferent to their international fate. It is an unprecedented event in world history when a numerous people, which considers itself a great people, a world power despite all kinds of qualifications, has in eight months dug itself a grave with its own hands. . . .

—Diary of Iurii Got'e, history professor and critic of the revolution and the Bolsheviks, November 16, 1917

Workers gather for a political meeting at a factory in Petrograd in 1917. By the fall factory workers in the capital demanded "All Power to the Soviets!"

What is the significance of this revolution? Its significance is, in the first place, that we shall have a soviet government, without the participation of the bourgeoisie of any kind. The oppressed masses will of themselves form a government. The old state machinery will be smashed to bits and in its place will be created a new machinery of government by the soviet organizations. From now on there is a new page in the history of Russia, and the present, third Russian revolution shall in its final result lead to the victory of Socialism.

One of our immediate tasks is to put an end to the war at once. But in order to end the war, which is closely bound up with the present capitalistic system, it is necessary to overthrow capitalism itself. In this work we shall have the aid of the world labor movement, which has already begun to develop in Italy, England, and Germany.

A just and immediate offer of peace by us to the international democracy will find everywhere a warm response among the international proletarian masses. . . .

In the interior of Russia a very large part of the peasantry has said: Enough playing with the capitalists; we will go with the workers. We shall secure the confidence of the peasants by one decree, which will wipe out private property of the landowners. The peasants will understand that their only salvation is in union with the workers.

We will establish a real labor control on production.

We have now learned to work together in a friendly manner, as is evident from this revolution. We have the force of mass organization which has conquered all and which will lead the proletariat to world revolution.

We should now occupy ourselves in Russia in building up a proletarian socialist state.

Long live the world-wide socialistic revolution.

The Socialist Revolutionaries were advocates of peasant socialism who believed that Russia could escape the evils of industrial capitalism if the peasants, with the help of factory workers, overthrew the tsarist regime. Their vision of a socialist Russia differed from that of their fellow revolutionaries, the Mensheviks, who were adherents of Marxian socialism. At the time of the February Revolution, the Socialist Revolutionaries and Mensheviks commanded the allegiance of peasants and workers, respectively, while the Bolsheviks were a fringe group with very little influence.

Views of the Revolution

Born in 1906, Zinaïda Shakhovskoi was a member of one of Russia's most distinguished noble families. Shakhovskoi's recollections illustrate the fears and anxieties that gripped the nobility as the revolution took its course and the peasants grew more aggressive and challenged the property rights of the gentry. In her memoirs Shakhovskoi describes what it was like to live through the February Revolution while a pupil at the Empress Catherine Institute for Young Noble Ladies in Petrograd.

February 26, 1917

. . . I must confess, this first day of the February Revolution seemed to us, the seventh-grade pupils, just an exceptionally exciting day which liberated us from the tedious obligation to behave ourselves in a lady-like manner—which meant walking demurely with hands gently crossed over our stomach and making deep reverences when we saw one of our teachers. Discipline was shattered, to our great delight. . . .

. . . But there came the day when even we, the youngest of the pupils, became aware that something tragic and final had befallen the Russian Empire and all of us. On March 3, all the pupils and

An aristocratic family dines on the terrace of its country estate on the eve of World War I. Many noble families living in Moscow, St. Petersburg, and other large cities derived much of their income and necessities of life from the land they owned in the countryside.

teachers were assembled in the hall as usual for the morning prayers read by one of the highest-ranking pupils. For the first time in about two centuries the prayer for the Tsar and his family was to be omitted, the Emperor having abdicated on the previous day. The girl, who was about 18, stumbled over her words and was unable to pronounce, "Let us pray for the Provisional Government." She started to cry. The teachers and mistresses took to their handkerchiefs and soon the four or five hundred of us were sobbing over something that was lost forever.

The next day the mothers came to take their daughters away; Catherine's Institute was seeing its last days.

Following our mother, my sister Natasha and I stepped out, for good, from the Catherine Institute. I hardly recognized the capital which I had last seen two months ago returning from my winter vacation. All the glamour had left Petrograd; many shops were closed and in front of the others was an unfamiliar sight: long queues were waiting. There were few carriages and no policemen to be seen at the crossings; the streets were full of disorderly soldiers, with a few gloomy civilians hurrying along. . . .

Many nobles fled Petrograd for what they believed would be the safety of their country estates. But as Shakhovskoi notes, the chaos of the city was duplicated in rural Russia, where peasants engaged in their own brand of revolution.

February 27, 1917

. . . The mail was functioning and my mother received letters both from my father, who was living on our family estate Matovo, district of Viniev, government of Tula, and from our estate-agent, who was in charge of another estate, Pronya, in the neighboring district of Epiphan. All seemed quiet at Matovo and my father insisted that my mother should come there with us as soon as possible. Quite another picture was conveyed by the estate-agent of Pronya, an estate not linked with our family by ancient ties, having been in our possession only since 1915. There the situation got out of hand: As soon as revolution was announced, the peasants came in force, broke the government seals on the reservoirs of spirits impounded in our distillery, and went for the liquor. Some of them drowned themselves in the huge containers, but others went on with their drinking spree, and upon leaving the place said that they would come back and burn down everything. The land-agent declared that, since he was unable to cope with the situation, he was leaving and returning to his native Baltic province. . . .

Iurii Got'e was one of Russia's most prominent historians when the tsar abdicated. In July 1917 he began to keep a diary that chronicles the events overcoming Russia. Got'e once belonged to the Kadet Party, but he was unaffiliated with any political group when revolution broke out. He wrote in his diary that he hoped the Provisional Government would give new life to the Russian military and enable Russia to achieve a victory over the Germans and Austrians. His hopes were sadly dashed by the continuing poor performance of the army, which he attributed to the subversive propaganda and agitation of Bolsheviks, and the widespread social and political unrest swirling around him. He grew disillusioned with the Provisional Government and alarmed that revolutionary events would destroy the country he so dearly loved. He did not mince words and made clear where his political sympathies lay. He frequently referred to the Bolsheviks and their peasant and worker supporters as "gorillas," and gave vent to anti-Semitic sentiments when he associated Russia's Jews with Bolshevism, a popular but unfounded stereotype that has lasted until this day. Got'e also reveals the responsibility he placed on himself and other educated Russians to preserve culture from the onslaught of illiterate and uncultured workers and peasants. Finally, his diary offers a glimpse into the impact of the revolution on daily life. The economic situation for most people had grown dire during the year.

8–16 July 1917. Finis Russiae. The army is an army no more. Russia has lost the capacity to defend herself. The fundamental cause, of course, is the century-long decomposition of the old regime. With its fall, it provoked the pendulum swing to the left and the rise to domination of forces that have developed in the underground and are fit only for destruction. The destruction of the army, undertaken in the name of underground slogans that were designed for the struggle against tsarism, has of course brought forth the fruit it was meant to yield: transformation of an army that had fought for two-and-a-half years into a crowd of propagandized bandits. . . .

The fate of Russia, an extinct dinosaur or mastodon, is to be transformed into a weak and poor country standing in economic dependence on other countries, most likely Germany. The bolsheviks as the true symbol of the Russian people—. . . : a mixture of stupidity, vulgarity, uncultured willfulness, lack of principle, hooliganism. . . .

Heart and soul have been torn out, all ideals shattered. Russia has no future. We have no present and no future. The only reason left for living is in order to feed and preserve our families—there is nothing else. The final fall of Russia as a great and unified power, as a result of internal, not external, causes, not directly to enemies but to our own flaws and inadequacies. . . .

26 July . . . Things are no better at the front. General Kornilov expects many more failures on all fronts. The account of the meeting

When it became illegal to criticize the Kremlin and its policies, people turned to the telling of jokes in privacy to close friends and relatives. Telling such anecdotes (and listening to them) was a dangerous activity that could lead to denunciation and prison; however, political jokes enabled people to express their frustrations with the imperfections of the economic system, food shortages, and the failings of Soviet ideology.

A doctor, an engineer, and a Communist were arguing about who was the first person on earth.

Doctor: "I was the first person, for without me, nobody could have made Eve from Adam's rib."

Engineer: "No, I was first, because without engineers, the world couldn't have been built from chaos."

Communist: "And who do you think created chaos?"

Democraps

In Russian *der'mokraty*, a play on the words "democrats" and "crap."

Born in 1868, the writer Maxim Gorky portrayed the world of Russia's poor to a reading public that knew little about that segment of Russian society. In his short stories, novels, autobiography, and plays, Gorky focused on social themes, and in his private life he became involved with the revolutionary movement. The tsarist government expelled him from Russia after the 1905 Revolution.

of statesmen in the Winter Palace produces a sorry impression. I was not left with the impression that Kerensky will be able to cope with his task. The disintegration of all of Russia is undoubtedly going forward with gigantic steps and the organic process of rebuilding some kind of remnants out of what used to be called Russia has yet to begin. . . .

24 September. The strike has begun. What will come of it and how will it influence the Russian democraps. I heard that expression yesterday, and I like it. In spite of the marvelous weather, I am sitting in my domestic retreat—the Moscow streets are physically repulsive to me, with their rude, unbridled, and idle crowd. . . .

Soon after the Bolshevik seizure of power Maxim Gorky realized that the revolution had veered off-course, with Lenin and other Bolshevik leaders responsible for the growing chaos and disorder.

November 7, 1917

. . . Lenin, Trotsky and their companions have already become poisoned with the filthy venom of power, and this is evidenced by their shameful attitude toward freedom of speech, the individual and the sum total of those rights for the triumph of which democracy struggled.

Blind fanatics and dishonest adventurers are rushing madly, supposedly along the road to the "social revolution"; in reality this is the road to anarchy, to the destruction of the proletariat and of the revolution. . . .

The working class cannot fail to understand that Lenin is only performing a certain experiment on their skin and on their blood, that he is striving to push the revolutionary mood of the proletariat to its furthest extreme and see—what will come of this?

Of course, he does not believe in the possibility of the victory of the proletariat in Russia under the present conditions, but perhaps he is hoping for a miracle.

The working class should know that miracles do not occur in real life, that they are to expect hunger, complete disorder in industry, disruption of transportation, and protracted bloody anarchy followed by a no less bloody and gloomy reaction.

This is where the proletariat is being led by its present leader, and it must be understood that Lenin is not an omnipotent magician but a cold-blooded trickster who spares neither the honor nor the life of the proletariat.

The workers must not allow adventurers and madmen to heap shameful, senseless, and bloody crimes on the head of the proletariat, for which not Lenin but the proletariat itself will pay. . . .

Some six weeks after the Bolsheviks assumed power, Gorky mused that the revolution had encouraged the cruel and violent tendencies of the crowd to dominate public life.

December 7, 1917

"The proletariat is the creator of a new culture"—a wonderful dream of the triumph of justice, reason, and beauty, a dream of man's victory over brute and beast is contained in these words; thousands of people of all classes have perished in the struggle for the realization of this dream. . . .

What will the revolution offer that is new, how will it change the bestial Russian way of life, and will it bring much light into the darkness of the people's life?

. . . Here is how democracy tries its sinners. A thief was caught near the Aleksandrovsky Market, the crowd there and then beat him up and took a vote—by which death should the thief be punished: drowning or shooting? They decided on drowning and threw the man into the icy water. But with great difficulty he managed to swim out and crawl up on the shore; one of the crowd then went up to him and shot him.

The middle ages of our history were an epoch of abominable cruelty, but even then if a criminal sentenced to death by a court fell from the gallows, he was allowed to live.

How do the mob trials affect the coming generation?

A thief, beaten half to death, is taken by soldiers to the Moyka Canal to be drowned; he is all covered with blood, his face is completely smashed, and one eye has come out. A crowd of children accompanies him; later some of them return from the Moyka and, hopping up and down, joyfully shout:

"They sunk him, they drowned him!"

These are our children, the future builders of life. The life of a man will be cheap in their estimation, but man—one should not forget this!—is the finest and most valuable creation of nature, the very best there is in the universe. The war has valued man cheaper than a tiny piece of lead; we were just indignant at this evaluation and reproached the "imperialists" for it—but whom shall we reproach for the daily, brutal massacre of people? . . .

Every night for almost two weeks crowds of people have been robbing wine cellars, getting drunk, banging each other over the head with bottles, cutting their hands with fragments of glass, and wallowing like pigs in filth and blood. . . .

CHAPTER 3

The Consolidation of Bolshevik Rule, 1918–1921

Young, homeless boys, barefoot and smoking cigarettes, play cards on the street. War and revolution left millions of children orphaned and homeless.

The Bolsheviks' first order of business was to issue a series of revolutionary decrees that satisfied the aspirations of workers, soldiers, and peasants. From the outset the new regime was intent on promoting the interests of the people in accordance with Marxist principles. The new leaders of Russia granted peasants the right to use all land, which was now nationalized, or brought under the control of the state. They also confirmed the practice of workers' control of factories and promised to enter into immediate peace negotiations with Germany after first arranging an armistice or cease-fire. They also guaranteed national minorities the right to self-determination, including political independence, and promised that elections to the Constituent Assembly, planned for late November, would proceed according to schedule.

The second order of business was the consolidation of Bolshevik rule through the establishment of soviet power outside the capital city, a process that took from a few days to several weeks. The Bolsheviks also demonstrated an unwillingness to share control with other revolutionary parties, which were wary of the Bolsheviks' attempt to monopolize power. In January 1918 Lenin barred delegates to the Constituent Assembly from meeting and unceremoniously shut down what would have been Russia's first genuinely, popularly elected national forum. Within months of seizing power, the Bolsheviks were well on their way to establishing a one-party dictatorship. It was clear that the Bolsheviks were not interested in sharing political power and would not tolerate criticism and opposition of any sort. They suppressed the free press, closing down journals and newspapers, and increasingly persecuted political parties of all stripes, including those on the left such as the Mensheviks and Socialist Revolutionaries. This was particularly so once representatives of these two parties did well in elections to local soviets in 1918 and 1919. Many Mensheviks and Socialist Revolutionaries chose to leave Russia, drop out of politics, or join forces with the Bolsheviks. By 1921 the Bolsheviks had forced all remaining prominent Mensheviks into exile, and in 1922 they staged a political trial at which some Socialist Revolutionaries were convicted of anti-Soviet activity and then exiled. By the early 1920s, then, the Bolsheviks were firmly ensconced in power and had established a one-party dictatorship.

Between 1918 and 1920 the Bolsheviks found themselves engaged in a brutal war of survival with the Whites, comprised of several armies under the direction of former tsarist military officers. The civil war was a particularly bloody affair, with both sides suffering enormous casualties and civilians caught in the middle of the hostilities. Both White and Red forces engaged in the arbitrary execution of real and suspected enemies and terrorized the enemy with displays of wanton violence and bloodletting such as beheadings and pouring water on naked prisoners, and then leaving them out in the cold to freeze to death.

The outbreak of civil war in mid-1918 prompted the fledgling government to adopt measures that not only helped the Bolsheviks maintain power but also contributed to the strengthening of their dictatorship. Despite all odds, the Bolsheviks prevailed for a number of reasons, not the least of which was that the various anti-Bolshevik armies did not coordinate their forces, which were frequently disorganized and marked by personal rivalries among the leaders. In addition, it was clear to the vast majority of peasants and workers that a White victory would mean the restoration of the old regime and the end of the social, political, and economic benefits brought about by the imposition of Bolshevik rule. Thus, most peasants and workers passively, and sometimes actively, supported the Bolsheviks.

Furthermore, the Bolsheviks ensured their victory by implementing policies designed to mobilize all the material and labor resources under their control for the war effort. Known as War Communism, these measures were an emergency program that required the regime *to assume greater control over all aspects of the economy in its fight for survival and to depend on a growing bureaucracy to implement its policies. War Communism entailed the confiscation of grain from the peasants, nationalization of industry, and the end of a market economy. Centralization of power in the hands of the Bolsheviks, renamed the Communist Party during the civil war, meant the end of grassroots participation of the common person in the affairs of state and death to soviet democracy. With their backs against the wall, the Bolsheviks believed it was imperative to defend the revolution at all costs, even if it meant antagonizing the very groups in society in whose name the revolution was carried out.*

The dire straits of the civil war led the Bolsheviks to renege on many of the promises and principles of 1917 and created the foundation of an authoritarian, one-party dictatorial state. The rulers of the world's first socialist government survived the crucible of the civil war, but the cost was the further deterioration of the economy and standards of living as well as the alienation of society. Six years of war, revolution, and civil strife had taken their toll on the Russian people, with between 15,000,000 and 20,000,000 casualties from war, disease, and starvation. Millions more had been wounded and maimed, while countless others found themselves homeless and on the move, as the Bolsheviks and Whites paid no attention to the impact their fighting had on civilians. Moreover, industrial output in 1920 was approximately one-fifth of the pre-World War I level, and agricultural production had dropped precipitously as a result of all the death and destruction. Factory workers were thrown out of work as one factory after another shut down, and food shortages prompted millions of urban residents to return to the countryside. In Moscow and Petrograd, for instance, the number of inhabitants in 1921 was half of what it was in 1917. The Bolsheviks now faced the daunting task of rebuilding the country.

Orphans

Known as *besprizorniki* (homeless waifs), orphaned children roamed the countryside and flooded cities, looking for food and shelter and resorting to crime, begging, sleeping in the streets, and prostitution. The government tried to accommodate them in children's homes, but the enormity of the problem overwhelmed the regime, whose resources were already stretched thin.

The Fate of the Royal Family

Tsar Nicholas II and Empress Alexandra, along with their four daughters and one son, were placed under "house arrest" after the collapse of the monarchy. A plan to exile the royal family to England fell apart after the British government, heeding the appeals of Russian socialists who feared that Nicholas might become a rallying point for counterrevolution, withdrew its offer for asylum. The Provisional Government then sent Nicholas and his family to the city of Tobolsk in Siberia, and in the spring of 1918 the Bolsheviks moved them to Ekaterinburg, located in the Ural Mountains. Worried about attempts to free Nicholas by monarchist enemies

As a child, Grigorii Valentinov left his parents during the famine and found his way to Moscow, where he took to a life of crime and became addicted to cocaine. He told a journalist the following:

I began to hang around train stations and markets, looking with dark thieving eyes for something to swipe. When evening comes there is nowhere to sleep. You have to sleep somewhere on the street, on the cold dirty grit. In the morning you get up filthy and go about business. Sometimes, when you are unable to steal anything, you go around hungry, mean, and depressed.

of the regime, the Bolshevik government adopted stringent measures to supervise the daily lives of the royal family. The soldiers charged with guarding them treated their prisoners with contempt and disrespect and constantly stole personal items from them. In July 1918, fearing that Ekaterinburg might fall to advancing anti-Bolshevik forces, local officials executed Nicholas, Alexandra, and their five children, along with the royal family's personal physician, Evgenii Botkin.

Several participants in the execution have described the scene. In 1919 Pavel Medvedev, commander of the guard at the house where the royal family was imprisoned, described the shooting of the Romanovs to a court run by the Whites who were temporarily in charge of Ekaterinburg.

None of the members of the imperial family asked anybody any questions in my presence. There were no tears, no sobbing, either. Having descended the stairs leading from the second entrance hall to the lower floor, we went into the courtyard and from there through a second door (counting from the gates) into the inner lodgings of the lower floor. Yurovsky showed the way. They were brought into the corner room on the lower floor adjacent to the sealed storage room. Yurovsky ordered that chairs be brought: his assistant brought three chairs. One chair was given to Her Majesty, the other to the sovereign, the third to the heir. Her Majesty sat by the wall with a window, closer to the back pillar of the arch. Behind her stood three daughters (I know them all very well by sight, as I saw each of them taking walks nearly every day, but I don't really know them by name). The heir and His Majesty sat side by side, almost in the middle of the room. Behind the heir's chair stood Doctor Botkin. The maid (I do not know her name—a tall woman) stood to the left of the door leading to the sealed storage room. One of the imperial daughters (the fourth one) stood with her. Two servants stood in the left-hand corner (from the entrance), by the wall adjacent to the storage room.

The maid had a pillow in her hands. The daughters brought little pillows with them also. One of the little pillows was put on the seat of Her Majesty's chair, the other on the heir's seat. It seems that all of them suspected the fate that was about to befall them, but no one made a single sound. Simultaneously, eleven people walked into the same room: . . . Yurovsky sent me out, saying, "Go to the street, to see whether anybody's there and whether the shots will be heard." I walked out into the courtyard enclosed by a tall fence, and I heard the sound of shots before I had reached the street. I immediately returned to the house (only 2 or 3 minutes had gone by), and when I entered that room where the shooting had taken place, I saw that all the members of the imperial family—tsar, tsaritsa, four daughters, and the heir— were already lying on the floor with multiple wounds to their bodies. The blood flowed in streams. The doctor, the maid, and the two servants were also dead. When I entered the room, the heir was still alive—moaning. Yurovsky walked up to him and shot him point-blank two or three times. The heir fell silent. The murder scene, the smell and sight of blood, made me nauseous. Before the murder, Yurovsky passed out Nagant revolvers to everyone. . . .

The children of Tsar Nicholas II and Tsarina Alexandra pose for a family portrait. All five were executed, along with their parents, in the summer of 1918 while under house arrest in Siberia.

Historians offer contrasting accounts of who ordered the execution. For many years scholars believed that Bolsheviks in Ekaterinburg acted on their own, without direct orders from Lenin and the government now housed in Moscow. In early 1918 fear of approaching German troops prompted the Bolsheviks to move government and party headquarters to the Kremlin, the site of tsarist power before Peter the Great moved the capital to St. Petersburg. However, recently revealed documents indicate that the top party leadership was planning to put Nicholas on trial, but the outbreak of civil war in mid-1918 and the very real threat that the Whites might overrun Ekaterinburg made a trial impractical. These materials strongly suggest but do not demonstrate conclusively that Lenin personally commanded the execution of Nicholas and his family. The most likely scenario is that Moscow ordered the authorities in Ekaterinburg to prepare for the trial of Nicholas, but also gave standing orders to execute the former tsar in the event the military situation in the Urals did not permit the holding of the trial. In any event, the murder of the royal family is considered to be one of the most infamous moments in the 20th century.

Yakov Yurovsky was in charge of the execution and in 1920 offered the Bolshevik government a graphic description of the execution and burial of the royal family. Killing the four daughters was difficult because they had sewn 18 pounds of diamonds and jewelry into their clothing. In addition, he explained why Tsar Nicholas and his family were murdered.

. . . A downstairs room was selected that had walls of plastered wood (to prevent [the bullets from] ricocheting); all the furniture was removed. The detachment was at the ready in the next room. The

Romanovs suspected nothing. The comm. [commandant] went to get them personally, alone, and led them downstairs to the room below. Nich. was carrying A. [Aleksei] in his arms; the rest carried little pillows and other small things with them. Walking into the empty room A. F. [Alexandra Fyodorovna] asked: "What, there isn't even a chair? One isn't even allowed to sit down?" The comm. ordered two chairs to be brought. Nich. seated A. on one, and A.F. sat down on the other. The commandant ordered the rest to stand in a row.

Tsar Nicholas II gardens with his family while under house arrest at his estate outside Petrograd. A devoted husband and father, Nicholas lacked the vision and skills needed to lead Russia through a time of social and economic change. He remained committed to the preservation of the autocracy and resisted reforms that would diminish his power.

When they had taken their places, he called in the detachment. When the detachment came in, the commandant told the R-ovs that, in light of the fact that their relatives in Europe were continuing their aggression against Soviet Russia, the Ural [Regional Soviet] Executive Committee had decreed that they were to be shot. Nicholas turned his back to the detachment, his face toward his family, then, as though collecting himself, turned to the commandant with the question: "What? What?" The comm. hurriedly repeated his statement and ordered the detachment to get ready. The detachment had been given instructions earlier on whom to shoot and were ordered to aim directly for the heart to avoid a large amount of blood and to finish them off more quickly. Nicholas, again turning to the family, said nothing more; the others made a few incoherent exclamations; this all lasted a few seconds. Then the shooting started; [it] lasted for two to three minutes. Nich. was killed on the spot by the comm. himself. A.F. died immediately after that and the other R-ovs (altogether 12 people were shot [in fact, 11 people were shot]): N., A. F., four daughters (Tatiana, Olga, Maria, and Anastasia), Doctor Botkin, the footman Trupp, the cook . . . another cook, and a lady-in-waiting. . . . A., three of his sisters, the lady-in-waiting, and Botkin were still alive. They had to be shot again. This surprised the comm. because they had aimed for the heart. It was also surprising that the bullets from the pistols ricocheted off something and jumped about the room like hail. When they tried to finish off one of the girls with bayonets, the bayonet could not pierce the corset. Thanks to all of this, the entire procedure, including "verification" (feeling the pulse, etc.), took around 20 minutes.

Opposition and Criticism

Soon after they seized power in October 1917, the Bolsheviks created a secret police organization to combat political opposition. Known as the "Cheka" (an acronym based on the first two Russian words of its official title, "Extraordinary Commission to Combat Counter-Revolution and Sabotage"), the secret police was directed by Felix Dzerzhinsky. They operated with virtually no restraints and paid little attention to the niceties of law and legality. At first the Cheka sought to weed out opponents, real and suspected, of the revolution, whom they threw into prison and sometimes executed, but they soon targeted any critic of the socialist regime and its policies. The secret police considered as "counter-revolutionary" any activity it deemed injurious to the cause of socialism and labeled as "enemies of the people" those accused of counter-revolutionary behavior. In 1918 the Cheka arrested 47,348 persons, and in 1919 detained 80,662 so-called counter-revolutionaries. The Bolsheviks released many of these prisoners after investigation, but they nonetheless executed some 10,000.

In a December 1917 letter to Dzerzhinsky, Vladimir Lenin outlined the reasons for establishing the Cheka. Placing the blame for serious economic and social problems on the shoulders of their genuine and alleged opponents allowed the Bolsheviks to argue that their policies were not the cause of some of the regime's problems.

In connection with your report today dealing with the struggle against sabotage and counter-revolution, is it not possible to issue the following decree: Struggle Against Counter-Revolution and Sabotage.

The bourgeoisie, landholders, and all wealthy classes are making desperate efforts to undermine the revolution which is aiming to safeguard the interest of the toiling and exploited masses. The bourgeoisie is having recourse to the vilest crimes, bribing society's lowest elements and supplying liquor to these outcasts with the purpose of bringing on pogroms. The partisans of the bourgeoisie, especially the higher officials, bank clerks, etc., are sabotaging and organizing strikes in order to block the government's efforts to reconstruct the state on a socialistic basis. Sabotage has spread even

Born the son of a wealthy Polish landowner in 1877, Felix Dzerzhinsky became a revolutionary when he was 18 years old. He embraced Bolshevism after the February 1917 revolution, rose to the top ranks of the party, and organized the secret police to combat counter-revolutionary threats to the fledgling Bolshevik government in December 1917.

In a June 1918 newspaper interview, Felix Dzerzhinsky, head of the secret police, noted, "We stand for organized terror—this should be frankly admitted. Terror is an absolute necessity during times of revolution. Our aim is to fight against the enemies of the Soviet Government and of the new order of life. Among such enemies are our political adversaries, as well as bandits, speculators, and other criminals who undermine the foundations of the Soviet Government. To these we show no mercy. We terrorize the enemies of the Soviet Government in order to stop crime at its inception."

In March 1918 Russia signed the Brest-Litovsk peace treaty with Germany and Austria, named for the Polish city where negotiations took place. Russia surrendered nearly a quarter of its territory and population and one third of its industry, and the Bolsheviks also agreed to recognize Ukraine, Poland, Finland, and the Baltic countries of Lithuania, Estonia, and Latvia as independent states. The unilateral withdrawal of Russia from the war angered the Allies, who sent troops to three Russian port cities to protect military supplies and help the Whites overthrow the new regime.

American troops enter Vladivostok, a port in the Russian Far East. After the Bolsheviks signed a peace treaty with Germany in early 1918, England, France, and the United States sent troops to prevent munitions and military equipment from falling into German hands. American troops remained in Russia until 1920.

to the food-supply organizations, and millions of people are threatened with famine. Special measures must be taken to fight counter-revolution and sabotage.

The Bolshevik seizure of power was more than a change in political regime: it had an impact on daily life that reflected social tensions and resentments between lower-class Russians and the well-to-do. For many people, the change in governments was an excuse for antisocial behavior and a way for the have-nots to get even with those with money, status, and privilege. The revolution was seen by many as a time to revel in the overthrow of the old and celebrate the coming of the new society, which often translated into drinking themselves into oblivion. A breakdown of social order was evident throughout 1917 and into 1918 as many peasants, workers, and other urban dwellers engaged in acts of wanton vandalism and hooliganism, not all of which were directed against the wealthy. Workers even meted out street-style punishment to other workers suspected of stealing.

Menshevik newspapers reported on civil disturbances, disease, and public drunkenness in the provinces in early 1918. In their destruction of furniture, art, and property, peasants rejected the alien values and beliefs of the urban, Western Europeanized upper classes.

From Danov come reports that the palace of the former governor of Riazan has been destroyed. . . . The furniture and art objects of the palace were valued at a million rubles. . . . Pictures of noted artists were burned. The peasant women grabbed the Sèvres vases and now use them for sour cream. . . . The stock farm was looted and the thoroughbred stock driven off. . . . Drunkenness and looting have spread. . . . In some cases the peasants have begun to attack each other.

From Kharkov come reports of the destruction of estates, houses, art treasures, grain, and livestock. . . . The Kropivnitsky collection of rare books, pictures, manuscripts, and notes is no more. This is a great loss. . . .

Not a single estate in Tula Province has escaped either partial or total destruction. . . .

Almost all the grain is turned into vodka. Practically every village has from fifteen to twenty distilleries. Rye sells at from forty-five to fifty rubles a *pud*, but if turned into home brew . . . it brings twice that amount. So much alcohol is distilled that there is enough for local consumption and for export. . . .

When under the influence of strong drink, men loot estates and destroy state and private forests. . . .

The villages are having a "big drunk." Village expeditions are sent to procure the "national wealth," as vodka is called. . . . These expeditions go armed with guns, revolvers, and clubs. . . . Not infrequently they run into "expeditions" from other villages and a pitched battle takes place. Wild, drunken orgies are the order of the day. Old men, young men, women, and minors drink. Even tiny children are given alcohol to put them to sleep so that their parents may drink undisturbed. Licentiousness and gambling keep company with this drunkenness. Venereal diseases are spreading fast. . . . Typhus is an everyday visitor in the village. . . .

Villagers tear down a house for firewood in Moscow during the civil war. Like food and other essentials, wood for cooking and heat was in short supply.

Like many other middle- and upper-class Russians, the history professor Iurii Got'e and his family were forced to share their living quarters with workers and their families and soldiers. Eventually they were forced out of their apartment and found refuge at a museum where he was associate director. For the Bolsheviks, the sharing of living space was a sign of social and economic justice. In this excerpt Got'e describes the effect of the changing political and social order on his family's life.

March 1, 1918. . . . There was a meeting of the building committee in the evening. I had not attended for a long time; but one should go—the dog deputies and their henchmen will soon make an assault on the bourgeoisie's apartments; a new tax is a possibility; so are attempts to squeeze in more tenants. They say, however, that one can buy them off, and the price is 500 rubles.

March 11, 1918. All day one has heard only about the "requisitions of housing," that is simply the eviction of people from their apartments with twenty-four, forty-eight, or seventy-two hours' notice, seizure of mansions, and similar acts for the good of the people. They are taking away everything that was left; after money—they are robbing personal property. Soon the haves will become beggars, and the robbers will make off with the spoils, . . .

Under the supervision of Bolshevik guards, two ex-tsarist officers clear the streets in Petrograd in 1918. For Russia's new rulers, the revolution was an opportunity to seek revenge against the representatives of both the tsarist regime and Provisional Government. Nobles and other well-to-do Russians unaccustomed to physical labor were required to do public labor such as sweeping streets and shoveling snow.

June 14, 1918. . . . I think that one of the most interesting phenomena of our present day is the universal weight loss that is occurring, and not just from hunger alone. True, hunger is felt by many, but by no means all, and not as yet in a severe form; and yet everyone has lost weight—some 15 percent, others 20 percent of their weight, yet others even more. Undoubtedly nervous tension is of great significance here. Thoughts and anguish undermine and desiccate human organisms; the grief of people who in full awareness see the abyss into which we continue to slide is so strong and so deep that it cannot fail to be reflected in their physical nature, just as the fact that the well-fed inhabitant can at any moment be stripped naked and robbed cannot fail to affect him. . . .

January 5, 1919. . . . My wife is being ordered to shovel snow tomorrow—that is yet another touch of contemporary life. We are surrounded by such "touches"; . . .

January 6, 1919. This morning I hauled sauerkraut down the streets of Moscow in the company of A. I. Iakovlev, just as much a university professor as I, . . . and then I scraped snow from the street. . . .

January 9, 1919. The specter of hunger is looming ever nearer and tighter. I took a stroll around Moscow today and was somehow especially horror-struck by this dead and murdered city; one thought—to flee, and more than ever before I have the firm view that [we] should prepare for departure.

February 24, 1919. The question of doubling up is being clarified: today we spent the last day in our dining room; tomorrow we will give it up either to Babogin . . . with three children and a witch for a wife, or to Rubtsov, an engineer with a big family. Such are the vicissitudes of contemporary life. The thought is growing ever stronger that the complete liquidation of the apartment is inevitable. . . .

February 25, 1919. The moving inside our apartment has been done; fatigue, disorder, dismay; all this is so barbaric and so unnecessary, and so contemporary. . . .

February 27, 1919. Two days were spent in moving, and here we are now, crowded into two rooms that barely accommodate that part of our belongings we need for living. Try in such conditions to study and contribute to scholarship, that is, to fulfill the obligation from which the Bolsheviks have not excused us. At first I was very sad to leave another third of the apartment and remain in the two back rooms; sad, because when we moved into this apartment, we thought it would be our apartment for life, because it suited us in all respects. The fact remains that it is impossible to live in such crowded conditions and a way out will have to be sought by moving into the museum, which I have refused to do for an entire twenty years.

February 11, 1921. The heat is being turned off here. Two months of extreme cold are in store. The task now is to supply enough fuel for the little stove in the bedroom. There you have the main concern of the day!

Living conditions were dire throughout Russia during the civil war. Alexis Babine, a Russian-born American who found himself teaching English at the university in Saratov, a city on the Volga River several hundred miles southeast of Moscow, confirms the breakdown of law and order and shows us how urban Russians took matters of justice in their own hands.

December 28, 1917. . . . The landlady . . . explained to me that the maid had gone to see a lynching. It turned out that at about 10 A.M. three robbers got into a house nearly opposite ours. The inmates managed to raise an alarm, one of the robbers was killed outright, one ran away, and one was caught by soldiers. The crowd that had assembled in front of the house roared for the last named—and our maid hastened there to see the execution.

Our servant soon returned with her story. When she got to the scene, soldiers were killing the second man with their bayonets. The body was put on a sleigh, and the face covered with a piece of fiber matting. But the matting would slip off and expose the blood-covered head and the face pierced with bayonets. That victim was a young man, almost a boy. . . .

The crowds are said to become perfectly frantic on such occasions and invariably demand immediate execution. A pious and

Children with their limbs shriveled to the size of sticks and their bellies horribly bloated by eating grass and herbs, which they were unable to digest, clustered 'round our windows begging piteously for bread—for life itself—in a dreadful ceaseless whine. We could not help them. Here and there it was possible to give one youngster a meal, but if we had distributed every scrap of food on our train, it would have been as nothing to feed this multitude.

—American industrialist Armand Hammer while traveling in the Soviet Union in 1921

Bodies of young and old, clothed and unclothed, were stacked high in the morgue during the terrible famine that gripped Russia in 1921–22.

charitable old lady who happened to be present at the lynching of a housebreaker goaded on the crowd, though under ordinary circumstances she would not hurt a fly. . . .

December 29, 1917. Yesterday's execution of the housebreakers was the work of women, exclusively, who surrounded the building after the alarm had been raised. They got hold of heavy sticks of wood and pounded the captives on their heads, even after they, dead, had been placed on a sleigh.

December 31, 1917. This morning I read a Bolshevik notice on a board fence . . . to the effect that searches of private residences will be made all over the city for concealed stores of provisions. . . .

January 15, 1918. The well-to-do people are being expelled from their residences to unsanitary basements and to hovels on the outskirts of the city, while the poor are encouraged to occupy the rich men's "palaces." But the benighted beggars prefer to remain in their izbas (huts) and leave the promised "palaces" to Bolshevik princes and their hirelings.

April 27, 1918. Lynch law has become quite fashionable in Russian villages. I have been told of a recent case when a man was sentenced by peasants for adultery, was killed and thrown into a grave, while the woman who betrayed her husband was put on top of her paramour and buried alive. . . .

December 29, 1918. Sunday. Last year the bourgeois tenants were driven out of the large two-story brick apartment house across the street from us, and the building was used as a barracks for "the pride and glory of the revolution." Soldiers began gradually to dismantle it of metal work and of everything else of value. The building had to be abandoned when cold weather came, and now only a ghastly ruin of a dilapidated brickwork remains: doors, window frames, windowsills, and everything else that could be used for firewood was carried off by neighbors—the normal, accustomed supply of cheap wood no longer coming in rafts from the far north, since the forests there had been declared the property of the Soviets, and since nobody wants to work for the Soviets.

June 9, 1920. My diet: black bread, butter, and Soviet coffee for breakfast (at 5:30 A.M..); potato or millet soup and some (very little) millet pudding or mashed potatoes for dinner (12:30 P.M.), and bread, butter, and Soviet coffee for supper. Sometimes I prepare a hasty Russian dish of mashed black bread seasoned with sunflower oil and diluted with water, . . .

In 1921 famine struck as a two-year drought combined with the already dismal state of affairs in agriculture to threaten the lives of tens of millions of people. The specter of starvation haunted the country until 1923 as some 5,000,000 people died; in the most affected regions, more than 90 percent of children under the age of 3 died. In some instances, parents took to killing their young children, and cannibalism was not an unknown phenomenon. The toll undoubtedly would have been higher had it not been for the efforts of future American president Herbert Hoover, who headed the American Relief Administration and directed the shipment and distribution of food to starving Russians. The American Relief Administration fed more than 10 million people daily and continued its activities until mid-1923.

James Goodrich, a former governor of Indiana, visited the famine-stricken area of the Soviet Union in the fall of 1921. His report to Hoover, which was also read to the Committee on Foreign Affairs of the U.S. House of Representatives, offers a very grim picture of the desperate situation in those regions affected by the famine.

I saw on every hand evidences of the greatest care that nothing having any food value be wasted. Cabbage leaves, melon rinds, and articles of this kind ordinarily thrown away are now utilized.

In one commune . . . I did not notice a single dog, a rather unusual condition for Russia, and on inquiry the local secretary of the commune told me that they had butchered about all of them and made them into bologna and sausage for use this winter. . . .

I could tell you stories of want, suffering, and death due to underfeeding and starvation. Of an old peasant found at Kazan last week along the roadside dead with a little dead child in his arms. Of another father at the same place without food, seeking, with three children, to enter a boat to go down the river, where he might find help, and when told but two of the children could go promptly threw the youngest in the river and boarded the boat, saying "If I cannot go, all three must die; it is better that one should die and the others

Family cannibalism during the famine of 1921–22.

February 14, 1922. Having run out of supplies, a woman in one of the famine-stricken districts began to use the body of her husband who had died of starvation for food. When local authorities got on to the fact and tried to remove what was left of the corpse, the wife and children of the dead man stuck to it in a state of wild frenzy shouting: "We won't give him up—we will eat him ourselves, he is ours."

February 22, 1922. A medical inspector of ours, driving through . . . village, caught glimpse of a couple of little girls running toward the road. He looked back and saw the girls pick up the fresh, warm horse dung and eat it.

—Diary of Alexis Babine, an American teaching in a provincial city

Red Army Oath

1. I, son of the laboring people, citizen of the Soviet Republic, assume the title of warrior in the Worker-Peasant Army.

2. Before the laboring classes of Russia and the entire world, I accept the obligation to carry this title with honor, to study the art of war conscientiously, and to guard national and military property from spoil and plunder as if it were the apple of my eye.

3. I accept the obligation to observe revolutionary discipline and unquestioningly carry out all orders of my commanders, who have been invested with their rank by the power of the Worker-Peasant government.

4. I accept the obligation to restrain myself and my comrades from all conduct that might debase the dignity of citizens of the Soviet Republic, and to direct all my thoughts and actions to the great cause of liberating the laboring masses.

5. I accept the obligation to answer every summons of the Worker-Peasant government to defend the Soviet Republic from all danger and the threats of all enemies, and to spare neither my strength nor my very life in the battle for the Russian Soviet Republic, for the cause of socialism and the brotherhood of peoples.

6. If I should with malicious intent go back on this solemn vow, then let my fate be universal contempt and the righteous hand of revolutionary law chastise me.

live," and they let him go his way. Of two peasant girls we found . . . their parents dead of cholera four days before, and they with nothing to eat for four days but cabbage leaves and carrots eaten raw, poor, hungry-looking, frightfully emaciated, half-naked waifs shivering in the cold raw wind, and I could tell you of these things until you would be sick at heart, as I have been, but that does not help to solve the situation.

Newspaper accounts of the time reveal the emergence of worker discontent and unrest by the early summer of 1918 and suggest that many workers who supported the Bolsheviks at the time of the seizure of power had now changed their minds. Workers resented the decision of the Bolsheviks to do away with workers' control and to interfere in elections to trade unions and soviets. Brief articles telling of strikes and victories of Menshevik and Socialist Revolutionary candidates in trade union and soviet elections appeared in non-Bolshevik publications throughout 1918 and 1919.

Kostroma. Of late a sharp change has been in evidence among the working masses. Recent elections to the City Soviet gave a majority to the Mensheviks. . . .

This change of attitude occurred under the influence of the food crisis. The largest factory in the city of Kostroma, which employs eight thousand workers, excluding [office] employees, is going to close next week because of shortage of money, fuel, and raw material. The demand for free trade in grain is finding more and more supporters among the workers. . . .

In the large factory village of Ozery . . . there recently took place an uprising of the workers against the Soviet. The events, according to official sources, were as follows:

Dissatisfied with the local Soviet authorities, a large crowd of workers, numbering about eight thousand, surrounded the building of the Soviet, in which at the time there were three members of the Executive Committee, . . . eight Red Army soldiers, and six militia officers. The members of the Soviet pleaded with the workers not to resort to violence, but in vain. . . . Thereupon those besieged began to fire on the crowd, which fell back somewhat. . . . A number of workers secured rifles and bombs from some source, climbed on the roof of the house next to the Soviet, and began to fire on the building of the Soviet. One of the bombs thrown into the Soviet premises exploded and destroyed the floor, a number of bookcases, and papers. . . .

Seeing that the Soviet refused to surrender . . . the assailants decided to set the building of the Soviet afire. . . . Soon the news spread that a train with Red Army soldiers . . . was nearing Ozery. Some of the workers rushed to the railroad to destroy the railway tracks, but this soldiers' train was already at the station. The soldiers rescued the Soviet. . . .

This article from a Menshevik newspaper in May 1918 describes how Bolsheviks in Tambov dealt with unfavorable results to elections to the soviet. Similar protests and actions occurred all over the country at this time, with the Bolsheviks relying on force to disband soviets with non-Bolshevik majorities.

April 1918. New elections to the city soviet ended in Tambov in the beginning of April. The Social Democrats [Mensheviks] and Socialist Revolutionaries won the majority of seats, not the Bolsheviks, who had held them before the elections. The Bolsheviks won only one-third of the seats in the soviet. The situation was unambiguous. Power in the city was slipping out of the Bolsheviks' hands. But it was not easy for the Bolsheviks to part with power, and they were ready to do anything to keep it despite the will of the Tambov workers. At the session of the newly elected soviet, the Bolsheviks declared an ultimatum: either they be assigned seven out of twelve seats on the Executive Committee or they would consider themselves "free to act." This ultimatum was turned down, and the Bolsheviks left the session, . . .

The next session of the newly elected soviet was scheduled for April 5. But when the members arrived for the session, all entrances to the . . . building, where the session was to take place, were blocked by armed militiamen. . . . They would not let anyone enter the building. The members of the soviet were searched and their deputy cards taken away and destroyed. Some members of the soviet managed, however, to enter the building and open the session. Then, on Bolshevik orders, armed men began to pull members of the soviet out of the assembly hall by force. They threatened them with weapons and turned off the electricity. The members of the soviet had no choice but to comply. . . .

Those who assumed dictatorial power wanted to make sure that the legitimately elected soviet, which they had disbanded, would not assemble again. . . .

March 1918. As is well known, Kovrov was the scene of outrageous and bloody events around March 20. A large rally of railway

A 1919 poster states: "Worker! The October Revolution Gave You the Factories and Free Labor." It reminds workers of the revolution's accomplishments and encourages them to receive training in the use of firearms and to remain vigilant against the threat of counter-revolution.

workers on March 12 demanded that new elections to the soviet take place immediately. After the rally, three comrades were arrested. Alarmed workers demanded that they be released immediately, but the authorities refused and declared that "any worker protest would be mercilessly suppressed by armed force." Then the workers decided to stage a peaceful procession. The general meeting of railway workers in Kovrov adopted a resolution: "An Appeal to Workers!"

> Freedom of press, freedom of speech, freedom of assembly, and inviolability of person—none of these exists anymore.... Workers cannot merely observe how, in their own name, those who in fact do not express the will of the working people are preparing the ruin of the revolution. The present soviet acts against the interests of the working class, and it must be replaced by the true representatives of the working people. Comrades! Begin new elections of your deputies to the soviet immediately.

The Red Guards opened fire on the peaceful demonstration. Martial law was imposed and arrests began. At the demonstration, the workers were marching in tight lines and singing revolutionary songs amid the uninterrupted crackle of rifle and machine-gun fire from the Red Guards.

It is not surprising that opponents of the Bolsheviks leveled a range of criticisms against the new regime, accusing them of undermining Russia's national greatness, selling out to the Germans, and implementing measures designed to destroy traditional Russian values. But many Bolsheviks did not refrain from expressing their concern. They noted that Lenin and his fellow leaders were making crucial mistakes that perverted the ideals of the revolution. At party meetings and in party publications, one group, known as the Workers' Opposition, criticized the increasing centralization of all economic and political power and control in the hands of the Party and the erosion of worker participation and involvement in the running of the economy and government. In particular, they decried the loss of trade union independence from the state and Party as well as the Party's practice of appointing officials, many of whom were not proletarians, rather than having workers themselves elect them.

The solution of this problem as it is proposed by the industrial unions, consists in giving complete freedom to the workers as regards experimenting, class training, adjusting and feeling out the new forms of production, as well as expression and development of their creative abilities, that is, to that class which alone can be the creator of communism. This is the way the Workers' Opposition handles the solution of this difficult problem from which follows the most essential point of their theses. "Organization of control over

N̶ot a single ... store of any kind was open and one marveled how the population managed to secure the barest necessities with which to sustain life ... At night the town was in total darkness.

—An American relief worker describing conditions in Feodosia, a port city on the Black Sea at the end of the civil war the ... economy is a prerogative of the All-Russian Congress of Producers, who are united in the trade and industrial unions which elect the central body directing the whole economic life of the republic" (Theses of the Workers' Opposition). ...

In order to do away with the bureaucracy that is finding its shelter in the soviet institutions, *we must first get rid of all bureaucracy in the party itself.* ...

The third decisive step toward democratization of the party is the elimination of all non-worker elements from all the administrative positions; ...

The fourth basic demand of the Workers' Opposition is this: *the party must reverse its policy to the elective principle.*

Appointments must be permissible only as exceptions, but lately they began to prevail as a rule. Appointments are very characteristic of bureaucracy, and yet at present they are a general, legalized and well-recognized daily occurrence. The procedure of appointments produces a very unhealthy atmosphere in the party, and disrupts the relationship of equality among the members by rewarding friends and punishing enemies as well as by other no less harmful practices in our party and soviet life. ...

The Embrace of Dictatorship

At the Tenth Party Congress, held in March 1921, Lenin and the majority in the Party decided to clamp down on internal opposition and ensure party discipline and authority through a resolution entitled "On Party Unity." The resolution forced the Workers' Opposition to disband and the Party henceforth banned factions, which meant that party members were unable to organize official platforms to challenge the policies adopted by the majority of the Party. This so-called "ban on factions" undermined internal party discussion and debate and contributed in no small manner to the emergence of Joseph Stalin as dictator.

The Congress directs the attention of all members of the Party to the fact that the unity and solidarity of its ranks, the guaranteeing of complete confidence between members of the Party and of work that is really enthusiastic, that genuinely embodies the unified will of the vanguard of the proletariat is especially necessary at the present moment, ...

On the other hand, even before the general Party discussion about the trade unions, some signs of factionalism were manifested in the Party. Groups grew up with special platforms and

A 1920 poster proclaims, "Only the Close and Unbroken Union of Workers and Peasants Will Save Russia from Destruction and Hunger." The government entreated workers and peasants to work together on behalf of the revolution: peasants would deliver food to workers, while workers would produce farm tools and machinery for peasants.

with a desire to maintain a separate existence to a certain degree and to create their own group discipline.

All class-conscious workers must clearly recognize the harm and impermissibility of any kind of factionalism, which inevitably leads in fact to the weakening of energetic work and to the strengthening of the repeated attempts of enemies who have crept into the governing Party to deepen the differences and to exploit them for counterrevolutionary purposes. . . .

The Congress gives instructions that all groups which have been organized on the basis of some platform should be immediately dissolved and commissions all organizations to watch out very closely, so that no factional demonstrations may be permitted. Nonfulfillment of this decision of the Congress must bring as its consequence unconditional and immediate expulsion from the Party.

The Russian born Emma Goldman, an anarchist who believed in the destruction of the state and government institutions, was exiled by the United States government to Russia. She arrived in early 1920, remaining there until the end of 1921. In her account of her life in Russia Goldman explains why she grew disillusioned with the new regime. Extremely idealistic, she catalogued what went wrong with the revolution, stressing that the Bolsheviks succeeded in replacing the tsar's dictatorship with their own.

The decision to record my experiences, observations, and reactions during my stay in Russia I had made long before I thought of leaving that country. In fact, that was my reason for departing from that tragically heroic land.

The strongest of us are loath to give up a long-cherished dream. I had come to Russia possessed by the hope that I should find a newborn country, with its people wholly consecrated to the great, though very difficult, task of revolutionary reconstruction. And I had fervently hoped that I might become an active part of the inspiring work.

In 1919 the United States expelled the anarchist Emma Goldman for her revolutionary beliefs. The American government sent her to Russia, where she became critical of the Bolsheviks' authoritarian methods of rule.

I found reality in Russia grotesque, totally unlike the great ideal that had borne me upon the crest of high hope to the land of promise. It required fifteen long months before I could get my bearings. Each day, each week, each month added new links to the fatal chain that pulled down my cherished edifice. For a long time I strove against the disillusionment. For a long time I strove against the still voice within me which urged me to face the overpowering facts. I would not and could not give up.

I saw before me the Bolshevik State, formidable, crushing every constructive revolutionary effort, suppressing, debasing, and disintegrating everything. Unable and unwilling to become a cog in that sinister machine, and aware that I could be of no practical use to Russia and her people, I decided to leave the country....

If I were to sum up my whole argument in one sentence I should say: The inherent tendency of the State is to concentrate, to narrow, and monopolize all social activities; the nature of revolution is, on the contrary, to grow, to broaden, and disseminate itself in ever-wider circles. In other words, the State is institutional and static; revolution is fluent, dynamic. These two tendencies are incompatible and mutually destructive. The State idea killed the Russian Revolution and it must have the same result in all other revolutions, unless the *libertarian idea prevail.*[sic] . . .

It is at once the great failure and the great tragedy of the Russian Revolution that it attempted (in the leadership of the ruling political party) to change only institutions and conditions while ignoring entirely the human and social values involved in the Revolution. Worse yet, in its mad passion for power, the Communist State even sought to strengthen and deepen the very ideas and conceptions which the Revolution had come to destroy. It supported and encouraged all the worst anti-social qualities and systematically destroyed the already awakened conception of the new revolutionary values. The sense of justice and equality, the love of liberty and human brotherhood—these fundamentals of the real regeneration of society—the Communist State suppressed to the point of extermination. . . .

Some two-and-a-half million Jews lived in the Russian Empire on the eve of World War I, and the vast majority of them eked out meager livings as workers in small workshops, shopkeepers, and petty traders. Russia's Jews welcomed the overthrow of the autocracy in early 1917, since the Provisional Government had lifted all legal disabilities and restrictions. Likewise, the Bolsheviks confirmed the political emancipation of the Jews and took a strong stance against anti-Semitism. Nonetheless, Jews continued to feel the brunt of popular hatred and were no strangers to periodic outbursts of anti-Semitic violence, known as pogroms. Many non-Jews unfairly viewed all Jews as responsible for the collapse of the autocracy and the victory of the Bolsheviks. Indeed, the labels "Jew" and "Bolshevik" were synonymous in the minds of many Russians. In the short story "Crossing into Poland," Isaac Babel, a Jew who fought for the Bolsheviks during the civil war, describes the tragedy that befalls a poor Jewish family caught in the fighting between Bolshevik and Polish armies during the civil war.

The commander of the Sixth Division reported that Novograd-Volynsk was taken at dawn today. The staff is now withdrawing from Krapivno, and our cavalry transport stretches in a noisy rear guard along the high road that goes from Brest to Warsaw, a high road built on the bones of muzhiks by Czar Nicholas I.

Fields of purple poppies are blossoming around us, a noon breeze is frolicking in the yellowing rye, virginal buckwheat is stand-

Many people believed that Jews were behind the Bolshevik victory and that Lenin was a paid German agent who did the bidding of Russia's enemies. No credible evidence substantiates such opinions. British citizens who had lived in Russia in 1917 and 1918 stated upon their return to London that:

Eighty-five per cent of the members of the soviets and ministries are Jews, many of whom have lived in America. Those men, like their leaders Lenin and Trotsky, have as their programme the total destruction of all organizations of civilization, . . . There is no doubt in the minds of all those who have returned from Russia that Lenin and Co. are obeying German orders. . . .

ing of the horizon like the wall of a faraway monastery. Silent Volhynia is turning away, Volhynia is leaving, heading into the pearly white fog of the birch groves, creeping through the flowery hillocks, and with weakened arms entangling itself in the underbush of hops. The orange sun is rolling across the sky like a severed head, gentle light glimmers in the ravines among the clouds, the banners of the sunset are fluttering above our heads. The stench of yesterday's blood and slaughtered horses drips into the evening chill. The blackened Zbrucz roars and twists the foaming knots of its rapids. The bridges are destroyed, and we wade across the river. The majestic moon lies on the waves. The water comes up to the horses' backs, purling streams trickle between hundreds of horses' legs. Someone sinks, and loudly curses the Mother of God. The river is littered with the black squares of the carts and filled with humming, whistling, and singing that thunders above the glistening hollows and the snaking moon.

Late at night we arrive in Novograd. In the quarters to which I am assigned I find a pregnant woman and two red-haired Jews with thin necks, and a third Jew who is sleeping with his face to the wall and a blanket pulled over his head. In my room I find ransacked closets, torn pieces of women's fur coats on the floor, human excrement, and fragments of the holy Seder plate that the Jews use once a year for Passover.

"Clean up this mess!" I tell the woman. "How can you live like this?"

The two Jews get up from their chairs. They hop around on their felt soles and pick up the broken pieces of porcelain from the floor. They hop around in silence, like monkeys, like Japanese acrobats in a circus, their necks swelling and twisting. They spread a ripped eiderdown on the floor for me, and I lie down by the wall, next to the third sleeping Jew. Timorous poverty descends over my bed.

Everything has been killed by the silence, and only the moon, clasping its round, shining, carefree head in its blue hands, loiters beneath my window.

I rub my numb feet, lie back on the ripped eiderdown, and fall asleep. I dream about the commander of the Sixth Division. He is chasing the brigade commander on his heavy stallion, and shoots two bullets into his eyes. The bullets pierce the brigade commander's head, and his eyes fall to the ground. "Why did you turn back the brigade?" Savitsky, the commander of the Sixth Division, shouts

In his diary entry for Feb. 25, 1918, Iurii Got'e described the Bolsheviks as "A bunch of scum consisting of Jew-internationalists, people without a fatherland, without honor, without law, crazed gorillas from the Russian workers and former soldiers . . . have decided the fate of Russia. . . ."

Survivors cart away the bodies of Jewish pogrom victims during the civil war. Anti-Bolshevik forces blamed Jews for the travails engulfing the country: in 1919 and 1920 some tens of thousands of defenseless Jewish men, women, and children living in Ukraine were slaughtered by anti-Bolshevik soldiers and peasants who held Jews collectively responsible for the revolution.

at the wounded man, and I wake up because the pregnant woman is tapping me on the face.

"*Pan*," she says to me, "you are shouting in your sleep, and tossing and turning. I'll put your bed in another corner, because you are kicking my papa."

She raises her thin legs and round belly from the floor and pulls the blanket off the sleeping man. An old man is lying there on his back, dead. His gullet has been ripped out, his face hacked in two, and dark blood is clinging to his beard like a clump of lead.

"*Pan*," the Jewess says, shaking out the eiderdown, "the Poles were hacking him to death and he kept begging them, 'Kill me in the backyard so my daughter won't see me die!' But they wouldn't inconvenience themselves. He died in this room thinking of me. . . . And now I want you to tell me," the woman suddenly said with terrible force, "I want you to tell me where one could find another father like my father in all the world!"

Peasant Resistance and the Crisis of Kronstadt

The establishment of Soviet power in the countryside did not go smoothly and was a costly affair. The Bolsheviks were intent on bringing the revolution to the village and set out to promote class warfare in the countryside by stripping wealthy peasants, known as *kulaks,* **of their property. The peasants, however, were for the most part immune from the entreaties of the Bolsheviks to engage in a civil war of poor peasant against rich peasant. They tended to act in unison in opposition to the state's policy of forced grain requisitioning. Lenin justified the use of violence against** *kulaks.* **In "Loot the Looters," a newspaper article from early 1918, Lenin employed simple, direct language to characterize opponents of Bolshevik policy and justify whatever measures he deemed necessary to get hold of the valuable grain to feed cities and the Red Army, which Trotsky had organized from the remnants of tsarist troops.**

The bourgeoisie . . . and the saboteurs are . . . conspiring against us. They know that they will be completely ruined . . . if the people succeed in dividing the national wealth which is now in the exclusive possession of the rich. . . .

That is where your function begins. You must organize and consolidate the Soviet power in the villages. You will encounter there the village-bourgeoisie—the *kulaks*—who will hinder your work in every way. But to fight them will be an easy matter. The masses will be with you. . . .

Make it clear to the peasant that the *kulaks* and the bloodsuckers must be expropriated in order to bring about a just and equitable distribution of goods. . . . The bourgeoisie are concealing in their coffers the riches which they have plundered, and are saying, "We shall sit tight for a while." We must catch the plunderers and compel them to return the spoils. . . .

That Bolshevik was right who in reply to a question whether or not it was true that the Bolsheviks are looters, said, "Yes, we loot the looters."

As early as 1918 peasants resisted Bolshevik policy, despite their initial support for the overthrow of the Provisional Government because of Bolshevik promises to permit peasants control of the land. Yet for the most part the peasants tended to endure the emergency measures because they feared that a White victory would take away the land. But by the

Fear as Weapon

Lenin did not shy away from the use of terror to ensure the peasants' compliance with Bolshevik policies. In August 1918 he sent this telegram to communist leaders in Penza, located several hundred miles southeast of Moscow.

Comrades! The revolt by the five *kulak* districts must be suppressed without mercy. The interest of the *entire* revolution demands this, because *we have* now before us our final decisive battle "with the *kulaks*." We need to set an example.

1) You need to hang (hang without fail, so that the *public sees*) *at least 100* notorious *kulaks*, the rich, and the bloodsuckers.

2) Publish their names.

3) Take away *all* of their grain. . . .

This needs to be accomplished in such a way that people for hundreds of miles around will see, tremble, know, and scream out: *let's choke* and strangle those bloodsucking *kulaks*.

Telegraph us acknowledging receipt and *execution* of this.

Yours, Lenin

P.S. Use your toughest people for this.

middle of 1920, with the Whites out of the way, the peasants bristled at the continued policy of grain requisitioning and rose up in rebellions that challenged the Red Army.

Peasant resistance to the Bolsheviks, as well as the Whites, grew into a crescendo of rebellions, culminating in a massive revolt in 1920–21 by peasants under the leadership of A. S. Antonov in the province of Tambov, a rich, grain-producing region southeast of Moscow. Numbering in the tens of thousands, Antonov's rebel army, nicknamed the "Greens" for their hideouts in forests, wanted to overthrow the Bolsheviks. In 1920 Antonov established the Union of Toiling Peasants, which voiced the rebels' demands in its party program. It took a major military campaign by Moscow to suppress the peasant rebels.

Needing to feed the Red Army, government officials, and factory workers, the Bolsheviks established armed food requisitioning brigades that ferreted out and seized all available grain and other foodstuffs from the peasantry. The policy antagonized the peasants, who eventually took up arms against the Bolshevik regime. It also discouraged peasants from growing food, thereby exacerbating food shortages in both town and country.

The Union of Toiling Peasants has set itself the task of overthrowing the government of the communist-bolsheviks, which has reduced the country to penury, ruin and shame. The Union, which organises volunteer partisan detachments, is waging an armed struggle in order to destroy this detestable government and its rule. Its aims are as follows:

1. Political equality for all citizens, without division into classes.
2. An end to the civil war and a return to civilian life.
3. Every effort to be made to ensure a lasting peace with all foreign states.
4. The convocation of a Constituent Assembly on the basis of equal, universal, direct and secret suffrage, without predetermining its choice of political system, and preserving the voters' right to recall deputies who do not carry out the people's will.
5. Prior to the convocation of the Constituent Assembly, the establishment of provisional authorities in the localities and the centre, on an elective basis, by those unions and parties which have taken part in the struggle against the communists.

6. Freedom of speech, the press, conscience, unions and assembly.

7. The full implementation of the law on the socialisation of the land, adopted and confirmed by the former Constituent Assembly.

8. The supply of basic necessities, particularly food, to the inhabitants of the towns and countryside through the cooperatives.

9. Regulation of the prices of labour and the output of factories run by the state.

10. Partial denationalisation of factories; heavy industry, coal mining and metallurgy should remain in state hands.

11. Workers' control and state supervision of production.

12. The opportunity for both Russian and foreign capital to restore the country's economic life.

13. The immediate restoration of political, trade and economic relations with foreign powers.

14. Free self-determination for the nationalities inhabiting the former Russian empire.

15. The initiation of wide-ranging state credit for restoring small-scale agriculture.

16. Freedom for handicraft production.

17. Unfettered teaching in schools and compulsory universal literacy education.

18. The volunteer partisan units currently organized and operating must not be disbanded until the Constituent Assembly has been convened and it has resolved the question of a standing army.

Tambov . . . Committee of the Union of Toiling Peasants

In April 1921 a Socialist Revolutionary paper published in Prague provided the following account of the uprising in Tambov.

In the Fall of 1920 the Tambov peasantry once more revolted and attacked the Soviet authorities with clubs and pitchforks. Ever since there has been a state of open rebellion; and, now subsiding, now flaring up again in full force, the struggle has been going on continuously, being carried on by partisan detachments. . . .

The occasion for that particular uprising among the peasants of Kamenka was furnished by the arrival of a requisitioning detachment which began to collect additional levies of grain. Seven members of the detachment were killed by the peasants, and the village then realized that it would not escape Bolshevik retaliation. Thereupon a peasant "Staff" was hastily organized, trenches were dug, and the villagers prepared . . . to repel the punitive expedition of the Bolsheviks. The latter was not slow in making its appearance. Soon there appeared 20 cavalrymen. . . . A brief fusillade of shots was exchanged, as a result of which the punitive expedition was beaten and fled. This first expedition was followed by a second and third one, with increasing numbers of soldiers, but these, too, were routed by the peasants. . . .

The most stubborn resistance of all was offered by the peasants of Kapteva village. Three times in succession they repelled the attacks of the Government troops, each time routing them completely. Meanwhile one village after another was overthrowing its Soviet and, arming itself with anything that came to hand,—rifles, pitchforks, but mostly clubs—it made preparations for battle. . . .

The strength of the rebels was growing from day to day. . . .

Encouraged by their successes, the peasants resolved to take Tambov. This army of peasants on the march to Tambov presented a striking appearance. Along the highway there was moving forward, amidst clouds of dust, silently and ominously, a multitude of thousands of peasants. They had their own cavalry as well as infantry. Most of them were only armed with weapons made by themselves, such as axes, pitchforks, clubs, etc.

The villages along the road welcomed the marching peasants with the ringing of churchbells, and furnished them with provisions and arms, adding detachments of their own to the army of peasants. As they were drawing nearer and nearer to Tambov, the insurgents were growing more and more numerous. All Bolshevik attempts to repel the peasants and to force them to give up their plan of marching on Tambov ended in failure. The insurgents advanced like an avalanche, easily beating off all attacks, and on the 1st of September they were already at Kuzminka, the last railway station before the city of Tambov. . . . The Bolshevik authorities at Tambov were in a panic. To their luck, however, aid arrived at this most critical moment from neighboring provinces, and the insurgents were forced to retreat from Tambov after having come to within 10 miles of the city.

For some time the Bolsheviks again became masters of the situation. New punitive expeditions were organized and sent to the insurgent regions, where they established a bloody reign of all-around

responsibility among the peasants for individual acts of hostility. Not to mention the large masses of peasants shot and killed, the exact number of which is beyond calculation, the punitive detachments also burned down to the ground several villages. . . .

Red Army soldiers attack the Kronstadt naval base in March 1921. Sailors at Kronstadt rebelled against the authoritarian rule of the Bolsheviks, who responded by ruthlessly suppressing the uprising.

The Bolsheviks found themselves confronted with another crisis after the threat of the Whites had dissipated by the fall of 1920. In the cities workers vented their frustration by engaging in strikes and protesting Communist control over soviets and trade unions. The mass discontent of the populace is best summed up in a popular accusation leveled at the regime, "I like the Bolsheviks but hate the Communists." In the minds of many confused workers and peasants, the Communists were viewed as usurpers of the revolutionary dreams and aspirations inspired by the Bolshevik revolution of 1917. Of course, the average peasant or worker did not understand that the Communists and Bolsheviks were identical and that the revolution had gone astray because the exigencies of civil war forced the Bolsheviks to make hard choices in order to save Soviet power.

Lenin and his fellow revolutionaries recognized the extent of popular discontent, but they took action only in March 1921 after sailors at

The Kronstadt rebellion was a sobering experience for the Party leadership. The civil war had clearly generated a crisis of authority for the regime, but the Communists felt they needed to suppress the sailors in order to stay in power. Red Army soldiers crossed the frozen waters separating Petrograd from Kronstadt and attacked the sailors. Both sides suffered extensive casualties. Over 2,000 sailors were captured, and the Communists executed several hundred of them for their roles in the uprising. The remaining sailors were imprisoned, where some were shot or died from disease, hunger, and hard work.

Oprichniki

The *oprichniki* served as the police force of Tsar Ivan the Terrible in the mid-16th century.

Kronstadt, a naval base on an island in the Gulf of Finland near Petrograd, turned against the regime. Ardent and loyal supporters of the revolution, the Kronstadt sailors sided with workers and peasants and soundly condemned the policies of the government that had become bureaucratized and dictatorial. They demanded free elections to the soviets and power-sharing by the Bolsheviks with other left-wing parties, and also called for the end of grain requisitioning. In short, the sailors wanted a return to the ideals and goals they believed the 1917 revolution embodied and condemned the Kremlin for abandoning the objectives of the revolution. The sailors expressed some of their goals in "What We Are Fighting For," a proclamation published during the uprising.

After carrying out the October Revolution, the working class hoped to achieve emancipation. The result has been to create even greater enslavement of the individual man. The power of the police and gendarme monarchy passed into the hands of the Communist usurpers, who, instead of giving the people freedom, instilled in them the constant fear of falling into the torture chambers of the Cheka, which in their horrors far exceed the gendarme administration of the tsarist regime. The bayonets, bullets, and gruff commands of the Cheka *oprichniki*—these are what the workingman of Soviet Russia has won after so much struggle and suffering. The glorious emblem of the workers' state—the sickle and the hammer—has in fact been replaced by the Communist authorities with the bayonet and barred window, for the sake of maintaining the calm and carefree life of the new bureaucracy of Communist commissars and functionaries.

But the most infamous and criminal of all is the moral servitude which the Communists have inaugurated: they have laid their hands also on the inner world of the toilers, forcing them to think in the Communist way. With the help of the bureaucratized trade unions, they have fastened the workers to their benches, so that labor has become not a joy but a new form of slavery. To the protests of the peasants, expressed in spontaneous uprisings, and those of the workers, whose living conditions have driven them out on strike, they answer with mass executions and bloodletting, in which they have not been surpassed even by the tsarist generals. Russia of the toilers, the first to raise the red banner of labor's emancipation, is drenched in the blood of those martyred for the glory of Communist domination. The picture has been drawn more and more sharply, and now it is clear that the Russian Communist party is not the defender of the toilers that it pretends to be. The interests of the working people are alien to it. Having gained power, it is afraid only of losing it, and therefore deems every means permissible: slander, violence, deceit, murder, vengeance upon the families of the rebels.

The long-suffering patience of the toilers is at an end. Here and there the land is lit up by the fires of insurrection in a struggle against oppression and violence. Strikes by the workers have flared up, but the Bolshevik *okhrana* agents have not been asleep and have taken every measure to forestall and suppress the inevitable third revolution. . . .

No, there can be no middle ground. Victory or death! . . . Here the new revolutionary step forward has been taken. Here is raised the banner of rebellion against the three-year-old violence and oppression of Communist rule, which has put in the shade the three-hundred-year yoke of monarchism. Here in Kronstadt has been laid the first stone of the third revolution, striking the last fetters from the laboring masses and opening a broad new road for socialist creativity. . . .

The present overturn at last gives for the toilers the opportunity to have their freely elected soviets, operating without the slightest force of party pressure, . . . At last the policeman's club of the Communist autocracy has been broken.

Okhrana

The *okhrana* was the secret police under the tsars.

CHAPTER 4

The Road to Socialism

Workers celebrate May Day (International Workers' Day) in 1925 on a float with a large bust of Lenin. The cult of Lenin quickly grew to enormous proportions, with large statues erected in most cities. Virtually every building and office had a bust or portrait of Lenin at the entrance, and his face remained on the currency and billboards that were ubiquitous in the Soviet Union until its collapse in 1991.

Between 1918 and 1921 the Communists overcame enormous odds to consolidate their control of the country. Not only had they survived the travails of civil war and peasant insurrection, but they had also defeated mutinous sailors at Kronstadt and refused demands to democratize the political system. However, the lesson of the mutiny, labor unrest, and peasant uprisings was not lost on the Bolsheviks, who, at the Tenth Party Congress, in session during the Kronstadt rebellion, implemented a reform program that scrapped the onerous features of War Communism and replaced them with the New Economic Policy (NEP, 1921–28). These concessions calmed the workers and peasants and helped to stabilize the social and economic situation in the country, but they were made in tandem with political maneuvers that assured the Bolsheviks, with fewer than 600,000 members in 1921, their grip on society.

In principle, the Soviet Union's government was headed by an executive branch (Council of People's Commissars, or Sovnarkom) and a legislative branch (Congress of Soviets, which elected a Central Executive Committee). But in reality the Communist Party, headed by the Politburo, dominated governmental institutions and ruled the country. The Party ensured its control by having its members occupy key positions in the government and having them take their orders from the Politburo. Party control was also manifested in the arts and intellectual life, notwithstanding its decision in 1925 not to be the arbiter of literature and other forms of art. The Party generally tolerated all artistic expression so long as it was not anti-revolutionary. It welcomed the efforts of artists, musicians, and writers, so-called "fellow travelers" who sympathized with the Bolshevik Revolution, even if they themselves were not members of the Party. Nevertheless, during the 1920s the Party imposed greater censorship, sought control of newspapers, and intervened more and more in the activities of artists and their organizations. The roots of the oppressive sterility and political correctness that all cultural and intellectual endeavors acquired in the 1930s can be found in the previous decade as the state became more interventionist and set out to centralize policies toward culture and the arts.

The NEP guided the Soviet economy and society until the late 1920s. At the Tenth Party Congress the regime decided to end grain requisitioning and permit individuals to market food and other consumer goods, all in the hope of encouraging the peasantry to prosper as well as feed people in the cities. The NEP resuscitated the economy and restored social and political stability to the country. The NEP economy was a mixed one, with both state and private sectors. The government retained control over large-scale industrial factories, foreign trade, transport, and banking, but it permitted individuals and families to own small retail and commercial stores and industrial enterprises. The restoration of a market economy bore fruit by the mid-1920s as the economy recovered to its pre-World War I levels of agricultural and industrial production.

But as food returned to store shelves and life acquired a degree of normalcy not known during many years of war, revolution, and famine, a variety of problems—ideological, political, and economic—continued to plague the Soviet Union during NEP. For many workers and party members, NEP promoted capitalism and was a clear retreat from the building of socialism. Lenin himself had acknowledged in 1921 that NEP was a compromise with capitalism, a strategic retreat required to give the regime a breathing spell during which it could regroup and create the social and economic foundations of a gradual transition to socialism and, ultimately, communism. The Party was in a quandary that required it to balance the interests of workers and peasants as well as to consider those of the state. Remembering the peasant unrest of the civil war, the Party chose to avoid antagonizing the peasantry. The regime adhered to the dictum of Nikolai Bukharin, a Politburo member and prominent advocate of NEP who encouraged the peasants "to enrich themselves." But by keeping to the spirit of NEP, the regime incurred the wrath of workers and rank-and-file party members who did not understand why the world's first socialist government pursued policies that favored peasants. This preferential treatment toward the peasants, whom Bolshevik ideology viewed with suspicion and even contempt because of the peasants' attachment to their private property (land), was bitter medicine for workers and party members to swallow.

[M]oney was once more becoming the touchstone of social life. . . . If money was reappearing, wouldn't rich people reappear too? Weren't we on the slippery slope that led back to capitalism?

—A young Bolshevik commenting on the ideological threat of NEP

The struggle to see who would succeed Lenin, who died in early 1924, as Party leader occurred against this backdrop of NEP. Joseph Stalin ultimately won the battle, largely because he controlled the massive party and government bureaucracies and had a firm grip on the daily operations of the Party. Leon Trotsky and others, while supporting the general contours of NEP, believed that the Soviet Union could not take the slow road to socialism and urged the regime to extract more taxes from the peasantry in order to finance rapid industrialization. To counter Trotsky's appeal and stature, Stalin created a flurry of excitement with his slogan "socialism in one country." Ever since 1917 a central core belief of Bolshevik ideology was that the revolution in Russia would founder without support of proletarians throughout the world. In the absence of world revolution, the Russian revolutionaries would remain isolated and vulnerable to the machinations of capitalist governments eager to see the world's first experiment in socialism fail. Foreign intervention during the civil war lent credence to this view, but the failure of workers in Europe and the United States to rise up and overthrow capitalism meant that the effort to build a socialist society in the Soviet Union would have to be put on the back burner until the international situation was more favorable.

Unwilling to wait until some future date when workers elsewhere carried out their own socialist revolutions, many workers and party members enthusiastically supported Stalin's policy of "socialism in one country" because it meant that their revolution was self-sufficient and did not depend on the actions of workers in other parts of the world. The slogan "socialism in one country" not only struck a resonant chord in society, but also fostered impatience with NEP. It was becoming increasingly clear to many in the party leadership that NEP was not well suited to building socialism in the near future because it promoted a prosperous peasantry and was not generating the resources needed for industrialization. "Socialism in one country" implied that the Soviet Union had to embark on the path to industrialization, but the simple fact of the matter was that the modernization of the economy was an elusive goal.

The Transformation of Culture and Society

Public praise and celebration of Lenin as Russia's great revolutionary leader began while he was alive, but his death in early 1924 and subsequent burial in a mausoleum on Red Square, next to the Kremlin, fostered the emergence of a cult of Lenin that served several political ends.

This is one of the last photographs of Lenin, taken in 1923. Lenin suffered the first of several debilitating strokes in 1922, and as his infirmities grew he found himself more and more isolated from the inner workings of the Politburo. Shortly before his death he did manage to dictate his "Last Testament" in which he advised his colleagues to remove Stalin as General Secretary. The remaining members of the Politburo ignored this request, largely because they were more concerned with undermining Trotsky's appeal as successor to Lenin.

First, adulation of Lenin provided the regime with a symbol of the revolution's promises and achievements and signified that the task of building a socialist society would continue even in the absence of the revolution's leader. Second, the contestants to succeed Lenin jockeyed for position by praising him and tying their political fortunes to how closely they could portray themselves as the most faithful disciple of Lenin and his teachings. The reverential worship of Lenin provided the foundation of the cult of Stalin that would emerge in the mid-1930s. Stalin gave a eulogy at Lenin's funeral in January 1924, a text that is striking for its ritualistic undertones. The repetitive phrasing and the multiple use of the word "commandment" at the end of the eulogy no doubt reminded those in attendance of a religious service. Henceforth, Stalin would take advantage of Lenin's death to enhance his status as Lenin's closest disciple and most worthy successor.

Comrades! We communists are people of a special mould. We are fashioned out of special stuff. We are they who form the army of the great proletarian general, the army of comrade Lenin. There is nothing higher than the honour of belonging to this army. There is nothing higher than the calling of a member of the party whose founder and leader is comrade Lenin. Not to every man is it given to be a member of such a party. Not to every man is it given to endure the tribulations and tempests which go with membership of such a party. Sons of the working class, sons of need and strife, sons of unexampled privations and heroic strivings—such are the men who, first and foremost, are fitted to be members of such a party. That is why the party of Leninists, the party of communists, is also called the party of the working class.

Leaving us, comrade Lenin enjoined on us to hold high and keep pure the great calling of member of the party. We vow to thee, comrade Lenin, that we will with honour fulfil this thy commandment.

Leaving us, comrade Lenin enjoined on us to keep the unity of our party as the apple of our eye. We vow to thee, comrade Lenin, that we will with honour fulfill this thy commandment.

Leaving us, comrade Lenin enjoined on us to keep and strengthen the dictatorship of the proletariat. We vow to thee, comrade Lenin, that we will not spare our strength to fulfill with honour this thy commandment.

Leaving us, comrade Lenin enjoined on us to strengthen with all our might the union of workers and peasants. We vow to thee, comrade Lenin, that we will with honour fulfill this thy commandment. . . .

Along with the socioeconomic and political transformation of the country, the Bolshevik Revolution held out the promise of profound changes in how people think and behave. The Bolsheviks believed that a new culture and society were in the making as a new Soviet man and woman emerged committed to the values of socialism. Socialist culture would embody the values of cooperation and collective endeavor, values opposed to the individualism that, from the perspective of the Bolsheviks, characterized capitalist society. In 1922 Nadezhda Krupskaya, Lenin's wife, published the brief essay "What a Communist Ought to be Like" in a journal for young members of the Communist Party. Like many other prominent party members, Krupskaya reflected upon the attributes and attitudes of the new socialist man and woman.

Russians wait of line in Red Square to view Lenin's corpse in 1925. The Party ignored the disapproval of Lenin's widow and built a mausoleum, where the leader of the Russian Revolution remains to this day.

A communist is, first and foremost, *a person involved in society,* with strongly developed social instincts, who desires that all people should live well and be happy.

Communists can come from all classes of society, but most of all they are workers by birth. Why? Because the conditions of workers' lives are such as to nurture in them social instincts: collective labor, the success of which depends on the separate efforts of each; the same conditions of labor; common experiences; the common struggle for humane conditions of existence. All this brings workers closer together and unites them with the bonds of class solidarity. Let us take the capitalist class. The conditions of life for this class

On the first anniversary of Lenin's death, Stalin wrote the following ode. Ilyich was Lenin's middle name, and its use by Stalin suggested his closeness to and affection for Lenin.

Remember, love and study Ilyich, our
    teacher, our leader.
Fight and defeat our enemies, home and
    foreign—the way that Ilyich taught us.
Build the new society, the new way of life,
    the new culture—in the way that Ilyich
    taught us.
Never refuse to do the little things, for from
    little things are built the big things—that
    is one of Ilyich's important behests.

are completely different. Competition forces each capitalist to see another capitalist primarily as an opponent, who has to be tripped up. . . . Of course, the common struggle against the working class unites capitalists, but that internal unity, that formation into a collective which we see among workers—they have nothing to divide among themselves—does not exist in the capitalist class, where solidarity is corroded by competition. That is why in the working class the person with well-developed social instincts is the rule, while among the capitalists such a person is the exception. . . .

The October Revolution opened for Russia an opportunity for widespread building in the direction of communism. But in order to utilize these possibilities it is necessary to know what one can do at the moment in order to make at least one first step toward communism, and what one cannot, and it is necessary to know how to build a new life. It is necessary first and foremost to know thoroughly that sphere of work which you have undertaken, and then to master the method of a communist *approach* to the matter. Let us take an example. In order to organize correctly medical affairs in the country, it is first necessary to know the situation itself, secondly, how it was organized earlier in Russia and is currently organized in other states, and thirdly, how to approach the problem in a communist manner, namely, to conduct agitation, to create . . . a powerful organization in regard to medical affairs. It is necessary not only to know how to do all this, but to be able to *do* it. Thus it follows that a communist must know not only what communism is and why it is inevitable, but also know his own affairs well, and be able to approach the masses, influence them, and convince them.

In his personal life, a communist must always conduct himself in the interests of communism. What does this mean? It means, for example, that however nice it might be to stay in a familiar, comfortable home environment, that if for the sake of the cause, for the success of the communist cause, it is necessary to abandon everything and expose oneself to danger, the communist will do this. It means that however difficult and responsible the task the communist is called upon to perform, he will take it upon himself and try to carry it out to the best of his strength and skill. . . . It means the communist puts his personal interests aside, subordinates them to the common interest. It means that the communist is not indifferent to what is happening around him and that he actively struggles with that which is harmful to the interests of the toiling masses, and that he on the other hand actively defends these interests and makes them his own. . . .

Trotsky was also concerned with the impact of the revolution on social relations. In his newspaper article "'Thou' and 'You' in the Red Army" from 1922, Trotsky discusses how the Bolshevik revolution was bringing about a change in how people treated each other. "Thou" or *ty* in Russian is used when addressing family members, children, and close friends and implies intimacy. However, social superiors might address inferiors (such as bosses talking to workers) with *ty* in order to demarcate class difference and social standing. "You" or *vy* in Russian indicates formality and social deference.

In Sunday's *Izvestiya* there was an article about two Red Army men, named Shchekochikhin and Chernyshev, who had behaved as heroes on the occasion of a fire and explosion at Kolomna. As the article recounts it, the commander of the local garrison approached the soldier Shchekochikhin and asked:

"Do you (*ty*) know who I am?
"Yes, you (*vy*) are the commander of the garrison."

I doubt that the dialogue has been recorded accurately in this case. Otherwise, one would have to conclude that the garrison commander does not use the proper tone in speaking to Red Army soldiers. Of course, Red Army personnel may use the familiar form in speaking to one another as comrades, but precisely *as comrades* and only as comrades. In the Red Army a commanding officer may not use the familiar form to address a subordinate if the subordinate is expected to respond in the polite form. Otherwise an expression of inequality between persons would result, not an expression of subordination in the line of duty.

Of course, the polite and familiar forms are only matters of convention. But definite human relationships are expressed in this convention. In certain cases the familiar form may be used to express close comradely relations. But in which? In those where the relationship is mutual. In other cases, the familiar form will convey disdain, disrespect, a looking down the nose, and a shade of lordly hauteur in one's relations with others. Such a tone is absolutely impermissible in the Red Army.

To some this might seem a trifling matter. But it is not! Red Army soldiers need to respect both themselves and others. Respect for human dignity is an extremely important element of what holds the Red Army together in terms of morale. Red Army soldiers submit to their superiors in the line of duty. The requirements of discipline are inflexible. But at the same time, the soldiers are conscious of themselves as responsible citizens called upon to fulfill the obligations of the highest sorts. Military subordination must be accompanied by a sense of the civil and moral equality of all, and that sense of equality cannot endure if personal dignity is violated.

Nearly three quarters of the inhabitants of the Russian Empire were members of the Russian Orthodox Church before the revolution. Religious leaders and organizations were wary of the Bolsheviks, who made no secret of their anti-religious views and intentions. They proclaimed the separation of church and state and guaranteed freedom of religious worship, but the regime also set out to weaken religion's hold on the populace. During the 1920s the regime was careful not to launch an all-out war against religious institutions, largely because it was afraid to alienate the peasants, the overwhelming majority of whom were devoted and loyal adherents of Russian Orthodoxy. Keeping to the conciliatory approach of the New Economic Policy, the party in 1923 instructed its members to avoid direct confrontation with peasants.

In these conditions the work of the Party for the final destruction of religious belief in all its forms among the workers and peasant masses inevitably acquires first of all the character of an intensi-

Ukrainian Jews view the destruction of the Torah scrolls in their synagogue, which were vandalized in the early 1920s.

fied, systematic propaganda, which clearly and persuasively reveals to each worker and peasant the falsehood and contrariness to his interests of all religions, which exposes the connection of various religious groups with the interests of the ruling classes, and which replaces the outmoded remnants of religious ideas with clear scientific views of nature and human society. In doing this, as stated in the Party program, it is necessary carefully to avoid any insult to the feelings of believers, which leads only to the strengthening of religious fanaticism. Deliberately coarse methods which often are practiced . . . do not hasten but instead hamper the freeing of the toiling masses from religious prejudices.

While acknowledging significant successes in this area, it is necessary, however, to underscore that the majority of the literature which has been published cannot appeal to a mass readership. It is necessary to publish pamphlets and leaflets for the average worker or peasant which, in a form they can understand, answer questions about the origins of the world, of life and the essence of human relations, expose the counterrevolutionary role of religion and the church. . . .

Notwithstanding its vow to respect freedom of religious worship, the state was keen on acquiring the wealth of the Church, and officials often received permission to close churches and to use church property for other purposes, including the melting down of bells for industrial use. This memorandum from Lenin, issued in March 1922, showed that the government was willing to seize church property despite the potential of angering the peasantry.

We must pursue the removal of church valuables by the most decisive and rapid fashion in order to secure for ourselves a fund of several hundred million gold rubles (do not forget the immense wealth of some monasteries and abbeys). Without this fund any government work in general, any economic build-up in particular, . . . are completely unthinkable. In order to get our hands on this fund of several million gold rubles . . . we must do whatever is necessary. . . .

One clever writer on statecraft correctly said that if it is necessary for the realization of a well-known political goal to perform a series of brutal actions, then it is necessary to do them in the most energetic manner. . . .

At the party congress arrange a secret meeting of all or almost all delegates to discuss this matter. . . . At this meeting pass a secret resolution of the congress that the removal of valuables, especially from the very richest abbeys, monasteries, and churches, must be carried out with ruthless resolution, leaving nothing in doubt, and in the very shortest time. The greater the number of representatives of the reactionary clergy and the reactionary bourgeoisie that we succeed in shooting on this occasion, the better because this "audience" must precisely now be taught a lesson in such a way that they will not dare to think about any resistance whatsoever for several decades. . . .

Many adherents to the revolution believed that building a new society entailed tearing down the old and the traditional. Yet destruction was tempered by efforts to preserve the past and to use it as a foundation for building a socialist culture. For Lenin and Anatolii Lunacharsky, the party official in charge of culture and education, socialism required an educated citizenry committed to the objectives of the revolution. To be sure, artists existed to publicize the goals and policies of the Bolsheviks, but

Even though the regime's treatment of organized religion in the 1920s was less aggressive than it would be in the 1930s, the Kremlin adopted policies to undermine Russian Orthodoxy, Judaism, and Islam during NEP. It closed churches, synagogues, and mosques and arrested clergy for preaching, according to the authorities, opposition to the "godless" Communists. The state also banned the teaching of Hebrew and outlawed the publication of books, journals, newspapers, and textbooks in Hebrew, thereby making it nearly impossible for Jews to study and observe their religion. The regime's antireligious policies did not eradicate religious belief, but they did seriously damage the foundation of organized religious life in the Soviet Union.

A song popular among members of the Komsomol (Communist Youth League) illustrates the campaign to have people declare their commitment to socialism by giving their children revolutionary names.

Give me a son, my darling,
And we'll take him to the club,
We will have a celebration,
And will name him "Kim [Communist International of Youth]."

Soldiers take art and religious items from a monastery in 1927. As part of its repression of religion, the government turned many churches and monasteries into warehouses, workers' clubs, and even interrogation centers, and tolerated the looting of valuables by soldiers.

Lenin and Lunacharsky took measures to safeguard the cultural and artistic heritage of tsarist Russia, seeking to make accessible to the public for the first time the treasured art collections housed in the palaces and museums of the former ruling class. In addition, Lunacharsky launched a campaign to stamp out illiteracy and expand educational opportunities for children and adults, both peasant and worker alike. Literacy rates shot up as a result of these efforts, and many workers found themselves promoted to supervisory positions after attending night school and acquiring new skills and knowledge. In a report at a party meeting at the end of 1920, the Commissariat of Enlightenment surveyed the Bolsheviks' policy toward the arts and stressed how it differed from that of the tsars.

In Tsarist Russia the enjoyment of art in all its forms was exclusively the privilege of the ruling classes. The "nation" only got wretched crumbs as a substitute. Knowing what a powerful means of agitation the theater is for the masses, the police state kept a vigilant eye upon the so-called people's theaters, fencing them round with a censorship and entirely subjecting them to the police authorities. Education, both musical, theatrical and artistic, was quite inaccessible to the masses.

It became the aim of the Soviet Government to make art accessible to all, to bind it up in the life of the laboring masses, to put it on a new foundation so that it should draw new forces from among the proletariat.

At the same time, while working persistently towards the creation of a new, purely proletarian art, we endeavored to familiarize the proletariat with the best achievements of former art. . . .

The Theatrical World. Much has been done in democratizing the theater. The repertoire of the biggest theaters has been greatly improved; in this connection, we are still working to acquaint the workers with the best models of the classic theater. By a recent regulation, a uniform price for seats at all theaters has been established; this measure is a step towards the complete abolition of all pay for theatrical shows. Considering the theater as an instrument of education and propaganda, we should make it free of charge, as we do the school. Parallel with the classical repertoire, there is slowly coming up a new revolutionary repertoire, . . .

On the other hand, among the working masses themselves, such a tremendous striving towards theatrical creation is evident that it has proved extraordinarily difficult to manage and direct all the theaters and groups that sprang up so naturally.

The Soviet government sent this train, named after Lenin and decorated with paintings and slogans, across the country to promote communism. Its staff distributed propagandistic literature, which was known as "agit-prop," short for agitation and propaganda.

The Musical World. In the musical field our path was generally the same as in the theatrical sphere, i.e., we aimed at drawing the wide labor masses to appreciate works of genuine musical art; extensive musical education was given and wide facilities for the production of new music, growing out of the proletariat itself and corresponding to the spirit of the time. . . .

Museum Department. One of the most brilliant pages in our art work is the activity . . . in the sphere of the safe-guarding of the monuments of art and of the past.

Since the Revolution, our museum collections have been growing all the time. All the treasures that had been hidden from the eyes of the masses in the palaces and manors have been collected and placed in the museums, being the property of all workers. . . .

The regime enlisted the support of artists to publicize the accomplishments of the revolution. In a society where many adults could not read, the Bolsheviks relied on visual representations of the revolution, particularly posters and film. In a 1919 essay Lunacharsky explained why the Bolsheviks nationalized the film industry and emphasized its importance for the instilling of socialist values.

The state cinema in Russia faces quite unusual tasks. It is not only a matter of nationalizing production and film distribution and the direct control of cinemas. It is a matter of fostering a completely new spirit in the branch of art and education. . . .

We must do what nobody else is either able or willing to do. We should remember that a socialist government must imbue even film shows with a socialist spirit. . . .

Furthermore, the main task of cinema in both its scientific and feature divisions is that of propaganda. . . .

Generally speaking, every art, as Tolstoy once remarked, is above all a means of instilling the artist's emotions into the masses. Education in the wider sense of the word consists in the dissemination of ideas among minds that would otherwise remain a stranger to them. Cinema can accomplish both these things with particular force; it constitutes, on the one hand, a visual clarion for the dissemination of ideas and, on the other hand, if we introduce elements of the refined, the poetic, the pathetic, etc., it is capable of touching the emotions and thus becomes an apparatus of agitation. . . .

[W]e must concentrate only on moments that are important for agitation and propaganda. We must convey the history of the beginnings of the growth of the state in such a way that basic Communist ideas . . . on the development of man and his different forms, on the unique form of the state—the dictatorship of the poor or of the proletariat—are made clear to every viewer. . . .

The history of political conflicts, in particular the history of the great French Revolution, and all kinds of important events of our recent revolutionary history, . . . must also be treated with all due care. . . .

[W]e must not hesitate too much and in choosing between two pictures of roughly the same importance and value we must make the one that can speak to the mind and the heart more vividly from the standpoint of revolutionary propaganda.

By 1920 nearly 500,000 proletarians were involved in *Proletkult* activities, ranging from writing workshops to producing plays for the stage that expressed the social, cultural, and political values and ideals of the working class. The government dissolved *Proletkult* in the early 1930s, along with other forms of artistic experimentation that violated the rigid cultural conformity imposed by Stalinist policies.

Party activists engaged in agitation and propaganda, or agit-prop, to stir up public interest in socialism. In some instances, trains decorated with revolutionary slogans and pictures would traverse the countryside, spreading the gospel of revolution through films, speeches, plays, concerts, posters, and pamphlets. In early 1920 Jacob Okunev, writer for *Soviet Russia*, published by the Friends of Soviet Russia, described one such train.

Lenin's train—that is what the peasants and workers call the train; it now carries the name of Lenin and recently returned to Moscow after a trip around the western part of the Soviet Republic.

A Moscow tram bears the slogans "Long Live the First of May" and "Long Live the Communists of the World" on May Day, 1920.

The train consists of 15 cars, decorated with paintings in bright colors, with forceful and unmistakably revolutionary inscriptions. It contains a moving picture apparatus and screen, a book shop, and a branch of the telegraph bureau, which posted the latest news at every station and sent out bulletins with the latest telegrams. . . .

Everywhere it passed, tens of thousands of leaflets and revolutionary pamphlets were handed out, socialist and revolutionary literature distributed, with books of all kinds, meetings arranged, lectures held, while propaganda instructed and animated the masses. . . . The speeches were made from the roofs of the cars, and revolutionary leaflets and pamphlets were scattered from the bookshop like snowflakes. . . .

At the present time, 5 more trains of this kind are being organized, also boats for a similar purpose . . . , and motor trucks which will make it possible to reach places where neither railroads nor waterways are available. Agitators will penetrate the most hidden nooks of Soviet Russia, there to sow the . . . fire of Revolution, to spread leaflets and pamphlets, and to waken the great masses of the peasants and the poor. . . .

The whole of Soviet Russia will soon be covered with a living net of similar trains and boats. Thanks to them, the center will come in contact with the farthest regions of the republic. It can listen to their wishes and answer their questions.

The revolution released the creative and spontaneous forces of artists in art, theater, cinema, literature, architecture, fashion, and music. Artists of all stripes gave free rein to their imaginations as they tried to lay the foundation of a culture that would represent the interests and values of the socialist revolution and its prime supporter, the proletariat. Some groups of artists, particularly writers, believed that all cultural endeavors should adopt a strictly proletarian point of view and vigorously act on behalf of the revolution. One of the more successful forms of revolutionary culture was the group known as *Proletkult* (Proletarian Culture, or the Association for Proletarian Culture and Education), dedicated to creating new forms of art and education that would express the spirit of the proletarian revolution. Leonid Krasin's report given in 1918 at a *Proletkult* meeting conveys the enthusiasm of those involved in building a revolutionary culture, in this case a new form of music that would express the class interests of the proletariat and stand in contrast to "bourgeois" musical forms.

I propose . . . that we first of all resolve to carry on the struggle against the anti-artistic music of restaurants, cabarets, gypsy music, and so on. This bourgeois music has poisoned real music. It is too widely spread; it has penetrated and poisoned the village. Gramophone records have spread it everywhere. It seems as though all measures are taken for its wider distribution. The struggle against it must be waged energetically, but it is a difficult struggle, since now everything is hurrying to dress itself in revolutionary garb. Writers of revolutionary songs too often write revolutionary words to the most banal tunes.

Proletkult must make music healthy and help the proletariat to take possession of purely musical culture. Everything which is valuable should be granted it, and it will take for itself that which it needs. Folk songs must be returned to the masses. We must bring up a proletariat that listens, understands and creates music.

I will tell you what the Moscow Proletkult has done in this regard. We pay the greatest attention to choral singing as a means for

The First Symphonic Orchestra without a Conductor was established in Moscow in the early 1920s by musicians committed to a leaderless work setting where equality and collective decision making—essential socialist values—were the norm. Authority was diffuse, with each musician learning the entire score and deciding how the piece should be played. In a sense, the conductorless orchestra harkened back to the workers' control movement of 1917. By the end of the 1920s eleven such orchestras existed throughout the Soviet Union, and inspired the formation of similar troupes outside the Soviet Union. They played in factories, military barracks as well as concert halls, and since the musicians were talented, the quality of their performances was quite high. A French pianist offered the following description of a performance he attended in 1917 while visiting Moscow:

The performers group themselves in a large circle, so as to be able to see each other easily, . . . The utmost concentration and attention is demanded of each player, all of whom are fully conscious of their responsibility in that magic circle. . . . Each member of the orchestra has his own important part to play, and glances, raising of the brow, and slight motions of the shoulders . . . are done by each instrumentalist, but so discreetly that the listener . . . seldom notices it. The rhythm of the interpreted work is completely felt by all, and the silence experienced by vigilance acquires for that very reason an unusual emotional importance. For the purpose of determining the rendering, a small group of performers meet and agree upon the nuances and other questions of interpretation. . . .

the harmonious union of all. Choral studios have been formed. In these studios only workers and their children are accepted. There they sing folk songs, learn the history of music, and so on. There is no comprehensive plan for all the studios: each one operates in its own way. Choirs are divided into those for listeners and participants, children and adults, men and women. The instructors are free professional artists and composers. . . .

The English theater expert Huntly Carter wrote extensively about the impact of the revolution on theater and cinema between 1917 and 1923. In a book he published in 1925, Carter emphasizes that the idea of participating in as well as watching amateur theater struck a responsive chord among workers, soldiers, and peasants.

All over Russia little co-operative groups of men, women and children are making theatres for their own use. These are the smaller organizations which have arisen from the private initiative of communists, workers, peasants, soldiers, and students without official aid. Their number is amazing. There are thousands in Moscow, Petrograd, and the cities, towns and villages throughout Russia. A glance at the pages of the *Proletkult Bulletin* for 1918, 1919, 1920 reveals column after column of notes on the theatrical work of countless working-class organizations scattered in all parts of vast Russia. The majority of these groups have formed theatres in clubs, rooms, cellars, in fact, every available place. Besides these there are a number of theatres established in factories. . . .

These theatres, barn, room, cellar, club, and factory, are largely the outcome of the 1917 Revolution, and a great many owe their existence to the proletkult movement. Many belong to the proletkult organization, and many more are influenced by its ideas. . . .

Generally speaking, all these small organizations conceive of the theatre as an instrument of self-expression. It is a place wherein the new working class population can, in their leisure moments, play at destroying the old Tsarist Russia and building up a new Russia more after their own likeness. The organization and work are mainly on voluntary and cooperative lines. Workers, peasants, and others come together, form a dramatic group, and together they support their particular theatre while co-operating in its work. The plays are mostly improvised, and many of the performances have a spontaneous co-operative character. . . .

The production of revolutionary episodes is as follows. The stage-manager relates to the dramatic circle the history of the movement to

Diversity characterized culture during the first decade of Soviet power. Experimental artists, musicians, and writers were free to express their ideas, but the average person found much of the revolutionary art too abstract and inaccessible. Instead, workers and peasants preferred revolutionary art, music, and literature that realistically portrayed the heroic exploits of people, especially soldiers and Party activists during the revolution and civil war. In addition, they continued to enjoy the classics of 19th-century Russian literature and became enthralled with science fiction, detective stories, and adventure novels.

which the episodes belong, then selects an interesting episode, and describes striking individual figures. Soon the circle is penetrated by the atmosphere of the time, and receives exact ideas concerning the social causes of this or that movement springing from the main one. Then the circle proceeds to produce a definite episode, using improvisation for the purpose. . . .

I began my evening with the performance at a Railway Men's Club. The piece was called "Once in an Evening." The story dealt with the rather hackneyed theme of a man who wants to start a revolution and has an obstacle to overcome. In this instance it is a prison where he is spending an enforced holiday. A woman comrade is working to set him free. The Governor of the prison, who knows all about the revolutionary plot, agrees to release the man if she will consent to be his mistress. But no sooner has the agreement been made than the woman learns that the Revolution has taken place. In the end the prison is set on fire, the bold bad general is roasted alive amid communistic cheers, and everything comes communistically right according to plan. The moral is that revolution will out in spite of bureaucracy.

A skit performed in a factory's cafeteria by the Blue Blouse Workers' Theater Group in 1924 was a product of *Proletkult*. In all probability, the show lasted one hour and focused on the day's news and current events. The theme of electrification was a prominent, newsworthy event since the regime was devoting extensive resources to providing electricity to all citizens of the Soviet Union.

Electrification

We, the workers and the peasants,
Swept the tsarist throne away.
We twist a socket in the ceiling
And it shines the night away!

He blew away like a cloud of dust,
His imperial majesty.
We twist a socket in the ceiling
And there's electricity.

Dear heart, wait a bit, you'll see,
The whole world will turn around:
Look it, there's a 'lectrical
Windmill working in our town.

A 1920 government poster entitled "Electricity to the Countryside" boasts of the efforts to modernize peasant life. By bringing electricity and other modern conveniences to the village, the regime hoped to win the support of the peasantry.

In the hut of the widow Natalka,
Something's shining through the night
I'll be darned, I'll be darned,
Moonlight sure don't shine that bright.

Electricity and steam
Reap and mow and forge for us.
Soon electricity, not brains
Will do our thinking for all of us.

The Association of Artists of Revolutionary Russia (AKhRR) in 1922 announced its goal of promoting a realistic treatment of the daily lives of workers, peasants, and soldiers.

The Great October Revolution, in liberating the creative forces of the people, has aroused the consciousness of the masses and the artists—the spokesmen of the people's spiritual life.

Our civic duty before mankind is to set down, artistically and documentarily, the revolutionary impulse of this great moment of history.

We will depict the present day: the life of the Red Army, the workers, the peasants, the revolutionaries, and the heroes of labor.

We will provide a true picture of events and not abstract concoctions discrediting our Revolution in the face of the international proletariat. . . .

It is this content in art that we consider a sign of truth in a work of art, and the desire to express this content induces us, the artists of Revolutionary Russia, to join forces; the tasks before us are strictly defined.

The day of revolution, the moment of revolution, is the day of heroism, the moment of heroism—and now we must reveal our artistic experiences in the monumental forms of the style of heroic realism.

By acknowledging continuity in art and by basing ourselves on the contemporary world view, we create this style of heroic realism and lay the foundation of the universal building of future art, the art of a classless society.

Celebrating Revolution

Significant resources were also devoted to staging public rituals and festivals celebrating the revolution. Mass spectacles commemorating the anniversary of the revolution began in 1918, with the 1920 festival in Petrograd including some 6,000 performers who re-enacted the October Revolution before an audience of tens of thousands. May Day festivities, which had begun in Europe in the 1890s to celebrate workers and their labor, and commemoration of the Bolshevik seizure of power developed into major holidays. Replete with fireworks, well-orchestrated marches, and displays of military hardware, May Day celebrations included speeches by prominent party and government dignitaries throughout the Soviet Union's existence.

In 1920 Huntly Carter witnessed the celebration of the storming of the Winter Palace. His account illustrates how actor and audience merged in the public festival. Indeed, the mass spectacle drew its power and sustenance by the role played by the audience.

Two large stages, White and Red, had been erected in front of the Winter Palace, the immense semi-circle of which formed the background of the play. To the right was a white one; to the left a red one. In the center they were connected by a high arched bridge. At the start 1,500 people were the actors. . . . But at the conclusion more than 100,000 were participating, pouring out from the . . . houses. The spectacle began at ten at night. A searchlight attached to the top of the Alexander Column lit up as bright as day the white stage to the right, on which the Provisional Government of Kerensky was holding a meeting. From the other side, from the invisible Red stage, an indistinct murmur was proceeding; it was the low murmur of Kerensky's word of command, as the ministerial council . . . had just resolved to pursue the war to a victorious termination. The searchlight was turned on to the Red stage. There one saw workmen and women, children and cripples reeling home tired from the factories; maimed soldiers toiling up to the bridge because the order had been issued that new armies were to be formed. At the same time on the White stage capitalists pushed sacks of money with their bellies towards Kerensky's throne, and ministers jumped from the ministerial bench and collected all the valuables in a heap, whilst from the dark side the cry of "Lenin" rose above the murmurs, at first in-

distinctly, then louder and louder. Next Kerensky was seen on his throne at the head of the ministerial bench gesticulating, waving his hands energetically and pointing to the money-bags. But the ministers remained undecided. They fidgeted about on their bench, as from the invisible Red stage the tumultuous sounds became more rhythmic and more collective; one could now hear the notes of a song, which might or might not be "The Internationale." Kerensky was still speaking and gesticulating to the ministerial bench, but the restlessness and indecision had become general. The whole row, clad in grey, were seen to bend over together to the right, then with a sudden jerk to the left. This was repeated several times with increasingly violent movements. . . . As the White stage became wrapped in darkness, the Red one was illuminated. Workmen, women and children, soldiers with arms, and people of all kinds were seen crowding round a gigantic Red Flag. The factories, the prisons—large red scenic constructions with barred windows, their interiors lit up with glaring red light—opened their doors wide. Crowds increasingly emerged from them, and clustered round the Red Flag. From the collective surging crowd "The Internationale" rose as a powerful

Alexander Column

The Alexander Column stands near the Winter Palace to honor Tsar Alexander I.

In 1920, a St. Petersburg theater produced "Storming the Winter Palace," a play that commemorated the Bolshevik seizure of power in 1917.

The Internationale

"The Internationale" is the song of the international socialist movement.

articulate chorus. The word "Lenin" was hurled to the sky as by one mighty shout from a hundred thousand throats. . . .

The Winter Palace now began to take a part in the play. All the first-story windows were suddenly illuminated by a most brilliant light. At the same time fighting on the bridge continued. Accompanied by the rattle of machine guns and wild firing, an action developed, and hand-to-hand fighting took place between the Red Army and the Whites, who had remained behind. Dead and wounded fell down the steps, tumbling over the parapet of the bridge on to the pavement of the square below. In the meanwhile the lights in the Winter Palace were turned on, turned off, and again turned on. For several minutes the battle raged on the bridge, till at last a decision was reached. The whole fighting mass of the Red Army, united and conscious of its strength, this mass singing "The Internationale," pressed down the steps towards the Winter Palace. Regiments emerged from side streets . . . , and joined those coming from the stage in tens and tens of thousands. . . .

A hundred thousand were approaching the Winter Palace. The immense square was crowded with marching, running, singing, shouting people, all pressing towards the Winter Palace. Rifle shots, the rattle of machine guns, the terrible thunder from the "Aurora"— all this was awful, arresting, almost indescribable. Then came rockets to announce the end. The guns of the "Aurora" became silent, the shouting died down, and the mass melted in the night.

No one who sees a mass spectacle of the kind can fail to be impressed by its magnitude, and the almost ecstatic spirit of the multitude. Of course, it bears various interpretations. The political-minded will see in it a habit of counter-revolutionists to avail themselves of the opportunity afforded by a "theatrical bombardment" to foment risings and to teach the method of carrying them out. The sociologist, the historian, the mystic, the moralist, the psychologist will each see it in his own way also. As for that rarity, the man of the theater possessing social ideas, to him it can appear only as a revelation, pregnant with suggestion towards that theater of the future which shall fully answer the need of spiritual social service.

Aurora

A volley from the battleship "Aurora" signaled the beginning of the Bolsheviks' attack on the Winter Palace in 1917.

Organizing the annual celebration of the revolution required the work of countless individuals, while the actual events saw the participation of thousands of people. The regime used a new means of communication, the radio, to reach Soviet citizens who lived far from the public spectacles that occurred in the streets of Moscow and Leningrad. Live radio broadcasts were one way to promote a sense of unity and common

experience. This radio broadcast of the 1925 celebration of the revolution in Moscow enabled listeners living thousands of miles from the capital to feel as if they were part of a nationwide celebration.

Comrade workers, peasants, and everyone else listening to this radio-newspaper in near and distant cities and villages of our Union. You are sitting by your radio receivers and loudspeakers and listening to Moscow. You want to know how Moscow is celebrating the eighth anniversary of the October Revolution. We won't be transmitting all of today's speeches, because they were already broadcast from Red Square and you've heard them. But we will tell you how Moscow is abuzz and enjoying itself today.

Let's begin from early morning. The day started out cloudy. There was a drizzle. But that had no effect on the mood. The city was sparkling with bright posters, fresh greenery, fiery flags, and the portraits of revolutionary leaders.

Life began early on the outskirts. Building decorations were hastily completed in several places. Every factory, every club, every co-operative was painstakingly decorated with bright-red cloth, slogans, and garlands of green. . . .

Petrograd workers celebrate May Day in 1920 by decorating a truck with ribbons and a bust of Lenin. Soviet citizens commemorated May Day and the October Revolution with festive parades featuring floats and banners that gave the towns and cities of the country a carnival atmosphere.

Workers began to gather for the demonstration at ten in the morning. Joyful laughter, merry jokes, and the cheerful exchanges of thousands of workers. . . . The human mass swiftly arranged itself in rows and columns.

By eleven o'clock, the streets and squares of Moscow were overflowing with people. Automobiles filled with children honked ceaselessly. Huge masses of people streamed into the center from the outlying districts. The merry chatter of the marchers was mixed with the happy hum of children's voices and cheerful orchestral strains. The air was filled with the Great Holiday's triumphant noise. . . . The holiday atmosphere was joyful.

Now let's take a look at the main streets leading to Red Square. Here the stream of people gets thicker. Endless columns of people go by. They stretch from all ends of Moscow, and it seems that no power can stop this endless stream.

Symbols of the revolution such as the hammer and sickle and the use of the color red (the color of European socialism) became common currency. In addition, new parents proclaimed their commitment to the new Soviet state by naming their children after revolutionary persons and events in Russia and elsewhere. Some adults got caught up in the fervor of the times and renamed themselves. Some common names were Vladlen (Vladimir Lenin); Ninel (Lenin spelled backwards); Melor (Marx, Engels, Lenin, October Revolution); Melsor (Marx, Engels, Lenin, Stalin, October Revolution); Robespierre, the famous French revolutionary of the 1790s; Revoliutsiia (Revolution); Traktor (Tractor); Elektrifikatsiia (Electrification); and Turbina (Turbine). Some revolutionary names were clearly the result of misunderstandings and ignorance about the meaning of foreign words, such as Vinaigrette and Embryo.

Plants, factories, institutions, organizations, and schools are all marching toward Red Square. Banners and posters flutter in the air. The children are especially animated. Hundreds of trucks transport them all over the city. The kids wave red flags and shout greetings to the passing columns. Joyful exclamations and anniversary salutations can be heard from every side street. Gaily decorated automobiles drive by. . . .

We're next to Lenin's tomb. A megaphone booms: "Long live the worldwide victory of workers!" The little red flag quivers and the proletarian tot yells in a bell-like little voice: "Hurrah!" . . .

The Debate about NEP

Industry and technology would one day be the backbone of a socialist economy in the Soviet Union, but the leadership could not agree on the policies needed to develop the country's industrial base. Leon Trotsky and others, known as the Left Opposition, believed that the government should promote rapid industrialization and finance economic development by taxing the peasants. The Left Opposition agreed that the NEP had to be maintained in order to keep the peasants placated, but it also worried that industrial workers were getting the short end of the stick in terms of government policies. In this essay entitled "Theses on Industry" from 1923, Trotsky argued that failure to adopt measures to promote industrialization would make it difficult to realize the dream of building a proletarian society.

The mutual relations which exist in our country between the working class and the peasantry rest in the last analysis on the mutual relations between industry and agriculture. In the last resort the working class can retain and strengthen its role as leader not through the State apparatus or the army, but by means of the industry which gives rise to the proletariat. The Party, the trade unions, the youth associations, our schools, etc., have for their task the education and preparation of new generations of the working class. But all this work would prove as if built on sand did it not have for its basis a continually expanding industry. Only the development of industry creates the unshakable basis for the dictatorship of the proletariat. At present agriculture is of primary importance in the economic life of Soviet Russia, although the technical level on which it stands is still very low.

Only in proportion as industry makes real progress and as the heavy industries—which form the only firm basis of the proletarian dictatorship—are restored, and in proportion as the work of electrification is completed will it become both possible and, indeed, inevitable to alter the relative significance in our economic life of agriculture and industry and to shift the centre of gravity from the former to the latter. The Party must work systematically and perseveringly, whatever the sacrifice or labour, to accelerate this process, especially as regards the rapid restoration of heavy industry.

How long the period of the predominant importance of peasant economy in the economic system of our federation will last will depend not only upon our internal economic progress, which in view of the general conditions mentioned above can be but very gradual, but also upon the process of development taking place beyond the boundaries of Russia, i.e., before all, upon the way the revolution in the West and in the East will proceed. The overthrow of the bourgeoisie in any one of the most advanced capitalist countries would very quickly make its impress upon the whole tempo of our economic development, as it would at once multiply the material and technical resources for socialist construction. While never losing sight of this international perspective, our Party must at the same time never for a moment forget or omit to keep in mind the predominant importance of peasant economy, when it is estimating the consequences of any step it is on the point of taking. . . .

Only such industry can prove victorious which renders more than it swallows up. Industry which lives at the expense of the budget, i.e., at the expense of agriculture, could not possibly be a firm and lasting support for the dictatorship of the proletariat. The question of creating surplus value in State industry is the fateful question for the soviet power, i.e., for the proletariat.

An expanded reproduction of State industry, which is unthinkable without the accumulation of surplus value by the State, forms in its turn the condition for the development of our agriculture in a socialist and not in a capitalist direction.

It is therefore through State industry that the road lies which leads to the socialist order of society.

In contrast to the position of the Left, Nikolai Bukharin, with the support of Stalin, argued for a more moderate pace of industrialization that did not rely on the peasantry to pay for it. Rather, industrial development could be financed by producing goods that the peasants would consume, thereby fueling further growth of industry. According to Bukharin, the regime had to be careful not to antagonize the peasants with onerous taxation. Memories of the peasant unrest of the civil war years inspired

The Kremlin commissioned the making of this porcelain plate in 1922 to praise the Communist International (Comintern), also known as the Third International, which was the umbrella organization of communist parties throughout the world. The plate reads, "We will kindle the whole world with the flame of the Third International."

Bukharin to caution against disrupting the stability of the NEP years. In 1926 Bukharin expressed his views in a report to the Leningrad party organization, warning also about sectionalism.

The first thesis advanced by the opposition is the assertion that our industry is retrogressing, and that the disproportion between agriculture and city industry is increasing, to the detriment of city industry.... The total balance is undoubtedly in favor of the growth of industry as compared with agriculture.

The second thesis advanced by the opposition in the sphere of economic policy in its relationship to the industrialization of the country is the thesis that we must now carry on a greatly intensified industrial policy, this to be accomplished in the first place by increasing the prices of our industrial products....

We believe this policy to be entirely *wrong*,...

How much can we take away from the peasantry, *to what extent* and *by what methods* can we accomplish the pumping-over process, what are the limits of the pumping over, and how shall we calculate in order to arrive at favorable results? This is the question. Here lies the difference between us and the opposition, a difference which may be defined by saying that the comrades of the opposition ... are desirous of putting so severe a pressure upon the peasantry that in our opinion the result would be economically irrational and politically unallowable....

The Central Committee ... has been faced by the fact that a number of comrades, including some holding extremely responsible positions, had actually taken such steps as the convocation of an illegal meeting against the party and its leaders. *Were we to tolerate such actions, our party would cease to exist tomorrow as a Leninist party.* We cannot tolerate this. We say to these comrades: Defend your principles, declare your standpoint, *speak in the party meetings*; but if you take to the forest, if you will not reply to our questions, ... if you choose the method of organizing a new party within our party, the method of illegal organization, then we shall fight you relentlessly....

In 1924 Stalin published *Problems of Leninism*, in which he expounded on the concept of "socialism in one country." Stalin challenged the Bolshevik belief that worldwide proletarian revolution had to occur before the Soviet Union could itself build a socialist society. It was clear that world revolution was not in the offing, but rather than admit that the revolution was foundering, Stalin argued that the Soviet Union could nevertheless embark on the path of building socialism. He denounced Trotsky, who still insisted that world revolution was a necessary condition of building

Pumping over

"Pumping over" refers to the transfer of resources from agriculture to industry.

a socialist society in the Soviet Union. Stalin correctly read the mood of many rank-and-file party activists who were eager to get on with the important task of creating a socialist society in the Soviet Union. "Socialism in one country" became an effective political slogan for Stalin by emphasizing that the Russian revolution was self-sufficient and did not depend on events elsewhere to succeed.

According to Trotsky, the necessary strength can be found only "in the arena of the world proletarian revolution."

But what if the world revolution is fated to arrive with some delay? Is there any ray of hope for our revolution? Trotsky offers no ray of hope; for "the contradictions in the position of a workers' government . . . can be solved *only* . . . in the arena of the world proletarian revolution." According to this plan, there is but one prospect left for our revolution: to vegetate in its own contradictions and rot away while waiting for the world revolution.

What is the dictatorship of the proletariat according to Lenin?

The dictatorship of the proletariat is a power which rests on an alliance between the proletariat and the laboring masses of the peasantry for "the complete overthrow of capital" and for "the final establishment and consolidation of Socialism."

What is the dictatorship of the proletariat according to Trotsky?

The dictatorship of the proletariat is a power which comes "into hostile collision". . . with "the broad masses of the peasants" and seeks the solution of its "contradictions" *only* "in the arena of the world proletarian revolution."

What difference is there between this "theory of permanent revolution" and the well-known theory of Menshevism which repudiates the concept of dictatorship of the proletariat?

Essentially, there is no difference.

There can be no doubt at all. "Permanent revolution" is not a mere underestimation of the revolutionary potentialities of the peasant movement. "Permanent revolution" is an underestimation of the peasant movement which leads to the repudiation of Lenin's theory of the dictatorship of the proletariat.

Trotsky's "permanent revolution" is a variety of Menshevism.

This is how matters stand with regard to the first peculiar feature of the October Revolution. . . .

After all this, what does Trotsky's assertion that a revolutionary Russia could not hold out in the face of a conservative Europe signify?

It can signify only this: firstly, that Trotsky does not appreciate the inherent strength of our revolution; secondly, that Trotsky does not understand the inestimable importance of the moral support which is given to our revolution by the workers of the West and the peasants of the East; thirdly, that Trotsky does not perceive the internal infirmity which is consuming imperialism today. . . .

There can be no doubt that the universal theory of a simultaneous victory of the revolution in the principal countries of Europe, the theory that the victory of socialism in one country is impossible, has proved to be an artificial and untenable theory. The seven years' history of the proletarian revolution in Russia speaks not for but against this theory. This theory is not only inacceptable as a scheme of development of the world revolution, for it contradicts obvious facts. It is still less acceptable as a slogan; for it fetters, rather than releases, the initiative of individual countries which, by reason of certain historical conditions, obtain the opportunity to break through the front of capital alone; for it does not stimulate an active onslaught on capital in individual countries, but encourages passive waiting for the moment of the "universal climax"; for it cultivates among the proletarians of the different countries not the spirit of revolutionary determination, but the mood of Hamlet-like doubt over the question, "What if the others fail to back us up?" Lenin was absolutely right in saying that the victory of the proletariat in one country is a "typical case," that "a simultaneous revolution in a number of countries" can only be a "rare exception."

Stop it, . . . don't make a fool of yourself. Everybody knows that theory is not exactly your field.

—David Riazanov, a Marxist theorist commenting on Stalin's "socialism in one country"

After Lenin's death Lev Kamenev and Grigorii Zinoviev, two influential men of the Politburo, allied with Stalin in order to ensure Trotsky would not assume the mantle of Lenin's successor. However, in 1925 Zinoviev and Kamenev began to put out feelers to Trotsky for help in forming the "United Opposition" in order to challenge Stalin's growing control of the party and government. Zinoviev and Kamenev agreed with Trotsky that Stalin and Bukharin were ignoring the difficulties of building a socialist society dominated by the peasantry. They also denounced the bureaucratization of party and government organizations, which adversely affected economic productivity, and the stifling of party democracy. Stalin used these developments to consolidate his grip on the levers of power. In 1926 the United Opposition issued a proclamation that outlined their concern with the growing concentration of power in the hands of Stalin and the lack of vigorous debate at the highest levels of the Party.

The immediate cause of all the sharpening crises in the party is in bureaucratism, which has grown amazingly in the period following the death of Lenin, and continues to grow. . . .

An official show prevails in the meetings, together with the apathy which is unavoidably connected with it. Frequently only an insignificant minority remains at the time of voting; the participants in the meeting hasten to leave so that they will not be compelled to vote for decisions dictated earlier. No resolutions anywhere are ever adopted otherwise than "unanimously." All this is gravely reflected in the internal life of the Party organization. Members of the Party are afraid openly to express aloud their most cherished thoughts, wishes and demands. . . .

In 1920 a party conference under Lenin's direction considered it essential to point out the impermissibility of the fact that in the mobilization of the comrades, party organs and individual comrades were guided by some considerations other than business ones. Any repression whatever against comrades because they think differently about one or another question or party decision is impermissible. The whole present practice contradicts this decision at every step. Genuine discipline is shaken apart and replaced by subordination to the influential figures in the apparatus. The comrades on whom the party can rely in the most difficult days are pushed out of the staff in ever greater numbers, they are thrown around, exiled, persecuted, and replaced steadily and regularly by casual people, untested, but who are distinguished by silent obedience. . . .

The bureaucratic regime has spread like rust into the life of every plant and workshop. If the members of the party are in fact deprived of the right to criticize by the district committee, the provincial committee, or the Central Committee, in the plant they are deprived of the right to subject the immediate authorities to criticism. Party members are scared. The administrator who is able as a loyal person to guarantee himself the support of the secretary of the next higher organization thus insures himself against criticism from below and not infrequently also from responsibility for mismanagement or actual stupidity. . . .

Only on the foundation of party democracy is healthy, collective leadership possible. There is no other path. In struggle and in work on this, the only correct path, our unrecriminating support is guaranteed to the Central Committee wholly and fully.

Stalin and Bukharin responded to the criticisms of the United Opposition by accusing Trotsky, Zinoviev, and Kamenev of undermining party unity and violating the 1921 ban on factionalism that they had supported. Consequently, in 1927 Stalin co-engineered the expulsion of Trotsky, Zinoviev, and Kamenev and their adherents from the Party. While Zinoviev,

Kamenev, and their followers were reinstated in the Party after they admitted their errors, supporters of Trotsky were exiled to distant regions of the country. Trotsky was exiled to Central Asia and in 1929 expelled from the Soviet Union. He eventually settled in Mexico, where he criticized Stalin from afar. At the Party congress in December 1927, Stalin gave a report explaining why the Party was correct to deprive the United Opposition of its membership.

Here, the opposition utterly break away from the Leninist principle of organization and take the path of organizing a second party, the path of organizing a new International.

Such are the seven fundamental questions which indicate that on all these questions the opposition have slipped into Menshevism.

Can these Menshevik views of the opposition be regarded as compatible with our Party's ideology, with our Party's program, with its tactics, with the tactics of the Comintern, with the organizational principles of Leninism?

Under no circumstances; not for a single moment!

You will ask: how could such an opposition come into being among us, where are their social roots? I think that the social roots of the opposition lie in the fact that the urban petty-bourgeois strata are being ruined under the conditions of our development, in the fact that these strata are discontented with the regime of the dictatorship of the proletariat, in the striving of these strata to change this regime, to "improve" it in the spirit of establishing bourgeois democracy.

I have already said that as a result of our progress, as a result of the growth of our industry, as a result of the growth of the relative weight of the socialist forms of economy, a section of the petty-bourgeoisie, particularly of the urban bourgeoisie, is being ruined and is going under. The opposition reflect the grumbling and discontent of these strata with the regime of the proletarian revolution.

Such are the social roots of the opposition. . . .

Why did the Party expel Trotsky and Zinoviev? Because they are the organizers of the entire anti-Party opposition (*voices*: "Quite right!"), because they set themselves the aim of breaking the laws of the Party, because they thought that nobody would dare touch them, because they wanted to create for themselves the privileged position of nobles in the Party.

But do we want to have a privileged nobility and an unprivileged peasantry in the Party? Shall we Bolsheviks, who uprooted the nobility, restore them now in our Party? (*Applause.*)

Comintern

The "Comintern" (Communist International) was established by the Bolsheviks to coordinate the efforts of communist parties all over the world in an effort to foment international proletarian revolution.

You ask: why did we expel Trotsky and Zinoviev from the Party? Because we do not want a nobility in the Party. Because there is one law in our Party, and all members of the Party have equal rights. (*Voices*: "Quite right!" *Prolonged applause.*)

If the opposition wants to be in the Party let them submit to the will of the Party, to its laws, to its instructions, without reservations, without equivocation. If they refuse to do that, let them go wherever they please. (*Voices*: "Quite right!" *Applause.*) We do not want new laws providing privileges for the opposition, and we will not create them. (*Applause.*)

The question is raised about terms. We have only one set of terms: the opposition must disarm wholly and entirely, in ideological and organizational respects. (*Voices*: "Quite right!" *Prolonged applause.*)

They must renounce their anti-Bolshevik views openly and honestly, before the whole world. (*Voices*: "Quite right!" *Prolonged applause.*)

They must denounce the mistakes they have committed, mistakes which have grown into crimes against the Party, openly and honestly, before the whole world.

They must surrender their nuclei to us in order that the Party may be able to dissolve them without leaving a trace. (*Voices*: "Quite right!" *Prolonged applause.*)

Either that, or let them leave the Party. And if they don't go out, we'll throw them out. (*Voices*: "Quite right!" *Prolonged applause.*)

That is how the matter stands with the opposition, comrades.

CHAPTER 5

Stalin's Revolution from Above, 1928–1932

A male peasant and his son (or perhaps his grandson) inspect the first tractor in their village in 1926. The regime publicized its efforts to modernize agriculture, though in many cases the tractors on display were not yet ready for use.

At the same time that he became the undisputed head of the party and leader of the Soviet Union, Stalin decided to push ahead with his plan to build a socialist society. Beginning in late 1928 the Kremlin adopted the twin policies of rapid industrialization and collectivization of agriculture. They were designed to transform the social and economic landscape of the Soviet Union and propel the country into the ranks of the modern industrialized world. Historians frequently refer to these programs as the second revolution that complemented the Bolsheviks' seizure of political power in 1917. The decision to embark on the path of rapid industrialization stemmed from ideological, political, and economic concerns. Many party leaders, including Stalin, had grown impatient with the New Economic Policy (NEP) and its policy of favoring the peasantry. The Soviet Union was the world's first socialist state, but Karl Marx had predicted that socialism would come first to a highly industrialized society where the proletariat comprised the majority. In the Soviet Union of the 1920s, the peasantry was numerically still the dominant social group, and NEP was neither stimulating industrialization nor the emergence of a proletariat. The Soviet countryside and city experienced vast upheavals as the country's leadership carried out monumental changes that radically altered the fabric of society. The human and financial costs were tremendous, but the achievements noteworthy.

Prior to collectivization each peasant family on its own tilled the land, which often consisted of scattered narrow strips. In collective farms (*kolkhoz*, singular form in Russian) all members would pool their tools and livestock and work together under the direction of farm managers, who took their cues from the state's economic planners. The consolidation of all the land at the disposal of the collective farm and the adoption of modern farming techniques and equipment would replace strip farming and hopefully lead to increased food production.

The hallmarks of Stalin's revolution from above were central state planning of all economic activity. Under the auspices of Gosplan (State Planning Committee), economists drew up the First Five-Year Plan in 1928; these plans became the basis of the command economy of the Soviet Union until its dissolution in 1991. In a command economy, all economic activities are determined by a central plan drawn up by the state, not by the operation of a market that pays attention to the law of supply and demand. All resources, both material and human, came under the purview of government and party officials who mobilized society for the project of state-directed modernization. Moreover, economic development would be financed on the backs of peasants and workers.

Party doctrine envisioned the end of traditional peasant agriculture and its replacement by large-scale collective farms that entailed the reorganization of peasant farming with an eye to making it more efficient and productive. Stalin hoped that collectivization of agriculture would provide the state with complete control over the fruits of the peasantry's labor and supply the resources necessary for feeding the newly emerging industrial workforce. The state also needed grain for sale abroad as payment for machinery and other items required for the industrialization drive. Collectivization ensured that Soviet authorities now could exercise greater control over agricultural production, since the peasants were no longer free to determine how much grain to grow or how much of it they would market. Instead, collective farms guaranteed the state a steady flow of agricultural output since the peasants were required to turn over a fixed amount of their output to the state no matter what they actually produced. This allowed the peasants to hold onto barely enough to ensure their survival.

Massive peasant resistance to collective farms spurred the regime to stage scenes showing peasants eagerly joining collective farms. The presence of armed soldiers to ensure compliance, not to mention the arrests, summary executions, and deportations of peasants, underscored the government's reliance on force and intimidation. The vast majority of peasants, both rich and poor, recognized the threat collective farms posed to their independence and believed that collectivization signified the return of serfdom, which had been abolished in 1861.

Collectivization led to food rationing throughout the country for several years in the 1930s. Membership in collective farms was compulsory, yet peasants resisted joining because they resented the state's interference with their traditional way of life and farming. They protested by engaging in minor rebellions, refusing to work hard, and slaughtering their cows, pigs, horses, and other livestock rather than give them to the collective farm. Scholars estimate that the peasants killed more than half their horses, sheep, and goats during the initial stages of collectivization. The collectivization process so disrupted agricultural production that famine broke out in 1932–33, resulting in the deaths of millions of peasants and alienating the vast majority of the peasantry. Collectivization undoubtedly broke the independent spirit of the peasantry, but all citizens of the Soviet Union suffered its legacy for the next several generations. Stalin's revolution in the countryside was an unmitigated fiasco from which the country never fully recovered.

The First Five-Year Plan set overly optimistic and unrealistic production goals that were nearly impossible to achieve. The country simply lacked all the resources required for investment in industry, and the state reacted by resorting to coercive measures to enforce labor discipline and stimulate productivity. The party exhorted society to complete the plan in four years, thereby prompting both workers and managers to sacrifice quality for the sake of production. The government appealed to the patriotism of Soviet workers, counting on them for enthusiastic support of the industrialization drive.

Stalin's revolution from above had mixed results. The First Five-Year Plan, which was followed by 12 subsequent ones, created the basis of an urban, industrialized Soviet Union that began to correspond more closely to the socialist society predicted by Marx, Lenin, and others. Between 1928 and the end of the 1930s the population of the cities nearly doubled and the production of heavy industrial goods such as steel, iron, coal, and electricity increased dramatically. By the end of the First Five-Year Plan in 1932 (Stalin declared it fulfilled one year ahead of schedule), unemployment had essentially vanished in cities.

The disadvantage of this industrial expansion was that the Five-Year Plans in the 1930s stressed quantity over quality; initially lowered the standard of living for most workers through rising prices; intensified pace of work, stagnant wages, and inadequate housing and urban amenities; and ignored the growing needs of Soviet citizens for consumer goods, a problem that continued to plague the country for decades to come. Still, there is no denying that the industrialization drive initiated in 1928 catapulted the Soviet Union into the world's second largest industrial power within several decades.

Beating Russia into the 20th Century

Stalin's decision to launch an industrialization drive required a renunciation of NEP. Fearing the danger such a policy would have on social and political stability, Bukharin began to criticize Stalin, warning him that he risked provoking the peasantry, who had grown accustomed to NEP.

In 1929 Stalin delivered a speech to the Party in which he reacted to Bukharin's opposition by labeling him a "Right deviationist."

The fight against the Right deviation is one of the most decisive duties of our party.... Does Bukharin's group understand that to refuse to fight the Right deviation is to *betray* the working class, to *betray* the revolution?

This badge was awarded to a "Shock Worker for Fulfilling the Instructions of Stalin." A shock worker was someone who exceeded the production targets set by the Five-Year Plan and was heralded as an exemplary builder of socialism.

In 1928 Bukharin established the "Right Opposition," comprising leading party members who opposed what they believed to be Stalin's risky policy. In a speech delivered in July 1928 to the Party's elite, Bukharin reiterated why he supported the continuation of NEP. He also expressed concern about the use of "extraordinary measures" reminiscent of War Communism, when the state forcibly seized grain from the peasants.

If we want to catch up with Western Europe—and we want to do this—if we want to increase the tempo of accumulation for socialist industry—and we want to do this—if we take into account our general economic backwardness, our poverty, then it is perfectly clear that great difficulties for our building stem from all this. We want to solve a series of great tasks at once: the maximum accumulation in socialist industry, the maximum increase in agriculture, the maximum consumption for the working class and the toiling masses in general,... These tasks cannot be solved simultaneously....

Can we have such difficulties this year as we had last year? We can. How will we react to this? We will turn to the application of extraordinary measures if such difficulties are met within the coming year, but if we apply them, will we do so to the same extent or not? It seems to me that this is the most agonizing and important question that faces us....

We must in no case turn toward allowing the expanded production of extraordinary measures.

Despite the pride Soviet officials took in the industrialization drive, many nevertheless urged a slowdown because of the strains placed on the economy. Stalin lashed out at those who opposed the tempo of industrialization. In a 1931 speech to factory managers, Stalin defended rapid industrialization and emphasized the link between Soviet industrialization and the defense of the Soviet Union from the threat posed by its capitalist enemies, particularly countries that had either conquered or defeated Russia in the past. Moreover, it was a war against Russia's past and for its future, and the language and rhetoric he used constantly focused on war and threats from abroad. Many observers cite the last paragraph to show that Stalin had an eye toward the forthcoming war with Germany, which began in 1941. However, in 1931, when Stalin delivered this speech to factory managers, Hitler and the Nazi party had not yet come to power in Germany and no one had an inkling that a second world war would break out by the end of the decade.

It is sometimes asked whether it is not possible to slow down the tempo a bit, to put a check on the movement. No, comrades, it is not possible! The tempo must not be reduced! On the contrary, we must increase it as much as is within our powers and possibilities. This is dictated to us by our obligations to the workers and peasants of the U.S.S.R. This is dictated to us by our obligations to the working class of the whole world.

To slacken the tempo would mean falling behind. And those who fall behind get beaten. But we do not want to be beaten. No, we refuse to be beaten! One feature of the history of old Russia was the continual beatings she suffered for falling behind, for her backwardness. She was beaten by the Mongol Khans. She was beaten by the Turkish beys. She was beaten by the Swedish feudal lords. She was beaten by the Polish and Lithuanian gentry. She was beaten by the British and French capitalists. She was beaten by the Japanese barons. All beat her—for her backwardness: for military backwardness, for cultural backwardness, for political backwardness, for industrial backwardness, for agricultural backwardness. She was beaten because to do so was profitable and could be done with impunity. Do you remember the words of the pre-revolutionary poet: "You are poor and abundant, mighty and impotent, Mother Russia."

These words of the old poet were well learned by those gentlemen. They beat her, saying: "You are abundant," so one can enrich oneself at your expense. They beat her, saying: "You are poor and impotent," so you can be beaten and plundered with impunity. Such is the law of the exploiters—to beat the backward and the weak. It is the jungle law of capitalism. You are backward, you are weak—therefore you are wrong; hence, you can be beaten and enslaved. You are mighty—therefore you are right; hence, we must be wary of you.

That is why we must no longer lag behind.

In the past we had no fatherland, nor could we have one. But now that we have overthrown capitalism and power is in the hands of the working class, we have a fatherland, and we will defend its independence. Do you want our socialist fatherland to be beaten and to lose its independence? If you do not want this you must put an end to its backwardness in the shortest possible time and develop genuine Bolshevik tempo in building up its socialist system of economy. There is no other way. That is why Lenin said during the October Revolution: "Either perish, or overtake and outstrip the advanced capitalist countries."

In 1932 a government-sponsored organization of foreign workers published this pamphlet for an English-speaking audience that explained how the Five-Year Plan operated in Lyubertsy, a factory district outside Moscow. Pamphlets such as this one publicized the achievements of the Soviet Union to non-Soviet audiences.

We are fifty or a hundred years behind the advanced countries. We must make good this distance in ten years. Either we do it, or they crush us.

The War Against the Peasantry and Church

Women played a prominent role in the peasants' opposition to collectivization, but party and government officials believed that female rebels had fallen under the sway of counterrevolutionary *kulaks*. According to those in charge of collectivization, women were ignorant and prone to irrational, disorderly behavior, thereby making them perfect dupes for kulaks. As a consequence, women who engaged in active resistance tended to avoid punishment since the officials believed they were not responsible for their actions. The peasant community counted on this official perception and response and sometimes avoided government retaliation.

The state's decision to use intimidation, coercion, and violence to ensure the compliance of the peasantry and end resistance to collectivization exacerbated the situation in the Soviet countryside. Millions of peasants were arrested and deported to far-flung reaches of Siberia and Central Asia. Entire peasant families were transported in freight cars, with many dying of disease and starvation en route to their place of exile. Those peasants fortunate enough to survive the arduous journey found themselves either languishing in the burgeoning forced labor camp system or forced to make ends meet in unfamiliar and inhospitable surroundings.

Party officials believed that *kulaks*, or well-to-do peasants, were behind the opposition to the transformation of agriculture. Specifically, they were accused of withholding grain from the market in order to sabotage the industrialization campaign. The party labeled *kulaks* a class enemy of the proletariat and the socialist state since they had the most to lose as landholders. *Kulaks* comprised only a small portion of the peasantry, but the party had a useful weapon: it could characterize as a *kulak* any peasant who resisted collectivization. Stalin launched a campaign in late 1929 and early 1930 to "liquidate the *kulak* as a class" as a method of frightening peasants to join collective farms. The anti-*kulak* offensive allowed Stalin to blame opposition to his policies on class enemies and marked the launching of a civil war against the peasants, a policy reminiscent of grain requisitioning during the earlier civil war. In this 1929 speech to students studying agriculture, Stalin made clear his position on how the Soviet Union could become an industrial powerhouse.

Can we advance our socialized industry at an accelerated rate while having to rely on an agricultural base, such as is provided by small peasant farming, which is incapable of expanded reproduction, and which, in addition, is the predominant force in our national economy? No, we cannot. Can the Soviet government and the work of Socialist construction be, for any length of time, based on two *different* foundations; on the foundation of the most large-scale and concentrated Socialist industry and on the foundation of the most scattered and backward, small-commodity peasant farming? No, they cannot. Sooner or later this would be bound to end in the complete collapse of the whole national economy. What, then, is the solution? The solution lies in enlarging the agricultural units, in making agriculture capable of accumulation, of expanded reproduction, and in thus changing the base of our national economy. But how are the agricultural units to be enlarged? There are two ways of doing this. There is the *capitalist* way, which is to enlarge the agricultural units by introducing capitalism in agriculture—a way which leads to the impoverishment of the peasantry and to the development of capitalist enterprises in agriculture. We reject this way as incompatible with the Soviet economic system. There is a second way: the *Socialist* way, which is to set up collective farms and state farms, the way which leads to the amalgamation of the small peasant farms into large collective farms, technically and scientifically equipped, and to the squeezing out of the capitalist elements from agriculture. We are in favor of this second way. . . .

Now, as you see, we have the material base which enables us to *substitute* for kulak output the output of the collective farms and state farms. That is why our offensive against the kulaks is now meeting with undeniable success. That is how the offensive against the kulaks must be carried on, if we mean a real offensive and not futile declamations against the kulaks.

That is why we have recently passed from the policy of *restricting* the exploiting proclivities of the kulaks to the policy of *eliminating the kulaks as a class.*

Well, what about the policy of expropriating the kulaks? Can we permit the expropriation of kulaks in the regions of solid collectivization? This question is asked in various quarters. A ridiculous question! We could not permit the expropriation of the kulaks as long as we were pursuing the policy of restricting the exploiting proclivities of the kulaks, as long as we were unable to launch a determined offensive against the kulaks, as long as we were unable to substitute for kulak output the output of the collective farms. . . . Now we are able to carry on a determined offensive against the kulaks, to break their resistance, to eliminate them as a class. . . . Now the expropriation of the kulaks is an integral part of the formation and development of the collective farms. That is why it is ridiculous and fatuous to expatiate today on the expropriation of the kulaks. You do not lament the loss of the hair of one who has been beheaded.

This 1930 poster proclaims, "We Will Annihilate the *Kulaks* as a Class." The government urged peasants to resist what it believed to be the machinations of the *kulaks*, who were accused of opposing collectivization and preventing the modernization of agriculture.

What is a skeleton?

A peasant from a collective farm who has given the state wool, lard, meat, and eggs.

—Popular riddle from the 1920s–1930s

In May 1929 this report about peasant unrest was provided to the top leadership of the Party. The language indicates a suspicious and condescending attitude on the part of the authorities as well as an unwillingness to acknowledge the deep resentment of collectivization on the part of the peasants.

Top Secret

Information Department of the Central Committee of the All-Union Communist Party (of Bolsheviks) *TsK VKP (b)*

Political Report No. 1

Mass Uprisings Among *Kulaks* in the Countryside (May 1929)

Recently, in connection with the intensified offensive against the *kulaks* on two fronts—the grain requisition program and the restructuring of rural society—*kulak* anti-Soviet activities have increased significantly. More to the point, the *kulaks* no longer confine themselves to acts of individual sabotage but are beginning to adopt more sophisticated, openly counterrevolutionary tactics in the form of mass demonstrations, frequently connecting these demonstrations against the ongoing campaign to close churches, mosques, Islamic religious schools, . . . etc. As a result, this network of underground *kulak* groups, which has already made its presence felt in the Soviet election campaign, today has surfaced with impudent mass demonstrations with corresponding slogans and demands. These actions vary: in grain-procurement areas, they are against surrendering grain; in consuming areas, they focus on the difficulties of obtaining foodstuffs; in areas where campaigns are under way to close churches, they are in support of faith, religion, the old way of life; and almost everywhere, they are against collectivization, against new forms of land distribution, against the social restructuring of the countryside. . . .

A typical uprising took place in the village of Mikhailovskii on April 11 and 12, where "a mob under the control of confirmed counterrevolutionary elements ruled the village for two days. 150 armed men were required to bring the mob to heel." . . .

The incident can be summarized as follows. The *kulaks* took advantage of a mistake committed by the authorities when the latter sealed the barns of 28 farms. . . . The *kulaks* managed to sway the most backward segment of the population, namely the women, and through them the men, with an openly counterrevolutionary platform and managed to disrupt the grain procurement drive. They beat up the chairman of the surplus confiscation commission, shut down auctions of kulak property, seized property which had already been sold at auction, and used the threat of mob violence to compel the authorities to release prisoners under arrest, unseal the barns, and provide guarantees of no reprisals for the uprising. . . .

In another village . . . on April 12 an inventory of the property of peasants caught with surplus grain led a mob of 200 individuals (primarily women) under the leadership of the *kulak* Rubanovich to surround the village Soviet building, lock the 24 members of the village Soviet inside, and demand a halt to grain requisition. And if the Soviet refused, the mob threatened to burn down the building. The timely arrival of a police squad kept the mob from carrying out their threat. As soon as the police arrived, the mob began to disperse. While pursuing the kulak Rubanovich, one policeman's horse got stuck in the mud, and a *kulak* tried to kill the policeman with a knife, but was prevented from doing so by another policeman, who shot and wounded the kulak with his revolver. Ten persons were arrested in connection with the case.

Pioneers marching to the fields in Ukraine sow the fields of a collective farm, 1930. Pioneers were youths aged 10 to 15 who belonged to a mass organization designed to indoctrinate the younger generation with the values of the revolution.

The regime's toleration of organized religion came to an abrupt end with the collectivization campaign. The Kremlin believed priests supported *kulaks* in the resistance against collectivization and would serve as the rallying point for the peasants' hatred of collectivization. The state closed churches and monasteries and arrested tens of thousands of Orthodox priests, many of whom were executed or died in prison. Closed churches were turned over to government use, generally as warehouses or clubs. In some cases, the secret police used a church for interrogation

purposes. Fewer than 1,000 churches remained in operation by 1939, or 2 percent of the 1920 level. Peasants saw the onslaught against the church as one aspect of the government's larger campaign to subjugate them and destroy their way of life. This report on a peasant village's response to the closing of its church highlighted the tensions that surrounded the campaign against religion.

On 7 April 1930 I, the Head of the Area AD [Administrative Department] and Head of the area Militia Yerokhin, having studied the materials on the case of the officials who permitted the disorders in the small town of Shumyachi, have established:

Approximately one month ago following the decree of the Regional Executive Committee the cemetery church in the small town of Shumyachi was closed, the bells were removed and the religious artifacts taken away. After this the former prayer building was rebuilt as a club. The rebuilding was completed by 30 March but given that the crosses remained on the church, the Chairman of the DEC [district executive committee] Comrade Kovalev, at a meeting on 29 March, with the Chairman of the administration of the fire service Comrade Komissarov, suggested that he take down the crosses from the closed church, completely ignoring the fact that 30 March was a market day. At about 11 or 12 o'clock Komissarov proposed to the head of the fire brigade Kazachenkov that he gather the brigade using the bells (the call signal for the brigade) without telling him why. On the assembling of the brigade Komissarov instructed Kazachenkov with a note . . . that part of the firemen should go to remove the crosses, but those without equipment refused and only 6 or 7 persons went to the church. The religious inhabitants of the town, who had already gathered in an illegal gathering about the profanation of the church and knowing that the assembled firemen had been directed to take down the crosses as the firemen had earlier taken down the bells and, in addition, it had been announced on posters that on 30 March the opening of the People's House (in the former church) would take place and the opening could not happen while crosses were still on the building, ran up to the church on hearing the call on the bells, bringing along with them indifferently-minded people from the market. When the church people had come running, hysterical women started to obstruct the tidying up of the club, throwing sticks, and tried to place their own lock on the door. The militia present managed to calm down the crowd and to detain the instigators of the disorders in order to establish culpability. . . .

(a) The Cathedral of Christ the Savior, the largest cathedral in Moscow, lies in ruins. In 1931 Stalin ordered its destruction because it was a vivid remnant of pre-revolutionary Russia that was visible from his office in the Kremlin. **(b)** An architect's model of the Palace of Soviets, topped by a hundred-foot-tall Lenin, that was supposed to replace the Cathedral of Christ the Savior. It was never built because, to the delight of religious believers and the disappointment of party officials, the building's foundation kept sinking into the ground. **(c)** The outbreak of World War II put an end to construction efforts, and in 1958 the regime decided to build what would be the world's largest open-air swimming pool on the site. **(d)** In the 1990s the Moscow city government closed the swimming pool and helped finance the rebuilding of the Cathedral of Christ the Savior.

The peasants ate dogs, horses, rotten potatoes, the bark of trees, grass— anything they could find. Incidents of cannibalism were not uncommon. The people were like wild beasts, ready to devour one another. And no matter what they did, they went on dying, dying, dying. . . . I was thirteen years old then, and I shall never forget what I saw. One memory especially stands out: a baby lying at his mother's breast, trying to wake her.

—Survivor of famine
in a Ukrainian village

Lev Kopelev was a well-known Soviet literary critic and political dissident. Like many other enthusiastic Soviet young men and women, Kopelev joined the Communist Party as a young man. He worked as a journalist and was one of the tens of thousands of urban youths whom the party sent to the countryside to help collectivize the peasantry. As a journalist, Kopelev's chief task was to report about the achievements of collectivization, but his responsibilities also included identifying peasants suspected of hoarding grain they were supposed to turn over to the government and assisting in their arrests. His views about the peasantry and collectivization help explain the fervor and self-righteousness with which Kopelev and other urban communists approached their tasks in the village. For them, the building of socialism acquired top priority as they zealously ferreted out so-called counterrevolutionary saboteurs and "enemies of the people." In his autobiography, Kopelev described what it was like to participate in the collectivization campaign in 1933.

The grain front! Stalin said the struggle for grain was the struggle for socialism. I was convinced that we were warriors on an invisible front, fighting against kulak sabotage for the grain which was needed by the country, by the five-year plan. Above all, for the grain, but also for the souls of these peasants who were mired in unconscientiousness, in ignorance, who succumbed to enemy agitation, who did not understand the great truth of communism. . . .

Every time I began to speak I wanted to prove to these people that they were making a serious mistake by hiding the grain, that they were harming the entire country and themselves. I tried to repeat myself as little as possible, though I was called upon to make a speech at several meetings a day. I told them how hard was the life of workers in the cities and at construction sites. They worked two and sometimes three shifts in a row, without a day off. Their wives stood in line, because there wasn't enough food, enough grain for bread. And all because our country was threatened on all sides by mortal enemies. And that meant we had to muster up our strength in order to fulfill the plans on time. And therefore grain was needed. . . .

I said only what I definitely believed. And every time I got carried away, screamed, waved my arms. They listened, it seemed to me, attentively. The women stopped whispering. No one left to have a smoke, exchanging curses with the officials at the door who held back those suspected of intending to sneak away. . . . And to be sure, I reviled and cursed the kulaks and their hangers-on every which way. And all those who out of malice or lack of social conscience were concealing grain I threatened with the people's contempt and the proletariat's avenging sword. . . .

I pleaded with a woman wiping her cheeks—which were wet with sweat and tears—with the ends of a fringed kerchief tied cabbagewise around her head:

"You yourself are a mother, you love your own children. Now just imagine how the mothers in the cities are crying now. They don't know what to feed their little ones. Have pity on them and on your own. Because the grain you've hidden you have taken away from your own children. And if they punish you, what will happen? Your children will be left hungry, without a mother."

We put out a news sheet at least every other day. Statistics on the grain delivery, reproaches to the unconscientious peasants, curses to the exposed saboteurs.

The individual farmers listed as holdouts were pressured in every way. Nightly meetings were held in their huts, visiting officials were billeted with them. . . .

The highest measure of coercion on the hard-core holdouts was "undisputed confiscation."

A team . . . would search the hut, barn, yard, and take away all the stores of seed, lead away the cow, the horse, the pigs.

In some cases they would be merciful and leave some potatoes, peas, corn for feeding the family. But the stricter ones would make a clean sweep. They would take not only the food and livestock, but also "all valuables and surpluses of clothing," including icons in their frames, samovars, painted carpets and even metal kitchen utensils which might be silver. And any money they found stashed away. Special instructions ordered the removal of gold, silver and currency. In a few cases they found tsarist gold coins—five-ruble, ten-ruble coins. . . .

Several times Volodya and I were present at such plundering raids. We even took part: we were entrusted to draw up inventories of the confiscated goods.

"The comrade chiefs from Kharkov can check to make sure everything was as it should be. Give the weights. We'll reweigh all your wheat in pounds. We won't take a grain of wheat for ourselves."

The women howled hysterically, clinging to the bags.

"Oy, that's the last thing we have! That was for the children's kasha! Honest to God, the children will starve!"

They wailed, falling on their trunks:

"Oy, that's a keepsake from my dead mama! People, come to my aid, this is my trousseau, never e'en put on!"

I heard the children echoing them with screams, choking, coughing with screams. And I saw the looks of the men: frightened, pleading, hateful, dully impassive, extinguished with despair or flaring up with half-mad, daring ferocity.

"Take it. Take it away. Take everything away. There's still a pot of borscht on the stove. It's plain, got no meat. But still it's got beets, taters 'n' cabbage. And it's salted! Better take it, comrade citizens! Here, hang on. I'll take off my shoes. They're patched and repatched, but maybe they'll have some use for the proletariat, for our dear Soviet power."

It was excruciating to see and hear all this. And even worse to take part in it. No, it was worse to be present without taking part than when you tried to persuade someone, to explain something. . . . And I persuaded myself, explained to myself. I mustn't give in to debilitating pity. We were realizing historical necessity. We were performing our revolutionary duty. We were obtaining grain for the socialist fatherland. For the five-year plan. . . .

Some sort of rationalistic fanaticism overcame my doubts, my pangs of conscience and simple feelings of sympathy, pity and shame, but this fanaticism was nourished not only by speculative newspaper and literary sources. More convincing than these were people who in my eyes embodied, personified our truth and our justice, people who confirmed with their lives that it was necessary to clench your teeth, clench your heart and carry out everything the party and the Soviet power ordered.

Peasant voices are heard rarely in the documents about collectivization, and so the letter written in July 1929 by the peasant M. D. Mikhailin to his son is particularly valuable. In it Mikhailin discusses the impact of grain requisitioning and asks his son, who lives in a city, to help explain the state of affairs.

16 July 1929

A letter from your parents.

Good day dear son, we are sending you greetings from all the family, and from the relatives and from the acquaintances. We have received your letter and the money, 15 rubles, for which we are very grateful. . . .

Though we will collect the grain, they will hardly give it to us, for we are having grain procurements here. They have imposed 20 poods on us, and we ourselves have been buying since the winter. With [us], they have confiscated a colt and four sheep; they take away everything from everyone in the village on credit. Whoever has two horses and two cows—they take away a horse and a cow and leave one horse and one cow per home. The rest they take away. They take away every single sheep. And whoever lacks a beast—they take whatever goods they have: clothes, furniture, and dishes. In Korolevka, from Uncle Vasia Badinov they took a horse, a cow, a heifer, a year-and-a-half-old bull, seven heads of sheep, a sowing machine, a samovar, a cloth coat, a feather bed, . . . and even wool; and from Len'ka they will probably take a cow and two year-and-a-half-old bulls. They go from house to house and look for grain everywhere; where they find a pood or half a pood, they take everything away, leaving only pood per eater. One can't buy grain anywhere, can't find [it], and can't sell [it]. They want to bring the new grain to one threshing-floor and thresh it all together there, and starting in the fall they want to give us a norm of one pood per month per eater, and all the rest they will take away and pour together in a common barn. Thus, Mitiunia, write to

Soviet officials sell the property of a dekulakized peasant family soon after its arrest and deportation in the early 1930s. The regime hoped to build support for its agrarian policies by rewarding peasants who joined collective farms.

us how this whole business should be explained; there are rumors that there will be a big war soon and if not war, that they want to drive everyone into a collective farm, and we will all work together.

   Write what is going on with you in the center. The people are greatly frustrated. They even don't want to sow grain. Write to us about all this, and write to us whether this decree has been sent out from the center, or it is the local authorities that manage things so; we know nothing about this. . . . When you receive this, write what rumors you have [heard]. Even though we have no grain, still we do not wander around looking for grain, we have savings from the spring, so that there will be enough till the fresh reap; soon we will reap the new grain. With this, good-bye. Write in response; we are all alive and healthy and wish you the same. We all together send you our greetings. Write as soon as possible what is going on there with you.

A woman walks into her neighborhood store and asks the two butchers: "Do you have any pork?"

The older butcher replies, "No. We haven't had pork in this store for 20 years."

"Okay," says the woman. "Do you have any lamb?"

"No," responds the butcher. "We haven't sold any lamb in 15 years."

"Well, what about turkey? Do you have any turkey?" asks the woman.

"No. We haven't had any turkey, or chicken for that matter, for 25 years," says the butcher with exasperation.

The woman turns around and leaves the store. The older butcher turns to the younger butcher and says: "Can you believe that woman? She's been shopping here for over 20 years and knows that we never have any meat. Why does she keep asking these questions? She should know better."

The younger butcher quietly says: "True, but she has a great memory."

Peasants also expressed their displeasure in songs and poems.

> I went into the *kolkhoz* slowly,
> and left it at top speed.
> I went into the *kolkhoz* in shoes
> and left it barefoot.
> I arrived at the *kolkhoz*
> with a new skirt.
> I left the *kolkhoz*
> completely naked.

The writer Vasily Grossman described the famine of the early 1930s from the perspective of a peasant woman in *Forever Flowing*. It was not published in the Soviet Union during his lifetime.

The starving people were left to themselves. The state had abandoned them. In the villages people went from house to house, begging from each other. The poor begged from the poor, the starving begged from the starving. . . . And the state gave not one tiny kernel to the starving. Though it was on the grain of the peasants that the state was founded, . . . under the government of workers and peasants, not even one kernel of grain. There were blockades along all the highways . . .; the starving people were not to be allowed into the cities. . . . And it was impossible to understand, grasp, comprehend. For these children were Soviet children, and those who were putting them to death were Soviet people. These children were Russians, and those who were putting them to death were Russians. And the government was a government of workers and peasants. Why this massacre?

It was when the snow began to melt that the village was up to its neck in real starvation.

The children kept crying and crying. They did not sleep. And they began to ask for bread at night too. People's faces looked like clay. Their eyes were dull and drunken. They went about as though asleep. They inched forward, feeling their way one foot at a time, and they supported themselves by keeping one hand against the wall. They began to move around less. Starvation made them totter. They moved less and less, and they spent more time lying down. And they kept thinking they heard the creaking of a cart bringing flour, sent to them by Stalin from the district center so as to save the children.

The women turned out to be stronger and more enduring than the men. They had a tighter hold on life. And they had more to suffer from it too. For the children kept asking their mothers for something to eat. Some of the women would talk to their children and try to explain and kiss them: "Don't cry. Be patient. Where can I get anything?" Others became almost insane: "Stop whining, or I'll kill you!" And then they would beat the children with whatever was at hand just to put an end to their crying and begging. And some of them ran away from their homes and went to their neighbors' houses, so as not to hear their children cry.

No dogs and cats were left. They had been slaughtered. And it was hard to catch them too. The animals had become afraid of people and their eyes were wild. People boiled them. All there was were tough veins and muscles. And from their heads they made a meat jelly.

The snow melted and people began to swell up. The edema of starvation had begun. Faces were swollen, legs swollen like pillows; water bloated their stomachs; people kept urinating all the time. Often they couldn't even make it out of the house. And the peasant children! . . . their heads like heavy bails on thin little necks, like storks, and one could see each bone of their arms and legs protruding from beneath the skin, how bones joined, and the entire skeleton was stretched over with skin that was like yellow gauze. And the children's faces were aged, tormented, just as if they were seventy years old. And by spring they no longer had faces at all. Instead, they had birdlike heads with beaks, or frog heads—thin, wide lips—and some of them resembled fish, mouths open. Not human faces. And the eyes. Oh, Lord! Comrade Stalin, good God, did you see those eyes? Perhaps, in fact, he did not know. . . .

And now they ate anything at all. They caught mice, rats, snakes, sparrows, ants, earthworms. They ground up bones into flour, and did the same with leather and shoe soles; they cut up old skins and furs to make noodles of a kind, and they cooked glue. And when the grass came up, they began to dig up the roots and eat the leaves and the buds; they used everything there was: dandelions, . . . and nettles and every other kind of edible grass and root and herb they could find. They dried out linden leaves and ground them into flour—but there were too few linden in our region. The pancakes made from the linden leaves were greenish in color and worse than those made of acorn flour.

And no help came! And they no longer asked for any. Even now when I start thinking about it all, I begin to go out of my mind. How could Stalin have turned his back on human beings? . . . After all, Stalin had bread. He had food to eat. What it adds up to is that

Famine Descends

Unreasonable grain delivery quotas, mismanagement of collective farms, poor weather, and peasant resistance had so disrupted agricultural production that peasants had virtually no food and lived in dire circumstances. Realizing that the supply of grain was needed to feed the cities and export abroad, Stalin redoubled the state's procurement efforts and created an artificially made famine that claimed some 6 million lives.

It is unlikely that Stalin deliberately planned the famine in Ukraine with his harsh grain collection requirements, but there is no denying that his agricultural policies since 1928 caused the disaster. The Kremlin made sure that not a whisper about Ukraine's misery would be uttered in the press. It imposed a veil of secrecy and prevented peasants from leaving the famine-struck region.

Two pedestrians pass the bodies of famine victims in Ukraine. In 1932–33 famine ravaged the Soviet Union, particularly Ukraine, and resulted in the deaths of millions.

he intentionally, deliberately, killed people by starvation. He refused to help even the children. And that makes Stalin worse than Herod. How can it be, I keep thinking to myself, that he took their grain and bread away, and then killed people by starvation? Such things are simply unimaginable! But then I think and remember: it did take place, it did take place! Then again I think that it simply could not really have happened.

Before they had completely lost their strength, the peasants went on foot across country to the railroad. Not to the stations where the guards kept them away, but to the tracks. And when the Kiev-Odessa express came past, they would just kneel there and cry: "Bread, bread!" They would lift up their horrible starving children for people to see. And sometimes people would throw them pieces of bread and other scraps. The train would thunder on past, and the dust would settle down, and the whole village would be there crawling along the tracks, looking for crusts. But an order was issued that whenever trains were traveling through the famine provinces the guards were to shut the windows and pull down the curtains. Passengers were not allowed at the windows. Yes, and in the end the peasants themselves stopped going to the railroads. They had too little strength left to get to the tracks—in fact, they didn't have enough strength to crawl out of their huts and into the yard. . . .

That whole winter they had wondered whether there would be a harvest. They had asked the old men what they thought, and they searched for good omens. Their whole hope was in the winter wheat. And their hopes were justified, but they were too weak to harvest it. I went into a hut. People lay there, barely breathing, or else not breathing at all, some of them on the bed and others on the stove, and the daughter of the owner, whom I knew, lay on the floor in some kind of insane fit, gnawing on the leg of the stool. It was horrible. When she heard me come in, she did not turn around but growled, just as a dog growls if you come near when he is gnawing on a bone.

Deaths from starvation mowed down the village. First the children, then the old people, then those of middle age. At first they dug graves and buried them, and then as things got worse they stopped. Dead people lay there in the yards, and in the end they remained right in their huts. Things fell silent. The whole village died. Who died last I do not know. Those of us who worked in the collective farm administration were taken off to the city.

The World of Five-Year Plans

In 1932 John Scott, a young American radical disturbed by the Great Depression and disillusioned with the failings of capitalist society, decided to move to the Soviet Union. He believed he could participate in what he and thousands of other left-wing Americans enthusiastically believed to be the world-historic experiment of building socialism. He departed for a city named Magnitogorsk, located at the south end of the Ural Mountains, that the Soviets had founded in 1929 as the site of the largest steel plant in the world. This industrial complex, along with a planned city, symbolized the transformation of Soviet society under Five-Year Plans. It also signified the contrast between the rural, agrarian past and the Soviet Union's headlong thrust into the world of industrialism and technology.

Scott despaired when many of his Soviet friends were arrested in 1937 because of a government witch-hunt for spies, saboteurs, and other enemies of the Soviet Union. He returned to the United States, much more sober and critical of Stalin's Russia, but nonetheless unshaken in his opinion that the Soviet Union could take pride in its achievements. In his memoir about life in Magnitogorsk, Scott describes living and working conditions in the "city of steel" and underscores the enormous human and material costs involved in building socialism. Not only does he discuss the shortcomings of the Soviet path to industrialization, notably the shortages of food and consumer goods as well as the waste, cruelty, and inefficiency of centralized economic planning, but he provides readers with a balance sheet of the pros and cons of life in the Soviet Union during the 1930s.

It was just about nine-fifteen when I finished one side of the pipe and went around to start the other. The scaffold was coated with about an inch of ice, like everything else around the furnaces. The vapor rising from the large hot-water cooling basin condensed on everything and formed a layer of ice. But besides being slippery, it was very insecure, swung down on wires, without any guys to steady it. It swayed and shook as I walked on it. I always made a point of hanging on to something when I could. I was just going

A customer pushes his plate back in disgust and asks the waitress, "Do you serve garbage like this every day?"

The waitress replies, "No, we're closed on Mondays."

—Popular joke from the 1920s–1930s

An agitator assures a meeting that after a few Five-Year Plans, not only will most Soviet citizens have their own cars, they'll have their own airplanes. A listener is so carried away with the idea that he whispers to his wife: "Won't that be the life, Manka? We can take the plane anytime we hear they're selling cabbages in Moscow."

to start welding when I heard someone sing out, and something swished down past me. It was a rigger who had been working up on the very top.

He bounced off the bleeder pipe, which probably saved his life. Instead of falling all the way to the ground, he landed on the main platform about fifteen feet below me. By the time I got down to him, blood was coming out of his mouth in gushes. He tried to yell, but could not. There were no foremen around, and the half-dozen riggers that had run up did not know what to do. By virtue of being a foreigner I had a certain amount of authority, so I stepped in and said he might bleed to death if we waited for a stretcher, and three of us took him and carried him down to the first-aid station. About halfway there the bleeding let up and he began to yell every step we took.

I was badly shaken when we got there, but the two young riggers were trembling like leaves. We took him into the little wooden building, and a nurse with a heavy shawl over her white gown showed us where to put him. "I expect the doctor any minute," she said; "good thing, too, I wouldn't know what the hell to do with him."

The rigger was gurgling and groaning. His eyes were wide open and he seemed conscious, but he did not say anything. "We should undress him, but it is so cold in here that I am afraid to," said the nurse. Just then the doctor came in. I knew him. He had dressed my foot once when a piece of pig iron fell on it. He took his immense sheepskin off and washed his hands. "Fall?" he asked, nodding at the rigger.

"Yes," I said.

"How long ago?"

"About ten minutes."

"What's that?" asked the doctor, looking at the nurse and indicating the corner of the room with his foot. I looked and for the first time noticed a pair of ragged *valenkis* sticking out from under a very dirty blanket on the floor.

"Girder fell on his head," said the nurse.

"Well," said the doctor, rolling up his sleeves, "let's see what we can do for this fellow." He moved over toward the rigger, who was lying quietly now and looking at the old bearded doctor with watery blue eyes. I turned to go, but the doctor stopped me.

"On your way out, please telephone the factory board of health and tell them I simply must have more heat in this place," he said.

Blast furnaces in Magnitogorsk symbolized the achievements of Soviet industrialization.

I did the best I could over the telephone in my bad Russian, but all I could get was, "Comrade, we are sorry, but there is no coal."

I was making my way unsteadily back to the bleeder pipe on No. 3 when Kolya hailed me. "Don't bother to go up for a while, the brushes burnt out on the machine you were working on. They won't be fixed for half an hour or so." I went toward the office with Kolya and told him about the rigger. I was incensed and talked about some thorough checkup on scaffoldings. Kolya could not get interested. He pointed out there was not enough planking for good scaffolds, that the riggers were mostly plowboys who had no idea of being careful, and that at thirty-five below without any breakfast in you, you did not pay as much attention as you should.

"Sure, people will fall. But we're building blast furnaces all the same, aren't we?" and he waved his hand toward No. 2 from which the red glow of flowing pig iron was emanating. He saw I was not satisfied. "This somewhat sissified foreigner will have to be eased along a little," he probably said to himself. He slapped me on the back. "Come on in the office. We are going to have a technical conference. You'll be interested." . . .

Scott took advantage of his time in Magnitogorsk to observe the industrialization process elsewhere in the region. In mid-1933 Scott and a dozen or so co-workers visited a nearby collective farm.

A half-dozen buildings had been constructed around a well. There was a store whose shelves were virtually empty, an administration building, a large dormitory, and a club dining-room. Over toward the river bed a cow barn and other farm buildings had been built. Most of the farm machinery stood out-of-doors. We saw it even before we alighted from the truck. There had not been enough lumber for buildings to house the machinery. Cows or men would die if they had no shelter in winter, but machines would not, said Petrov.

We were given a very good lunch, the best that I had had for months. Then we went to work. A dozen young open-faced boys took us out to show us the tractors. I remember the enthusiasm of one of them. "Come on and fix this tractor first," he told us, dragging us over to the corner of a ragged-looking wheat field where a tractor listed hopelessly against a little knoll. We asked him what was so urgent about this particular machine.

He grinned. "Very good tractor," he said, pointing to a hole in the top of the radiator beside the radiator cap.

We did not understand, to the obvious disappointment of the driver. "How is it that these foreigners, these highly qualified specialists cannot see the technical possibilities of that hole?" he said in an undertone to another local farm boy. Then he told us. "Marvelous for boiling potatoes. Even two or three at a time. We used to have fights to decide who would drive this tractor. Then it was decided that the driver who fulfilled his norm by the highest per cent would get it."

Out of twelve tractors only three were working. The rest were in various stages of disintegration. Some had cracked blocks, stripped gears, burned-out bearings. Some were merely out of time, or the plugs were gummed up with carbon from the bad-quality fuel. At the end of three days we had nine tractors running. These nine included the good parts from the other three. I remember Petrov's face when we showed him a pile of junk which was the other three

Petrov

Petrov was head of the collective farm.

tractors. To him it was quite normal to leave machinery out in the dust or snow all year round. . . .

We would have turned our attention to some of the other farm machinery had it not been for the fact that several of the German mechanics were badly needed back in Magnitogorsk. Petrov reluctantly let us go. Before we left, we had a little class with the farm personnel, which consisted of a score of absolutely green shepherds, . . . They had never seen any kind of machinery or equipment before coming to the farm. They had been taught that when you pushed the pedal the tractor moved. That was the extent of their technical education. Matters such as lubrication and timing were completely beyond their ken. We tried our best to explain some simple points, but I am afraid very little of what we said was understood. . . .

While in Magnitogorsk Scott fell in love with and married a Russian woman, Masha. Contrary to Masha's initial impression of her future husband, Scott came from a prosperous family. He attended boarding schools, including one in Switzerland, before he enrolled at the University of Wisconsin in 1929. Masha symbolized the social mobility open to many Soviets, including women and peasants, who took advantage of educational opportunities in the 1930s. She came from a poor peasant family and, after receiving a higher education in Moscow, moved to Magnitogorsk in 1933. Scott, Masha, and their two children left for the United States in 1941.

Masha's first impressions of me were more interesting than mine of her. She wrote as follows in her haphazard diary:

"When I first went to work . . . I was filing a pile of applications from the previous year when I came across one written in such an impossible handwriting that I could hardly read it. I finally made out the name John Scott, and further learned that he was an American and had recently arrived in the Soviet Union. I had never seen an American and was much interested by the prospect of seeing this John Scott, who had, no doubt, come from the land of capitalist oppression to find a home in the land of Socialism. I imagined him as being tall, handsome, and very interesting. I asked Anya, the other secretary, to point him out to me.

"The next evening a stringy, intense-looking young fellow came into the office and sat down near the stove. He was dressed in ragged brown working clothes and had a heavy brown scarf around his neck. His clothes and his big tattered *valenkis* were absolutely grimy with blast-furnace dust. He looked very tired and lonely. When Anya

A 1931 poster encourages an accelerated pace of industrialization. The text reads: "Full Speed Ahead for the Fourth and Final Year of the Five-Year Plan."

told me in a whisper that it was John Scott, I didn't believe her at first. Then I was very disappointed, and then I became sorry for him.

"The first American I had ever seen, he looked like a homeless boy. I saw in him the product of capitalist oppression. I saw in my mind's eye his sad childhood; I imagined the long hours of inhuman labor which he had been forced to perform in some capitalist factory while still a boy; I imagined the shamefully low wages he received, only sufficient to buy enough bread so that he could go to work the next day; I imagined his fear of losing even this pittance and being thrown on the streets unemployed in case he was unable to do his work to the satisfaction and profit of his parasitic bosses." . . .

All Soviet citizens were expected to contribute to the building of socialism, since the fulfillment of the Five-Year Plans depended on the mobilization of both human and material resources. As a 1931 elementary school book about Five-Year Plans illustrates, the government exhorted even children to do their share in the construction of a socialist Soviet Union.

Do not imagine that the Five-Year Plan is wholly the work of grown-ups.

Every child can be a builder of the Five-Year Plan.

"The Lysvensky Factory Children's Brigade constructed a water and a wind mill and started a dynamo."

"On the Briansk road ten miles from Moscow in the village Peredelkino, the Khamovnichensky Region Children's Brigade electrified their camp. They dammed a small river, set up a water wheel, attached to it a small dynamo from a cinema apparatus, stretched wires to the camp, and henceforth illuminated their tents with electricity during the darkness of the summer nights."

"The youngsters of Ribinsk, while studying their own region, found deposits of lime which is entirely suited for use as fertilizer. The Novosiberian . . . Children's Brigades discovered resources worth many millions of pounds sterling. They went on a scouting expedition and stumbled upon beds of coal and iron."

"On the outskirts of Moscow a children's city working independently built a . . . road approximately three hundred yards long and planted apple trees on either side."

"The children of the Zherdevsky Collective Farm collected apple-cores and planted the seeds. They thus started a fruit orchard. Next year they will supply every household with valuable cuttings."

All these accounts I have taken from the report of the Children's Brigade Rally. There are dozens of such items in the report.

You thus see how children can help achieve the Five-Year Plan. Fulfill your own little plan and then the big plan will be fulfilled before the assigned time. Whether it will be a task which requires a few days or a few weeks matters not: it will be your contribution.

Here it is—the Children's Five-Year Plan:

(1) To discover beds of lime and phosphorus.

(2) To gather useful junk: rags, ropes, wool, bones, scraps of metal, and so on. All of these things will come in handy in our factories. Every child should collect not less than forty pounds a year.

(3) To build wireless sets and loud-speakers. Within the next few years seventy-five thousand wireless sets should be installed in villages. Not one school should be without a loud-speaker.

(4) To learn to get full marks for sorting grain grown on your parents' farms, for seed.

(5) To gather ashes for fertilizing fields. Each Children's Brigade should gather two tons of ashes a year.

(6) To destroy ten marmots a year in the regions infested by these animals; to clear one-fifth of an acre of land of parasites; to destroy all injurious insects on one fruit tree and on ten vegetables; to catch or destroy five rats and ten mice.

Kapiton Klepikov worked in a textile mill and fell afoul of the regime several times in the 1920s for voicing his frustration with poor living and working conditions. In a speech delivered at a meeting of trade unionists in 1926, Klepikov criticized the Party: "They told us before that under the old regime nothing was done in outlying worker districts (such as ours). And now, under the Soviet regime, almost nothing is done. We're wallowing in filth. . . . They say that nothing can be done, but in the past everything was cheaper and better. . . . Now all the achievements of the October Revolution have come to naught." In 1930 he was again arrested and refused to recant his views: "The October Revolution gave me the right as a worker to express my personal convictions openly." He received five years in a labor camp for his words and actions.

(7) To build one starling house and two feeding houses a year; to raise the number of starling houses to a million and a half and of feeding houses to two millions. Birds are our allies: they will help us destroy parasites.

(8) To organize in five years, five thousand children's bird preserving clubs, to found five thousand collective bird preserves, and to build five thousand chicken houses.

(9) To add two good laying hens to the possessions of every peasant household.

(10) To plant ten trees each in five years; to create Children's Brigade forests of seventy-five million trees.

(11) To destroy bedbugs, cockroaches, and flies in five hundred thousand houses. Each troop should clean up ten houses.

(12) To teach the illiterate to read and write. Each troop should endeavour to wipe out illiteracy in its region.

These are only some of the chief tasks for children. If you wish to learn the details, read "The Report of the Children's Brigade Rally."

Grown-ups will build large electric stations; children can build small ones. Grown-ups will build large houses; children can build starling houses and bird-feeding houses.

And do not imagine that these are trifles.

If children fulfill their Five-Year Plan, they will save from parasites grain worth £400,000.

Alexei Stakhanov was a miner whose feat of overfulfilling his work quota served as a model that other workers were encouraged to emulate. He and other so-called "Stakhanovite" workers received public acclaim and material awards such as radios, new apartments, and cars.

If children add two good laying hens each to the possessions of each household, they will make a present to the State of five billion eggs, £20,000,000.

From pennies, millions are composed; weak hands, if they be many, can move mountains and plant forests of trees.

In 1929 and 1930 Maurice Hindus, an American journalist, visited his native village in Ukraine and chronicled the impact of collectivization. He also spent time in Moscow, where he noticed enormous pride, industriousness, and determination. For many, the benefits of building socialism, especially for future generations, far outweighed the sacrifices required of them by the Party and state. Communists and their sympathizers believed the Soviet people were fighting a war with the outmoded past. Consequently, all necessary measures to break with tradition and create the basis of the socialist utopia were justified.

"Moscow spurted with a new energy that was almost desperation. It had clutched time by the throat, so to speak, in the hope of disciplining it to its own far-flung uses and missions. Work, construction, the machine—these were its new deities, and fiercely it exacted unswerving allegiance to them. It had no use for anyone who would not bring . . . his best gifts. It never before had been so brutally intolerant of the doubter, the intruder, the laggard, of everyone who would not forget the rest of the world and himself, even his very soul, and push on with this work, this construction, this machine—the biddings of these new gods. The five-year plan in four—this was the new slogan and the new ambition, and from hundreds of posters and banners floating from buildings, plastered on corner posts, staring from street cars, stuck onto automobiles, the words flashed their imperious message. Anybody who questioned the wisdom or the possibility of packing a generation of industrial development into four years, an enterprise so gigantic that the mere thought of it made one's head swim with wonder and dismay, was . . . a defeatist, a traitor . . . anything but a true soldier of the Revolution and of the one and only cause."

The regime kept a close eye on conditions throughout the country and monitored the attitudes and morale of Soviet citizens. While open protest and strikes were not common, the authorities worried that discontent could manifest itself in anti-government behavior and perhaps open political opposition. The state relied on political surveillance to collect such information, but workers and peasants also wrote letters to high-ranking party officials and to newspapers expressing their honest opinions and grievances with Soviet power. A report on the political attitudes of transportation workers, written in June 1933, is one of many such reports that acknowledged the disgruntlement of workers and were candid in their explanation of workers' discontent.

Negative attitudes have become widespread among all categories of transportation workers.

These attitudes are primarily in response to inadequate supplies, the pressure which has been applied in the grain procurement drive and its resultant problems, and delays in wage payments.

Some typical negative attitudes are reflected in the quotes provided below.

The speaker at a meeting is talking on the theme "We Will Catch the Capitalist Countries." An audience member asks: "When we catch them, can we stay there?"

"The Seven Wonders of Soviet Power"

1. There is no unemployment, but no one works.
2. No one works, but the plan is fulfilled.
3. The plan is fulfilled, but there is nothing to buy.
4. There is nothing to buy, but there are lines everywhere.
5. There are lines everywhere, but we are on the threshold of abundance.
6. We are on the threshold of abundance, but everyone is unhappy.
7. Everyone is unhappy, but they all vote, "Yes."

—Yulius Telesin, "Tysiacha i odin anekdot"

Workers

"It's disgusting, they aren't giving us our pay. We need another revolution to wipe out every last one of them (the Communists)." (Malapura, a machinist at the Artemovsk Depot)

"Soviet power is driving the workers into the grave. No matter what we do, it's not enough, and don't even ask about eating. In the old days the gentry made us work, but at least they let us eat." (Balabas, a coppersmith at the Izium Steam Locomotive Repair Works)

"In the country they're taking away the peasants' last bit of grain. It's outright robbery." (Matkovskii, a worker at the Komarovtsy Station. . . .)

"Did we really fight so that the workers and the peasants could live the way they're living today? There's nothing but bureaucracy and red tape. The peasants have been driven off and robbed of everything. If I get my chance, I'll pick up a rifle again and kill the high-ranking bastards who reduced the country to this condition." (Kalashnikov, a metalworker. . . .)

"Let's stop kidding around. The people are starving. The working-class sees everything quite clearly and won't follow you any more." (A comment by Markin, a metalworker . . . at a workers' meeting). . . .

White-Collar Workers

"This isn't a government, it's a gang. They've reduced the peasants to a condition where they have nothing to live on. They've taken their last bit of grain, they've taken all the potatoes, and they've left the peasants to the mercy of fate." (Bubyrev, an assistant station master. . . .)

"The people in power are a bunch of saboteurs who don't know how to plan. They're exporting everything to foreign countries, which means things won't get any better over here." (Pogorelov, a conductor. . . .)

"Nobody feels like doing anything on an empty stomach. If we got our supplies and our food quicker, then we might be able to fulfill the five-year plans. It's fine for Stalin with his full stomach to sit in Moscow and think up things. Let him try to live on our rations." (Tsvetkovskii, a telegraph operator. . . .)

In protest of food shortages, overcrowding, and harsh work rules, many workers reacted to the hardships caused by the first Five-Year Plan by engaging in work slowdowns and strikes. Many leaders acknowledged that the government's policies were responsible for these difficulties and suggested that Stalin moderate the goals of the Second Five-Year Plan. Stalin agreed to slow down the plan's tempo somewhat, but he still faced criticism by party members who believed his policies were foolhardy and leading the country to disaster. In 1932 Mikhail Riutin, a party leader in Moscow, circulated a petition highly critical of Stalin's style of leadership. Riutin and the others who signed the petition were expelled from the party. Riutin also received a 10-year prison sentence.

Comrades!

The party and proletarian dictatorship have been led by Stalin and his clique into an unprecedented blind alley and are suffering through a terribly dangerous crisis. With the aid of deceit, slander, and making fools of party people, with the aid of incredible violence and terror, under the flag of the struggle for the purging of the principles of Bolshevism and party unity, while relying on the centralized, powerful party apparatus, Stalin has for the last five years cut off and removed from leadership all the best genuine Bolshevik cadre of the party, established in . . . the entire country his own personal dictatorship, broken with Leninism, embarked on the path of the most unbridled adventurism and wild personal arbitrary rule, and placed the Soviet Union on the brink of a precipice. . . .

[F]or the past few years under Stalin the situation in the Soviet Union has . . . systematically and gigantically worsened each year. The disintegration and disorganization of the entire country's economy, in spite of the construction of dozens of the largest enterprises, have reached unprecedented proportions. . . .

The adventurist rates of industrialization, that entail the colossal lowering of the wages of workers and employees, excessive open and concealed taxes, inflation, rise of prices and the fall of the value of money; the adventurist collectivization with the aid of incredible violence, force, terror, dekulakization, which was directed actually primarily against the middle and poor masses of the countryside, and, finally, the expropriation of the countryside by all types of means of collection and forcible procurement have brought the entire country to the deepest crisis, the monstrous pauperization of the masses, and famine in both towns and countryside. . . .

Trade Commissar Mikoyan brags to Health Commissar Semashko: "When you took over, malaria raged and it still does; when I took over, there was bread, meat, and sugar—but no more!"

By a system of threats, terror, and deceit, the party has been compelled to play the role of the silent, blind weapon of Stalin for the achievement of his personal ambitious schemes. The party masses in their overwhelming majority are disposed against the Stalinist policy, but they have been beaten and persecuted by the party apparatus. Any keen Bolshevik party idea has been stifled by the threat of expulsion from the party, removal from a job, and deprivation of all means of existence; all things genuinely Leninist have been driven underground; genuine Leninism has to a significant degree become a forbidden, illegal study. . . .

The construction of the Belomor Canal in 1934 required workers to toil in harsh conditions. Here, two prisoners saw wood in knee-deep snow.

The shortage of machinery and labor prompted the government to use prisoners—both common criminals and those convicted of political offenses—to work on various projects, particularly those in inhospitable regions where workers did not volunteer to go. The government had no qualms about using forced labor and tried to put a positive spin on this system by stressing that such work helped rehabilitate the prisoners and turned them into productive citizens. One particularly infamous project that employed the labor of tens of thousands of prisoners was the White Sea–Baltic Canal (Belomor Canal), an enterprise designed to connect the northern port of Archangel on the White Sea to Leningrad and the Baltic Sea so that ships no longer had to travel all around Norway, Sweden, and Finland.

Maxim Gorky returned to the Soviet Union after having spent most of the 1920s abroad. He had apparently reconciled himself to what he believed to be the shortcomings of the revolution, but the industrialization program of the 1930s elicited his support. In 1935 he edited a book celebrating the Belomor Canal. At least 10,000 prisoners died from disease, malnutrition, and the harsh working conditions. Ironically, the canal was never used because it was too shallow.

But two problems remained unsolved. In the first place the demands of the new enterprises under the Five-Year Plan were so enormous that there were hardly enough hands to do the work, particularly too little skilled labour. No one who was good for anything could be spared. That was one side of the problem. On the other hand, there was a contrary problem: what was to happen to the thousands of men and women who had been sent for two, three or sometimes ten years to a labour camp? What was to happen to them during their time of detention and what was to happen to them afterwards? Were they to remain branded as criminals for the rest of their lives?

Stalin proposed that the construction of this Canal should be entrusted by the Communist Party to the G.P.U.

It was in 1926 that . . . Stalin first raised the question of work with criminals and homeless waifs. Stalin was the initiator . . . of the policy of reform through labour. Stalin it was who started the idea of building the White Sea–Baltic Canal with prisoners, because under his leadership such a method of reform appeared possible. Work in the U.S.S.R. has in reality become a matter of honour, a matter of glory, a matter of valour and of heroism. Over the entire country there is this new attitude towards work. Labour is no longer a hateful means of existence, but the rational expression of a happy life. . . .

And by whose work is all this to be accomplished? This sounds the most Utopian part of the plan, for the work is to be a double one; the task is to be attempted not by tried heroes of the revolution, but by the very men who set themselves to work against it; the men who are to forge this new tool for the Five-Year Plan are themselves to be re-forged.

G.P.U.
G.P.U., initials of State Political Administration, successor to the Cheka.

Российская Социалистическая Федеративная Советская Республика.

ПРОЛЕТАРІИ ВСЕХ СТРАН
СОЕДИНЯЙТЕСЬ !

ГОД
ПРОЛЄТАРСКОЙ
ДИКТАТУРЫ.
ОКТЯБРЬ 1917 - ОКТЯБРЬ 1918

Women's Liberation in the Soviet Union

Part and parcel of the Bolshevik revolution was a promise to emancipate women. According to Marxist theory, only a socialist revolution would provide the conditions under which women could be liberated. Just as capitalism guaranteed that workers would do the bidding of the ruling bourgeoisie, so too did it make sure that women would remain under men's thumbs. By ridding society of capitalist exploiters and ending women's economic dependence on men, socialism would enable women to participate as free and equal contributors to society. Marxist theory explicitly condemned marriage and the family as bourgeois, prophesizing that both would wither away under communism. Ideally, children would be cared for by the state, not by individual families. Radicals envisioned a society that based itself upon collective relationships rather than private couples.

Soon after the Bolsheviks assumed control of Russia, they tried to make good on some of socialism's promises to women. Before the first year of the revolution was over, a remarkable new law proclaimed full

Alexander Apsit, "Workers of the World Unite!" (1918)

This poster celebrated the first anniversary of the October Revolution. Standing atop discarded symbols of the old regime is an armed male blacksmith. At his right is a male peasant who appears to be looking at the worker for guidance. Two lines of red flag-wielding figures are woven across the scenery. The most prominent woman among them is wearing the telltale red kerchief of a female communist. Yet she is leaning on a man. The future, it would seem, belongs to the baby boy in her arms.

equality of the sexes. Bolshevik family legislation incorporated many elements of "bourgeois" feminists' demands—legal equality, equal rights, the principle of equal pay for equal work—and went even further, legalizing abortion, granting divorce at the request of husband or wife, decriminalizing prostitution and homosexuality, and ending the distinction between legitimate and illegitimate children. The Party also established the Zhenotdel (Women's Section), whose mission was to bring the revolution to women and foster women's participation in revolutionary politics.

But Soviet women after the revolution nonetheless continued to confront a recalcitrant reality. To be sure, the emancipated Bolshevik woman existed, but she was much less ubiquitous than posters, films, and other Soviet propaganda let on. Patriarchal habits and values had extremely deep roots in Russian society, and they blocked women's aspirations in spite of the new laws. Women throughout the Soviet Union also held themselves back from participation in the new order, afraid to use their voices and step onto what used to be exclusively male turf.

Other obstacles also thwarted women's emancipation. Most daunting was the social and economic situation. War, revolution, and famine had left millions of women abandoned and widowed. The New Economic Policy (NEP) had dire consequences for women in particular, as female unemployment reached higher levels than did male unemployment in cities. To make matters worse, the state did not enforce the law requiring equal pay for equal work. Nor did the authorities live up to their promise to provide state-sponsored childcare, public laundries, communal kitchens and nurseries, the services women needed to be free from what Lenin called "barbarously unproductive, petty, nerve-racking, stultifying and crushing drudgery." Consequently, women who did not have a man to boost the household income had difficulty making ends meet.

The spiraling divorce rate made matters worse. By easing divorce, Soviet law had taken Marxism's disdain for marriage and the family seriously. Yet it had destabilized the one institution that seemed to provide security in such tumultuous times. In the 1920s many of the women who engaged in free relations with men found themselves pregnant and alone. At the same time, many husbands felt free to indulge themselves with younger, willing women, leaving their wives and children behind. As much as the new divorce laws proved liberating for women trapped in bad marriages, they hurt those women who had hoped to stay married.

Massive industrialization at the end of the 1920s and in the 1930s helped bring women into the paid workforce. To enable mothers to leave their children, *the state finally started building nurseries and childcare centers.* Nevertheless, when they came home from work, women remained responsible for shopping, cooking, cleaning, laundry, and raising children. Lingering traditions of sexual inequality where a wife remained subservient to her husband guaranteed that women would continue *both to reproduce and to fulfill domestic obligations.* By promoting rigid gender roles, the state received two forms of labor from women for the price of one. *Soviet power indeed put women to work, but it also reinforced women's double burden.* In the 1970s a Soviet pop star summed up the position of women in the U.S.S.R. when she cried over and over in a popular song, "I'm exhausted!"

The Soviet government devoted enormous resources to producing posters, whose main *purpose was to communicate messages the regime thought were important.* As a form of propaganda, posters strove to reach the ordinary person in a straightforward manner. They sought to mobilize the populace for the tasks of building socialism, to familiarize viewers with the regime's policies, and to sway them to the government's point of view. Some posters also advocated on behalf of the "new *Soviet woman.*" Hundreds of organizations and institutions produced posters in the years after the revolution, but it was not until the 1930s that the regime gave the State Publishing House, which replaced the various publishers that existed in the 1920s, control over the production, printing, and circulation of all posters. Some posters in the 1930s received print runs of over 100,000, with some reaching a quarter million.

When poster artists drew human figures, they tended to draw ideal types—that is, men and women who looked healthy and robust and committed to revolutionary change. But less conscious decisions also moved the artists' hands. For example, artists obeyed traditional conventions when they drew women as much smaller than men, or when they chose to represent one figure (usually male) as active and another figure (usually female) as passive or on the receiving end of a male's activity. Similarly, artists tended to place children alongside women, not men. *Most Soviet-era posters, especially when they portrayed workers, contained representations of men only.* Despite an understanding that both women and men made up the proletariat, Soviet artists associated proletarians with traits usually ascribed to men: strength, power, and virility. By contrast, Soviet artists associated peasants with traits usually ascribed to women: fertility, closeness to nature, and nurturance. *In sum, posters represented both revolutionary and traditional attitudes toward gender.*

Women as Inconsequential

"May 1st is a Holiday for All Toilers" (1920)

In a May Day poster from 1920, we see workers marching to the left under banners that proclaim "May 1st is a holiday for all toilers," "Long live the toilers' army," and "Long live the Third International." Almost all of the workers are men, but this group, judging by their different hats, clothing, and skin tones, is an international one. The men's faces are determined, even angry. Some wield large mallets and sickles, all of which look like weapons of working-class revolution. Among the 40 or so figures, just two appear to be female, one of whom stands in the background under a red banner whose May Day message is partially obscured. The most prominent woman is last in a line of some 20 men, and she is being supported, perhaps even pulled, by a man. The red kerchief marks her as a supporter of the revolution, but she also appears to be a reluctant one: her expression is neither angry nor determined; she wields nothing; and she is behind the men both literally and metaphorically.

not a lot of women figure were drawn

"Bravely, Comrades, In Step" (1918 or 1919)

The most dominant figure in this poster is female, but she is an allegorical representation of Liberty, reminiscent of female images from the French Revolution. Clad in a pink gown that reveals part of her right breast, "Liberty" is holding a rifle in one hand and a billowing red flag in the other. She is surrounded by non-allegorical figures, all but one of whom are male. Across the top, columns of male workers march forward, holding the tools of their trades like weapons. Two more male workers, one who has broken free of chains around his wrist and the other who is holding a bayonet, stand to Liberty's left and right, looking up at her as if to hail the freedom that she represents. Encased in oval-shaped bubbles are also male figures. The one on the left appears to be breaking through to a new world with his axe; on the right, a male peasant and male worker greet each other from the factory and field. At the bottom left, a (female?) figure is thrusting a red flag atop barricades, and at the bottom right, symbols of the old regime are going up in flames. The lyrics from Leonid Radin's late-19th-century revolutionary anthem, "Bravely, comrades, in step!" are printed beneath the illustrations. Like the poster, with its emphasis on male bonding, the song refers to "brotherly union and freedom."

Dmitrii Moor, "May First is an All-Russian Workday" (1920)

With one exception, the figures in this poster are men actively engaging in manual labor. The sole woman represented here is toiling, but like many women in other posters she is an assistant and at the receiving end of male activity, relegated to helping men at work. She is holding a piece of metal in place so that the central male figure can pound it with his sledgehammer.

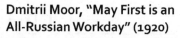

Vera Korableva, "Comrade, Come Join Us on the Collective Farm!" (1930)

This poster clearly publicizes the state's campaign for collectivization. Drawn by a female artist, it features both a male and female peasant. The red-kerchiefed woman is taking an unusually active role, for it is she who is presumably shouting the poster's slogan. Perhaps she is chiefly calling to other women, because Soviet collectivizers perceived women to be the greatest foes of collectivized agriculture. But, typically, it is the man who is driving the tractor, just as it is he who towers over her.

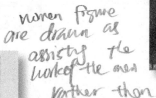

Nikolai Kogout, "We Defeated the Enemy with Our Weaponry" (1920)

At center, a muscular, powerful male worker is poised to pound his sledgehammer. His Red Army cap is on the ground and three rifles with bayonets are just to his left. On the receiving end is a strong-looking female worker who is wielding the tongs that hold the metal he is about to pound. Her kerchief is not colored red in the poster, but she is unmistakably a comrade. Unlike most posters that feature a man and woman as the central figures, she is portrayed as his size; even their arms are of equal girth. But characteristically, it is the male who is actively engaged in motion and the female who is the passive recipient of that movement. She appears to be an assistant, not a leader.

In the background are a dozen or so workers, all of whom are actively laboring and all of whom appear to be men. Their landscape is industrial, with a crane, wires, smokestacks, a bridge, and factory prominently displayed. The slogan reads, "We defeated the enemy with our weaponry. We shall obtain bread with our labor. Everyone to work, comrades!"

Emancipated Women

Anonymous, "What the October Revolution Has Given to the Woman Worker and Woman Peasant" (1920)

Created in 1920 by an anonymous artist, this oft-duplicated poster represented many of the promises of the revolution to women workers. Dressed in a blacksmith's apron and wielding the hammer, symbol of the proletarian revolution, the female figure in the poster is pointing to various buildings that signified women's emancipation. A maternity hospital is at the top. Below it is the Soviet of Workers' and Peasants' Deputies. Just beneath that on the right is an adult school, and next to it is a kindergarten. The women and children at bottom are heading into a library, and at their right is a communal cafeteria. At bottom center is a Women Workers' Club. The figure is standing on boulders with the slogan, "Land to the peasant, factories to the worker."

Mikhail M. Cheremnykh (1931)

This image appeared on the cover of a 1931 issue of the Soviet journal called *The Atheist at the Workbench*. Neither allegorical nor marginal, this red-kerchiefed female worker, whose sleeves are rolled up to reveal muscular arms, is holding a heavy hammer with one hand and kicking aside religious objects with her left foot. A good Soviet citizen, she has forsaken religion in accord with the accompanying slogan: "Drawing millions of women into active work for socialist construction is a completely necessary precondition for the victory of socialism." Although this appears to be a positive image of Soviet womanhood, there is nevertheless an underlying message associating women with religion, something considered a capitalist remnant that would have no place in communist society. The slogan also contains a utilitarian theme: rather than achieving emancipation in the socialist system, women were holding back socialism's triumph if they did not pick up the hammer (i.e., engage in paid labor).

Gustav Klutsis, "We Will Provide Millions of Qualified Workers' Cadres for 518 New Factories and Plants" (1931)

This poster also provides an interesting contrast to works that marginalize and minimize women workers. Although the figures in this poster are both male and female, the women dominate in both number and size. Indeed, women predominated among the millions of new workers who poured into the industrial labor force during the first and second Five-Year Plans.

Peasant Women

Maria Voron, "Reaping at a Shock Work Pace Means a Bolshevik Harvest" (1934)

In contrast to the determined female workers of the 1920s, the figure at this poster's center is an unthreatening female peasant. Yet she is sporting a red kerchief that is tied behind her head in the style of urban women, thereby marking her as a modern collective farm worker rather than a typical female peasant. In the background we see women making bundles of wheat, carrying wheat, and stacking wheat. The men are engaged in very different pursuits: the two at the top left are operating agricultural machinery. At the right we see a man in uniform, clearly a Soviet commissar, who is examining the flour that the peasant seems to have shown him. This poster suggests that a sexual division of labor persisted in the countryside, and that in the 1930s Soviet propaganda was not challenging that division.

Maksim Ushakov-Poskochin, "Woman Peasant, Strengthen the Union of the Workers and Peasants. It Will Make the U.S.S.R. Invincible" (1925)

The red-kerchiefed figure in the foreground is carrying books with prominently displayed titles. One is called *The Female Worker and the Female Peasant*. Another is the history of the Russian Communist Party. The third visible to us is entitled *Ilyich's Precepts,* after the affectionate name by which many Soviet citizens referred to Lenin. Behind her is another woman who is clearly discussing her reading materials with a female peasant and a girl. In the background are village buildings that have been altered by revolution: the one on the left is a thriving cooperative, as we can tell by the activity around it. Above on the right is a peasant hut that has been transformed into a library and to its right, the local soviet. The smaller figures all seem to be laboring, engaged in peasant work according to conventional male and female divisions. They include a woman hauling water from a well, women distributing goods, with men driving the village's sole tractor.

V. Livanova, "The All-Union Agricultural Exhibit Opens in Moscow, 1 August 1939" (1939)

At the center of this poster from a 1939 agricultural exhibition is a drawing of the well-known 530-foot statue that stood for many years in a Moscow park and served as the logo for Mosfilm (Moscow Film Studio), the way that a roaring lion was used by Metro-Goldwyn-Mayer. It first appeared at the Soviet Pavilion of the 1937 Paris World's Fair. At left, representing the Soviet proletariat is a tall male blacksmith holding a hammer above his head. To his right is a smaller female peasant whose raised sickle completes the representation of the Soviet Union as a marriage of industry and farm, worker and peasant. Both figures appear powerful and dynamic, yet the decision of the sculptor, Vera Mukhina, to have a man serve as the proletarian and a woman as the peasant reproduced several conventional wisdoms of Soviet society. As a proletarian, the male was both dominant and more important. As a peasant, the female was less powerful and more subservient. She also retained an association with fertility.

Women as Backward

Anonymous, "Having Eliminated Capitalism, the Proletariat Will Eliminate Prostitution" (1923)

The dominant figure in this poster is the large male worker at right. In one hand he is holding a hammer. With the other he is clasping the hands of a tiny, barefoot woman who is half his girth and stands barely level with his chest. She is dressed in modest clothes and her hair is tied back modestly in a bun. Most striking is her face: it is looking directly at his, and it is tilted upwards, as though in supplication. At their feet are hideous, leering caricatures of men, clearly the capitalists whom the proletariat, as the slogan says, have defeated. Behind a brick wall above the men, a group of hooded, female-looking figures emerge from an archway. Their heads are bowed down. Perhaps they, like the main female figure, are prostitutes who, with the help of big, strong male workers, can now leave their trade behind. Two slogans at right confirm this impression. The first says, "Prostitution is the greatest injustice of humanity." The one at bottom reads, "(Male) worker! Take care of the woman worker."

Alexander Samokhvalov, "Long Live the Komsomol" (1924)

Created in honor of the seventh anniversary of the October Revolution, this poster features two workers against an industrial background. The man, like many of the male proletarians in Soviet posters, stands tall. He is facing forward and bearing the weight of a red flag. By contrast, the female worker appears somewhat off balance and unsure. Looking behind her, rather than forward to the bright future, she seems to be leaning on the red flag rather than helping her comrade carry it. Bolshevik leaders often associated women with "backward" viewpoints, seeing them as obstacles to revolutionary change. Although the woman in this poster is part of the revolution, the fact that she is looking backward suggests that she is caught between the old and the new. The Komsomol was the Communist Youth League.

Elizaveta Kruglikova, "Woman! Become Literate!" (1923)

This poster reproduces the style of a traditional Russian woodcut, the kind of representation that would be familiar to the intended rural audience. It portrays a peasant woman and her daughter in a peasant hut. The mother is wearing bast shoes, an apron, and a kerchief markedly different from the tight red kerchiefs on communist women. Her barefoot daughter is seated on a chair, and she is holding a math book of some sort. On the nearby table, in addition to the traditional peasant samovar and teacups, are a pen, an inkwell, and another book. The slogan at the bottom reads, "Oh, mama! If you were literate, you would be able to help me!" The message here is clear: peasant women were supposed to seek an education, if only to make themselves useful to the next generation. The portrayal of a mother and daughter in this poster is significant. Far more women than men were illiterate in the first years of the revolution, particularly among the peasantry.

BÖJÜK STALİNƏ EŞQ OLSUN!
СЛАВА ВЕЛИКОМУ
СТАЛИНУ!

CHAPTER 7

Soviet Society and Culture in the 1930s

A poster from 1938, written in both Russian and Azeri, the language spoken in the Soviet republic of Azerbaijan, states, "Glory to the Great Stalin!" Stalin is depicted amid young marchers waving red flags, soldiers, airplanes, and tanks near the Kremlin in the upper-left corner.

In 1935 Stalin announced in a speech to a group of combine drivers that "life has improved, comrades, life has become more joyous." To be sure, most aspects of Soviet life contradicted the rosy picture painted by Stalin, but the regime was intent on presenting an image of a stable and prosperous society that had weathered the storms of the "revolution from above" and overcome the upheavals of collectivization, dekulakization, and forced industrialization. Stalin overlooked the disjuncture between reality and image when he proclaimed in 1936 that socialism had been achieved. In conjunction with the transformation of the economy brought about by Five-Year Plans, the Kremlin set about to impose social and cultural values that glorified the accomplishments of Soviet socialism and urged society to mobilize behind the goals of the state. The shortcomings and failures of Soviet society were covered over with an optimistic gloss emphasizing the achievements of Soviet power, which were supposedly the envy of the capitalist West, which was still mired in the Great Depression.

Beginning in the late 1920s the regime mobilized cultural and intellectual life to serve its interests and bolster Stalin's dictatorial grip on power. The transformation of Soviet society envisioned in the first Five-Year Plan required the mobilization of all human and material resources toward the primary goal set by the state: breakneck industrialization at all costs. All cultural and intellectual endeavors had to be devoted to building socialism, and this policy spelled a death knell for those artists, writers, and other intellectuals whose experimental and avant-garde endeavors now had no place in the society that Stalin and his supporters were creating. A new doctrine—socialist realism—was the linchpin of this new cultural and intellectual order. Socialist realism as applied in art, literature, and cinema did not offer a realistic portrayal of Soviet life, but instead depicted what Soviet society ought to be. Socialist realism may have helped the regime mobilize cultural forces behind its policies and values, but the doctrine also had a stultifying effect on intellectual life that was reinforced by the purges and fear of arrest and prison. The regime decreed that art had to be simple and accessible to the common person, and artists and intellectuals learned that their careers (and even their lives) depended on producing paintings, films, novels, poems, and music that were hackneyed, predictable, and uninspiring and satisfied the Party line. The result was a deadening homogenization of Soviet culture and society.

Public veneration of Stalin was a crucial ingredient to the emergence of the Stalinist political and cultural order. The Stalin cult emerged in 1929 on the occasion of Stalin's 50th birthday and marked his victory over his opponents in the Party. But the cult did not blossom fully until the mid-1930s. The cult built on the one surrounding Lenin and entailed the adulation of Stalin as Lenin's most worthy successor. It proclaimed that of all of Lenin's close political associates, only Stalin was capable of filling the shoes of Lenin and fulfilling the goals of 1917. The cult portrayed Stalin as an intrepid and undaunted leader who was leading the Soviet Union into the bright future of socialism, a fearless fighter who vanquished all those who stood in his way, a charismatic vozhd' (leader) who possessed superhuman qualities.

The cult served the purposes of both Stalin and the regime. Given the tumultuous impact of Five-Year Plans, the Stalin cult provided the Soviet people with a sense of direction and stability and deflected the problems created by the Stalinist system away from the architect of the system—Stalin—to supposed "enemies of the people." The cult made the decisions and policies of Stalin and the Kremlin unassailable and placed their shortcomings and failings at the feet of others, thereby providing yet another reason for political repression and purges while protecting Stalin and his associates from blame and responsibility. One crucial ingredient of the cult was the rewriting of history. If Stalin were to occupy the position of the omniscient, infallible leader of the Soviet Union, then any aspect of his life that revealed his faults, weaknesses, and mistakes had to be expunged.

Though the Kremlin deliberately manufactured the cult for its own reasons, the cult struck a responsive chord among most Soviet citizens, including peasants who, for the most part, did not have reason to worship Stalin. The cult spoke to a pressing need among Soviets for a leader who could act as an anchor during the challenges brought about by the regime's headlong rush into modernity. Popular reception of the Stalin cult was also conditioned by pre-revolutionary political traditions that venerated the tsars and frequently attributed god-like qualities to them.

With its cultural policies in the 1930s, the Soviet leadership made a conscious decision to abandon many of the ideals of the 1917 revolution. Society in the 1930s had a distinctly Stalinist flavor, one that was more conservative, rigid, and disciplinary than the one envisioned by Bolshevik visionaries a decade or two earlier. In many respects, the jettisoning of many revolutionary dreams and aspirations in the realms of culture and society was reminiscent of pre-revolutionary patterns, thereby appealing to many people who were much more traditional in their outlook than those Bolshevik visionaries who set out to recreate the world. The mundane triumphed over the imaginative and creative, and all artistic and intellectual ventures were geared to glorifying the 1917 revolution and building a socialist society.

The straitjacketing of cultural life did not meet with disapproval from most quarters of Soviet society. Many Soviet citizens supported the adoption of conservative social and cultural values and policies because they shared the sentiments embodied in them. Stalin's cultural policies engendered a sense of pride, accomplishment, and stability, the last being a quality sorely missing from a society enduring the growing pains of urban growth and industrial development. Moreover, many people benefited economically and socially from Stalin's revolution from above, and were committed and loyal supporters of the Soviet system as it developed in the 1930s. The state's policies to develop the economy gave rise to upward social mobility as sons and daughters of workers and peasants took advantage of expanding educational and employment opportunities. For those fortunate enough to escape the grasp of the secret police and to evade the maelstrom of collectivization, Stalin's Soviet Union had a lot to offer, notwithstanding the material deprivations caused by the shortcomings of the planned economy. In that respect, many Soviets were grateful to Stalin and Soviet power.

The Cult of Stalin

The cult served the purposes of both Stalin and the regime. Public adulation of Stalin not only satisfied the *vozhd*'s ego but also helped the regime to establish emotional ties between individual citizens and Stalin and, by extension, to the entire Soviet enterprise of the 1930s. In early 1935 the writer A. O. Avdienko, speaking in adulatory, religious terms at the Eighth Congress of Soviets, linked his personal happiness and success to Stalin.

The rewriting of history is evident in these two photographs of Stalin inspecting the Moscow–Volga Canal in 1937. The photo at left shows Stalin with secret police chief Nikolai Ezhov. After Ezhov's removal as head of the secret police soon after the photo was taken, his image was airbrushed from future copies of the photo, shown at right.

Thank you, Stalin. Thank you because I am joyful. Thank you because I am well. No matter how old I become, I shall never forget how we received Stalin two days ago. Centuries will pass, and the generations still to come will regard us as the happiest of mortals, as the most fortunate of men, because we lived in the century of centuries, because we were privileged to see Stalin, our inspired leader. Yes, and we regard ourselves as the happiest of mortals because we are the contemporaries of a man who never had an equal in world history.

The men of all ages will call on thy name, which is strong, beautiful, wise and marvelous. Thy name is engraven on every factory, every machine, every place on the earth, and in the hearts of all men.

Every time I have found myself in his presence I have been subjugated by his strength, his charm, his grandeur. I have experienced a great desire to sing, to cry out, to shout with joy and happiness. And now see me—me!—on the same platform where the Great Stalin stood a year ago. In what country, in what part of the world could such a thing happen.

I write books. I am an author. All thanks to thee, O great educator, Stalin. I love a young woman with a renewed love and shall perpetuate myself in my children—all thanks to thee, great educator, Stalin. I shall be eternally happy and joyous, all thanks to thee, great educator, Stalin. Everything belongs to thee, chief of our great country. And when the woman I love presents me with a child the first word it shall utter will be: Stalin.

O great Stalin, O leader of the peoples,
Thou who broughtest man to birth.
Thou who fructifiest the earth,

Thou who restorest the centuries,
Thou who makest bloom the spring,
Thou who makest vibrate the musical chords . . .
Thou, splendour of my spring, O Thou,
Sun reflected by millions of hearts . . .

Stalin's political biography was rewritten to glorify his actions during and after 1917, even when Stalin's actual behavior was far from blameworthy. All of Stalin's contributions to the seizure and consolidation of power were blown out of proportion or falsified. Likewise, the heroic exploits of other revolutionary leaders who had fallen into disfavor such as Trotsky were distorted so as to elevate Stalin's status into that of Lenin's closest political ally and confidant. Indeed, references to Trotsky and Bukharin were eliminated from all books, and it became common for published materials of purged individuals to be taken out of circulation. According to Sarra Mebel, who was born in 1917 and spent all her adult life in Moscow, she never saw a photograph of Trotsky until a visit to the United States in 1989.

In 1938 Stalin instructed the party to commission the writing of his official biography. _Stalin: A Biography_ is an excellent example of how the cult was codified. The 1949 edition effusively praised Stalin for his intellect and leadership, putting him on a pedestal as the greatest person who ever lived.

Millions of workers from all countries look upon Stalin as their teacher, from whose classic writings they learn how to cope with the class enemy and how to pave the way for the ultimate victory of the proletariat. Stalin's influence is the influence of the great and glorious Bolshevik Party, which workers in the capitalist countries look to as a model to follow. . . .

Stalin is the brilliant leader and teacher of the Party, the great strategist of the Socialist Revolution, military commander, and guide of the Soviet state. An implacable attitude towards the enemies of Socialism, profound fidelity to principle, a combination of clear revolutionary perspective and clarity of purpose with extraordinary firmness and persistence in the pursuit of aims, wise and practical leadership, and intimate contact with the masses— such are the characteristic features of Stalin's style. After Lenin, no other leader in the world has been called upon to direct such vast masses of workers and peasants. He has a unique faculty for generalizing the constructive revolutionary experience of the masses, for seizing upon and developing their initiative, for learning from the masses as well as teaching them, and for leading them forward to victory.

Stalin's whole career is an example of profound theoretical power combined with an unusual breadth and versatility of practical experience in the revolutionary struggle. . . .

Everybody is familiar with the cogent and invincible force of Stalin's logic, the crystal clarity of his mind, his iron will, his devotion to the Party, his ardent faith in the people, and love for the people. Everybody is familiar with his modesty, his simplicity of manner, his consideration for people, and his merciless severity towards enemies of the people. . . .

Stalin is the worthy continuer of the cause of Lenin, or, as it is said in the Party: Stalin is the Lenin of today. . . .

In the lore and art of the people, Stalin's name is ever linked with Lenin's. "We go with Stalin as with Lenin, we talk to Stalin as to Lenin; he knows all our inmost thoughts; all his life he has cared for us," runs one of the many Russian folk tales of today.

The name of Stalin is a symbol of the moral and political unity of Soviet society.

With the name of Stalin, all progressive men and women, all the peace-loving democratic nations associate their hope for lasting peace and security.

The Kremlin devoted enormous resources to spreading literacy, education, and health care to millions of indigenous peoples, many of whom were nomads who lived in the far reaches of the Soviet Union. Realizing that propaganda about Stalin would not be understood by many of these nomadic tribes, the regime decided to address these peoples in terms that made sense to them, using mythology, in this case worship of the sun, to convey its message about Stalin and the revolution.

And there came a time when a hero (who, although living far away from the Nanai people, saw and knew everything) took the sun into his hands, and turned it in such a way that its warmest rays shone where it was dark, and where downtrodden peoples were suffering. And they then knew well-being, warmth and happiness. The name of the hero was Lenin. When a great disaster befell the earth—when Lenin died—bad people were pleased. They thought that the sun would stop shedding its light on the people, but their glee was shorter than the space of a minute, because the people's sun was guarded by another hero. He is the nearest friend and companion of Lenin, and

This 1941 poster depicts Stalin in a Napoleonic pose, arm folded inside his coat. The text reads, "Stalin will lead us to victory!"

Nanai
Nanai are an indigenous people who live near the Soviet-Chinese border.

his name is Stalin. Nobody can equal the strength of that hero. His eyes see everything that goes on on earth. His ears hear everything that people say. His brain knows all that people think. His heart contains the happiness and the woe of all peoples. The depth of his thought is as deep as the ocean. His voice is heard by all that inhabit the earth. Such is the greatest of the very greatest in the whole world. And he took the sun out of Lenin's hands, and lifted it very high. And since then happiness shines on earth, because it is impossible for the sun not to shine.

"Glory to Stalin Shall be Eternal," written by the poet M. S. Kriukova in 1939, not only mythologizes Stalin but emphasizes how he was the legitimate successor to Lenin. It also hails the role Stalin played in fulfilling the promise of 1917, namely economic development, urbanization, and well-being.

Then the strong chains fell from the earth.
The whole earth lit up with light,
The ice of centuries melted and disappeared,
And the working people became free.
The leaders began construction work,
Soviet construction work.
But a misfortune suddenly happened—
Death felled Lenin.
While he was dying he called
His true friend, glorious Stalin:
"Take over, take over all my business,
Lead the people to bright happiness,
Teach them, help them."
Stalin gave him his faithful word,
It was strong as steel.
He set out on the road of Lenin
And in the steps of the Bolsheviks.
The wise leader began to adorn the country,
He rebuilt everything all anew.
Prosperous kolkhozes appeared in the villages,
Everyone started working with machines.
Everyone started to live well.
The fruit orchards began to bloom,
The people began to sing gay songs,
Little children were happy.
He built cities that amazed people.
The roofs of the buildings reached high to the skies.

Thank-you Note

An illiterate woman dictated this 1939 letter to her son.

"I want to share my feelings: I live very well and think that I will live even better. Why? Because I live in the Stalin epoch. May Stalin live longer than me! . . . All my children had and are getting an education thanks to the state and, I would say, thanks to the party, and especially comrade Stalin, for he, along with Lenin, opened the way for us simple people. . . . I myself, an old woman, am ready to die for Stalin and the Bolshevik cause."

Under the watchful eyes of Lenin, Stalin, and Vyacheslav Molotov, minister of foreign affairs, a beekeeper uses his spare time to take advantage of the cultural offerings of the reading room on the collective farm where he works in 1939. The revolution led to increased levels of literacy, and many workers took pride in attending night school and acquiring an advanced education.

And the equipment in the buildings is so marvelous. . . .
It's impossible to sing, to describe
Everything about Stalin-light,
About his great kindness and glorious deeds.
Glory to Stalin shall be eternal!
May he live and prosper for many years.
For the peace of the White Sea
And great honor of the Moscow River.

Many Soviets sincerely believed in the Stalin cult and genuinely revered the *vozhd'* for his leadership and inspiration. In that regard, much of public reverence shown to Stalin in public displays was heartfelt and genuine. Many others had nothing but contempt and hatred for Stalin and his policies. To be sure, many did not express their grievances out of fear. But the secret police nevertheless relied on paid and unpaid informers to keep abreast of individuals who uttered critical words about Stalin, the Party, and Soviet power. The poet Osip Mandelstam read the following poem at a gathering in 1933 and soon found himself in prison, where he died. The "broad-chested Ossete" at the end of the poem refers to Stalin, who was said to have Ossetian forebears, a people who live in the Caucasus Mountains of northern Georgia. In the version obtained by the secret police, the second stanza read: "All we hear is the Kremlin mountaineer, The murderer and the peasant-slayer."

We live, deaf to the land beneath us,
Ten steps away no one hears our speeches,

But where's so much as half a conversation
The Kremlin's mountaineer will get his mention.

His fingers are fat as grubs
And the words, final as lead weights, fall from his lips,

His cockroach whiskers leer
And his boot tops gleam.

Around him a rabble of thin-necked leaders—
fawning half-men for him to play with.

They whinny, purr or whine
As he prates and points a finger,

One by one forging his laws, to be flung
Like horseshoes at the head, the eye or the groin,

And every killing is a treat
For the broad-chested Ossete.

The Stalinist Revolution

Stalin's decision to adopt conservative social policies was in keeping with his revision of some of the hallowed principles of Marxism. Just as the doctrine of "socialism in one country" betrayed the Bolsheviks' commitment to internationalism and world revolution, so too did Stalin's musings on class struggle, social inequality, and state power in the 1930s indicate that he was less interested in maintaining ideological purity than in creating a dictatorship based on coercion. In 1931 the Soviet Union ended the practice of equalizing wages regardless of skill and productivity and reintroduced wage incentives as well as piece rates to boost labor productivity. According to Marx, the coming of socialism would lead to the "withering of the state" and the end of class struggle. But in his speech at the Seventeenth Party Congress, held in 1934, Stalin made it clear that efforts to build a socialist society entailed the intensification of class conflict and the strengthening of the state and its institutions. These assertions helped Stalin justify the immense bureaucracy that emerged to administer the Five-Year Plans and supervise all aspects of social and cultural life. They also offered an explanation of political repression and the emergence of a privileged elite who enjoyed a standard of living higher than that of the average worker and peasant.

Stalin embraces young Gelya Markizova after she gives him a bouquet of flowers at a 1936 reception in the Kremlin. The photograph promoted Stalin's image as the "Friend of the Little Children." Ironically, the girl's father, accused of espionage, was shot the following year and her mother was murdered under mysterious circumstances.

It goes without saying that a classless society cannot come of itself, spontaneously, as it were. It has to be achieved and built by the efforts of all the working people, by strengthening the organs of the dictatorship of the proletariat, by intensifying the class struggle, by abolishing classes, by eliminating the remnants of the capitalist classes, and in battles with enemies both internal and external.

The point is clear, one would think.

And yet, who does not know that the promulgation of this clear and elementary thesis of Leninism has given rise to not a little confusion and to unhealthy sentiments among a section of Party members? The thesis that we are advancing towards a classless society—which was put forward as a slogan—was interpreted by them to mean a spontaneous process. And they began to reason this way: If it is a classless society, then we can relax the class struggle, we can relax the dictatorship of the proletariat, and get rid of the state altogether, since it is fated to wither away soon in any case. They dropped into a state of . . . ecstasy, in the expectation that soon there will be no classes, and therefore no class struggle, and therefore no cares and worries, and therefore we can lay down our

Watch Out

People who voiced concerns about shortages of food and consumer goods while standing in line in stores were subject to arrest if informers or plainclothes agents of the secret police were listening. At the end of September 1938 in Leningrad, several thousand people stood in lines for shoes and clothing. A bedraggled shopper complained, "You stand in a queue and don't get anything." A police agent took the trouble to make a note of it.

arms and retire—to sleep and to wait for the advent of a classless society. . . .

It goes without saying that if this confusion of mind and these non-Bolshevik sentiments obtained a hold over the majority of our Party, the Party would find itself demobilized and disarmed. . . .

These people evidently think that socialism calls for equalization, for levelling the requirements and the individual lives of the members of society. Needless to say, such an assumption has nothing in common with Marxism, with Leninism. By equality Marxism means, not equalization of individual requirements and individual life, but the abolition of classes, . . . Furthermore, Marxism proceeds from the assumption that people's tastes and requirements are not, and cannot be, identical, equal, in regard to quality or quantity, either in the period of socialism or in the period of communism.

In June 1934 *Pravda*, the newspaper of the Communist Party, published "For the Fatherland!," an editorial penned by Stalin that highlights the need to emphasize Russian patriotism and nationalism. This article indicated the regime's rejection of a fundamental tenet of Marxism, namely its commitment to internationalism.

For proletarians and kolkhozniks, for honest Soviet specialists, there is nothing more beautiful and more clear than their own country liberated from the yoke of landowners and capitalists.

The best traditions of the Civil War and of the struggle with the interventionists, when the workers and peasants were armed to defend their rights to a new life, are now being multiplied in the progress of techniques and Socialistic culture. That is why the Soviet Union has become an impregnable fortress and is capable of crushing all those who would dare to attempt to violate the sanctity of its boundaries.

For our fatherland! This call fans the flame of heroism, the flame of creative initiative in pursuits and all fields of our rich life. For our fatherland! This call arouses millions of workers and alerts them in the defense of their great country.

The defense of the fatherland is the supreme law of life. And he who raises his hand against his country, he who betrays his country should be destroyed. . . .

For high treason, for acts detrimental to the country's military might, or state independence, or inviolability of her territories, for espionage, for divulging military or state secrets, for deserting to the enemy, or escaping across the border, the Soviet court will punish the guilty by shooting or by confiscating all his property. In the case of a civilian, some leniency will be shown according to circumstances, and for the death penalty will be substituted the confiscation of his property or imprisonment for ten years. For a person in military service, however, for treason there will be only one measure of punishment—execution by shooting with confiscation of all his property. Individual members of his family are also responsible for the acts of traitors. In the case of the escape or flight across the border of a person in military service, all mature members of his family, if they are implicated in aiding the criminal, or knew of his intentions and did not report them to the authorities, are punished by imprisonment for five to ten years with confiscation of all their property.

The other members of the family of the traitor and all his dependents at the time he committed treason are subject to disfranchisement and exile to some remote region in Siberia for five years.

Traitors should be punished unmercifully. On the other hand, if a person in military service was aware of a plot to betray the government or of an act of betrayal and did not report this to the authorities, he is subject to imprisonment for ten years. One cannot be a neutral observer where the interests of the country or the workers and peasants are concerned. This is a terrible crime; this is complicity in the crime.

This decree . . . gives the workers of the great Soviet Union a new weapon in their hands in the struggle against the enemies of the proletarian dictatorship. The one hundred and seventy million working people who regard the Soviet land as their own mother who has nursed them to a happy and joyous life will deal with the traitors of their fatherland with all their force.

For the fatherland, for its honor and glory, might and well-being!

In 1936 the government banned abortion, a practice that had been legalized soon after the revolution. To prepare the public for the ban, the government published a draft of the law and solicited feedback from the populace. In May 1936 *Pravda* published the following editorial, which reflects the regime's embrace of attitudes that tightened divorce proceedings, rejected the Bolsheviks' earlier pronouncement that the family would disappear under socialism, and strengthened women's primary responsibility for the family. Ominously, it claims that family members are to be held responsible for each other's behavior. It not only reveals the regime's emphasis on family stability and parental responsibility, but underscores the government's fears about falling birthrates. For the leadership, solid families meant more children. More children meant a larger population, and a larger population meant more workers and soldiers.

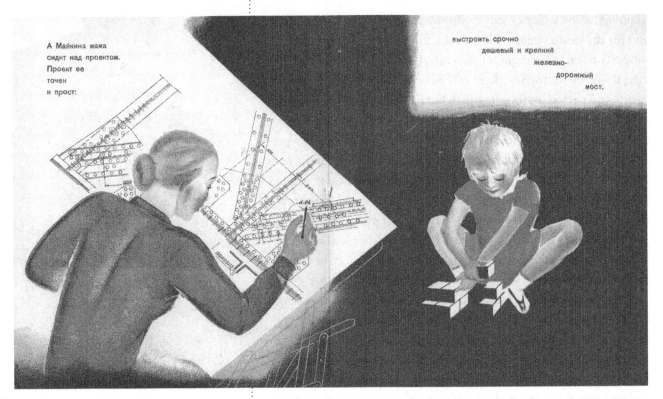

А Майкина мама
сидит над проектом.
Проект ее
точен
и прост:

выстроить срочно
дешевый и крепкий
железно-
дорожный
мост.

Mommy's Bridge, a 1933 book for preschoolers, showed women participating in the industrialization process, but it tried to demonstrate that working women could also be good mothers.

Horrified at the frequency of abortion and divorce, and supported by those who lamented the chaotic state of family relationships, Stalin took legislative steps to promote family stability. In 1934 the state clamped down on men who did not make their alimony payments, and the concept of illegitimacy resurfaced in a 1944 law that declared children illegitimate who were born outside a registered marriage.

The published draft of the law prohibiting abortion and providing material assistance to mothers has provoked a lively reaction throughout the country. It is being heatedly discussed by tens of millions of people and there is no doubt that it will serve as a further strengthening of the Soviet family. Parents' responsibility for the education of their children will be increased and a blow will be dealt at the lighthearted, negligent attitude toward marriage.

When we speak of strengthening the Soviet family, we are speaking precisely of the struggle against the survivals of a bourgeois attitude toward marriage, women and children. So-called "free love" and all disorderly sex life are bourgeois through and through, and have nothing to do with either socialist principles or the ethics and standards of conduct of the Soviet citizen. Socialist doctrine shows this, and it is proved by life itself.

The *elite* of our country, the best of the Soviet youth, are as a rule also excellent family men who dearly love their children. And *vice versa*: the man who does not take marriage seriously, and abandons his children to the whims of fate, is usually also a bad worker and a poor member of society.

Fatherhood and motherhood have long been virtues in this country. This can be seen at the first glance, without searching inquiry. Go through the parks and streets of Moscow or of any other town in the Soviet Union on a holiday, and you will see not a few young men walking with pink-cheeked, well-fed babies in their arms. . . .

More than once the enemies of the people suggested to us the foul and poisonous ideal of liquidating the family and disrupting marriage. The bourgeoisie has tried to use it as a weapon in the class struggle against socialist progress. It is enough to recall with what persistence they spread the slander about the "nationalization of women." And during the great move to collectivize, the kulaks again broadcast this favorite bourgeois allegation. The kulaks used it to scare the peasants: "In the collective farms you will all sleep under the same 30-yard-wide blanket."

The bourgeois who establishes his family order with the aid of a knout, the bourgeois for whom his own family is but a thin veneer covering prostitution and sexual debauchery, naturally thought that everyone would fall for his lie about "free love" in the country where the exploitation of man by man has been abolished and women have been liberated. But he failed. . . .

Knout
A *knout* is a leather whip.

There is no point in denying that in towns and villages there are still men and women whose attitude towards family and children is superficial and devil-may-care. Marriage and divorce are, of course, private affairs—but the State cannot allow anyone to mock at women or to abandon his children to the mercy of fate. The irresponsible profligate who gets married five times a year cannot enjoy the respect of Soviet youth. Nor can a girl who flutters from one marriage into the next with the swiftness of a butterfly enjoy respect. Men and women of this sort merely deserve social contempt. Marriage is a serious, responsible business and one that must not be approached lightheartedly. . . .

Not all Soviet citizens welcomed the ban on abortion. Before the government enacted the legislation, it solicited public opinion. People met at work and on collective farms to discuss the pros and cons of the proposed ban on abortion. Newspapers received thousands of letters expressing the views of men and women from a cross-section of the socioeconomic spectrum. A letter written in May 1936 by a woman engineer appeared in *Izvestiia*, the official newspaper of the government, and focused on the negative consequences of a prohibition on abortion.

"Abortions cannot be categorically forbidden."

I am non-party, married, with a 5-year-old son. I work as an engineer and have been and still am in a responsible position. I regard myself as a good citizen of the U.S.S.R.

I cannot agree with the prohibition of abortions. And I am very glad that this law has not entered into force but has been submitted to the workers for discussion.

The prohibition of abortion means the compulsory birth of a child to a woman who does not want children. The birth of a child ties married people to each other. Not everyone will readily abandon a child, for alimony is not all that children need. Where the parents produce a child of their own free will, all is well. But where a child comes into the family against the will of the parents, a grim personal drama will be enacted which will undoubtedly lower the social value of the parents and leave its mark on the child.

A categorical prohibition of abortion will confront young people with a dilemma: either complete sexual abstinence or the risk of jeopardizing their studies and disrupting their life. To my mind any prohibition of abortion is bound to mutilate many a young life. Apart from this, the result of such a prohibition might be an increase in the death-rate from abortions because they will then be performed illegally.

As for the increase in alimony, the enforcing of payment, the development of a network of maternity homes, crèches and kindergartens,—all these must be welcomed. Aid to large families should, I think, begin with the fourth or fifth child, while the amount of the subsidy could be decreased.

Several weeks later *Pravda* published another editorial underscoring a father's social and financial responsibility to his children and stressing that men should not abandon their families. In particular, the editorial declared that fathers who fail their children are also failing their duties as a citizen.

Social education is being widely developed in this country. The State is coming to the aid of the family. But the State in no way relieves the mother or the father of their care of the children. Under Soviet conditions the father is the social educator. He has to prepare good Soviet citizens: that is his duty, that is also his pride—and the Soviet land has heard many proud declarations by fathers and mothers about the sons and daughters they gave to the Soviet fatherland, about gallant pilots and parachutists, engineers, doctors, teachers. . . .

A man who cowardly and basely abandons his children, shuns his responsibility, hides in corners and puts all the paternal duties on the mother's shoulders, shames the name of a Soviet citizen. Evading the payment of alimony is not a weakness, though it is treated with such leniency by some of our institutions. It is a crime, and not only the man who befouls the name of Soviet citizen, but all those who protect him are guilty of this crime. . . .

A Soviet child has a right to a real father, an educator and friend. A father who abandons his children is guilty both before them and before the socialist State which has entrusted the children to his care. An irresponsible attitude towards marriage and family is a bad recommendation as a citizen.

Socialism provides every toiler with a happy, beautiful life. For the first time in history it creates for the workers a possibility of fatherhood and motherhood in the fullest sense of the word. It therefore makes serious demands on mother and father. A bourgeois attitude towards the family cannot be tolerated.

. . . "Paternal pride"—these words sound real only in the Soviet land. . . .

ДЕТИ СОВЕТОВ

ОГИЗ - МОЛОДАЯ ГВАРДИЯ 1931

This 1931 children's book was entitled "Children of the Soviets." Well-known authors such as Vladimir Mayakovskii, Kornei Chukovskii, and Samuil Marshak introduced young readers to non-political subjects such as ice cream, the circus, and other aspects of everyday life and political issues such as Soviet holidays, the Red Army, and May Day celebrations.

Stalin called writers "engineers of human souls," and the regime used literature as a propaganda tool. In a speech delivered in 1934, Andrei Zhdanov, a Party leader delegated by Stalin to establish greater Party control over literature, outlined the purpose and goals of Soviet literature and introduced the term "socialist realism" to describe the art that the regime wanted to encourage. During the 1930s the Kremlin established ideological control over every branch of cultural endeavor. After 1945 Zhdanov headed the Party in Leningrad and orchestrated the regime's campaign against Western culture and its influences.

Comrade Stalin has called our writers "engineers of human souls." What does this mean? What obligations does this title impose on us?

First of all, it means that we must know life so as to depict it truthfully in our works of art—and not to depict it scholastically, lifelessly, or merely as "objective reality"; we must depict reality in its revolutionary development.

In this respect, truth and historical concreteness of the artistic depiction must be combined with the task of the ideological transformation and education of the working people in the spirit of

There was an original column marching in the May Day demonstration. It consisted of people over 100 years of age who carried the placard: "Thank you, dear Stalin, for our happy childhood." Stalin is a little confused. He stops the column and says: "But I wasn't around back then." "That's precisely why our childhoods were happy."

Socialism. This method of artistic literature and literary criticism is what we call socialist realism. . . .

To be an engineer of human souls means to stand with both feet on the ground of real life. And this, in turn, denotes a break with the old-style romanticism that depicted a nonexistent life with nonexistent heroes and that spirited the reader away from the contradictions and oppression of life to an unreal world, to a world of utopias. Romanticism cannot be alien to our literature, which stands with both feet on the firm basis of materialism; but it must be a romanticism of a new kind, a revolutionary romanticism. We say that socialist realism is the basic method of Soviet artistic literature and literary criticism, and this presupposes that revolutionary romanticism must enter literary creativity as an integral part, because the whole life of our Party, of our working class and its struggle consists of a combination of the most severe, most sober practical work with supreme heroism and grand prospects. Our Party has always derived its strength from the fact that it united—and continues to unite—particular activity and practicality with grand prospects, with a ceaseless aspiration onward, with the struggle for the construction of a Communist society. *Soviet literature must be able to show our heroes, must be able to catch a glimpse of our tomorrow. This will not be a utopia, because our tomorrow is being prepared today by our systematic and conscious work. . . .*

The regime recognized the value of cinema as a form of mass communication and invested money and talent to develop a world-class film industry. The 1934 film about the civil war hero Vasily Chapaev received critical acclaim for its adherence to the principles of socialist realism. In the book *A Cinema for Millions*, which appeared in 1935, Boris Shumiatskii, head of the Soviet film industry, praised the film for its matter-of-fact portrayal of Chapaev in his heroic struggle to defeat the Whites. According to the Kremlin, heroes need not be perfect, but they must acknowledge their shortcomings and work to overcome them. Just as the building of socialism is a struggle requiring the work of all Soviet citizens, so too is the development of individuals committed to the principles and ideals of the revolution.

In 1934 the best film produced by Soviet cinema in the whole period of its existence was released: *Chapaev* as a film represented the real summit of Soviet film art.

The film is distinguished by its *exceptional* simplicity. This simplicity, which is characteristic only of high art, is . . . organic to *Chapaev*. . . .

The strength of *Chapaev* lies in the profound *vital truth* of the film. The directors . . . have depicted superbly the positive heroes and the positive features but they have not been afraid to show in their film a number of the negative aspects that existed in the Red Army at that time. . . . But these negative features are depicted realistically and truthfully. The film depicts in every negative feature the traces of its demise. . . .

The central character of the film, the wonderful figure of the heroic divisional commander Chapaev, is drawn in rich and vivid colors. Chapaev is not embellished. There is no touching up of his character. Chapaev is politically illiterate; he does not realize that there is no difference between a Bolshevik and a Communist, . . . he does not know the history of the Party. . . .

Chapaev learns avidly himself and at the same time teaches others. . . . His lesson on a commander's place in battle, his elaboration of plans of attack on the Whites, his astounding tenacity and sharp-wittedness that do not leave him for a moment, all these are extraordinarily precious and convincing strokes in depicting the image of the Bolshevik captain.

Teenagers participate in the 1934 election campaign in Moscow. Their banner reads, "Long Live the Soviets" and "Long Live the Communist Party."

Chapaev is stern: he does not hesitate before the fire of an enemy ready to stab the Revolution in the back, but Chapaev is a marvelous comrade. Chapaev is a sensitive and sympathetic human being. He dreams, loves a good song, laughter, jokes. . . .

G. and S. Vasiliev cleverly and sensitively and with the great tact of the artist, stroke by stroke and dash by dash, depict the character of Chapaev and show how this spontaneous Communist grows into a genuine Bolshevik, a disciplined member of Lenin's Party. Essentially, the whole film is about this: the growth of Chapaev and his comrades-in-arms under the attentive, careful and concerned guidance of the Party. The whole film is about our Party training the Red Army. . . .

Soviet citizens did not spend all their time working and reading Party propaganda. Nor did they spend every waking hour worrying about purges and the supposed enemies in their midst. People played, laughed, and fell in love. When not busy with work and family and domestic affairs, people could take advantage of a variety of forms of relaxation and entertainment such as attending sporting events and concerts and going to the theater and the movies. With literacy on the rise, more and more Soviets took the time to read one of the myriad newspapers and magazines published to satisfy the people's thirst for knowledge and information. The regime understood the necessity for rest and recreation and saw to it that not all forms of entertainment were didactic, merely serving the political ends of the government. Enamored with Soviet socialism, head of Johns Hopkins' Institute of the History of Medicine Henry Sigerist published a book in 1939 in which he describes the health-care system of the Soviet Union. He wrote that the Kremlin's commitment to the physical and mental well-being of its citizens can be seen in the resources devoted to the establishment of parks, most notably Gorky Park in central Moscow, where people seeking a break from the concerns of daily life could go to relax and unwind. Gorky Park is still a major attraction today.

This poster advertises the 1934 film "Chapaev," based on a novel about the exploits of Vasily Chapaev, a legendary commander of the Red Army during the Civil War. Some 30 million people saw the film during its first year of release, and it won the award for Best Foreign Film given by the U.S. National Board of Review in 1935.

The Maxim Gorky Park, beautifully located along the Moscow River and covering an area of about 750 acres, has playgrounds for all sports and every evening you can see thousands of young people in training. Most popular is the parachute-tower. Parachute jumping has become a regular craze in the Soviet Union, and it was embarrassing to me to have to confess repeatedly that I had neither jumped from an aeroplane nor had I ever felt the desire to do so. Dancing and singing are very popular in the park. Young physical-culture and music students lead the groups in such dancing and singing. All kinds of amusements are provided but the atmosphere is totally unlike that of Coney Island or of other Western amusement parks. You will not find the blinding floods of light, nor hear the deafening noises and the shrieking laughter customary in such places. The senses are not lashed by violent means. The light is soft neon light, the crowds move gently. American visitors often report that the Russians cannot possibly be happy because they do not laugh. They do laugh and very heartily, but it is not that raucous laughter that so often scarcely conceals the tears. The Slavs and Anglo-Saxons have very different temperaments. The Russian folk-songs, as a rule, are in minor tune. Besides, there is no alcoholic hilarity in these parks.

A large section of the Maxim Gorky Park provides cultural and educational facilities. Libraries are scattered all over the place and they distribute 2,000 volumes a day. On the shore of the lake is a pavilion with newspapers and magazines that can be read in comfortable armchairs. Lectures are held and exhibitions are displayed. Chess-players can meet their partners in a special pavilion. The foreign workers have their international club. Several theatres and cinemas give performances every night. The Green Theatre, an open-air theatre, attracts large numbers of people. I saw Dzerzhinski's opera *Tikhii Don* (And Quiet Flows the Don) performed there by a cast of one thousand for an audience of twenty thousand. In ten days 200,000 Moscovites had enjoyed the opera. . . .

A special feature of the Maxim Gorky Park is its Children's Village where children not only find playgrounds but also technical, chemical, and photographic laboratories, and art studios in which study and play are combined harmoniously. A great deal is done in the Soviet Union for the rest and recreation of children. . . .

An average of 120,000 people visit the Gorky Park daily. On free days corresponding to our Sundays there may be as many as 250,000. And yet the park is so large, so widely extended that whoever seeks complete rest and solitude will find it. Festivals are held in the park. Students of the Moscow schools meet there at the end of the academic year. Workers of a factory may celebrate the fulfillment of their plan of production in the park. Carnival festivals are held, with fireworks, music, . . .

Moscow, however, has more than one park. Each of them has a character of its own, as have the parks in the various cities. In the South they are conspicuous for their luxuriant vegetation. In small towns the park may be very modest, but I have spent many pleasant evenings in such small parks where the music consisted of a brass band or only a few accordion and balalaika. The spirit was the same everywhere. And what impresses the foreign visitor most is the feeling of social security expressed on all the faces. These people are adjusted to their environments. After a day's work they rest and relax. They need not worry about their job. There is no doubt that these Parks of Culture and Rest are institutions of great hygienic significance.

The revolution promised to create a society inhabited by men and women who turned their backs on individualism and embraced the welfare of the

In the 1930s musical comedies, modeled on those produced in Hollywood, were popular. In A Cinema for Millions, *published in 1935, Boris Shumiatskii rejected criticism of the musical comedy as having no place in socialist realist art.*

In a country building socialism, where there is no private property or exploitation, where the classes hostile to the proletariat have been liquidated, where the workers are united by their conscious participation in the construction of socialist society and where the enormous task of liquidating the remnants of the capitalist past is being successfully accomplished by the Party even in people's consciousness—in this country comedy, apart from its task of exposure, has another, more important and responsible task: the creation of a cheery and joyful spectacle. . . . even the hostile reviews . . . cannot completely deny the good things there are in the film: its cheerfulness, its joie-de-vivre and its laughter. The victorious class wants to laugh with joy. That is its right, and Soviet cinema must provide the audience with this joyful Soviet laughter.

Balalaika

A balalaika is a small, triangular stringed instrument.

Stalin, the Politburo, and their entire retinue are cruising along the Volga on a steamship. Suddenly, the ship begins to sink. If it goes down instantly, who will be saved?

The peoples of the U.S.S.R.

Kolkhozniks from the sticks are touring Moscow. The guide is reciting standard materials about the "accomplishments of the Soviet system," about its "concern for the human being," about the "expanding needs of Soviet people" and the "abundance of consumer goods."

One of the kolkhozniks says: "Comrade Leader, I spent the whole day yesterday walking around the city, and I didn't see any of the things you're talking about."

The guide replies with irritation: "You should spend less time walking around and more time reading newspapers."

collective. Self-sacrifice was a necessary part of this socialist ethos, and the Soviet regime in the 1930s devoted immense resources to building a propaganda machine to reach all members of society. Not surprisingly, the Kremlin focused enormous attention on fashioning a younger generation that, untouched by the legacy of tsarism and capitalism, could be more easily inculcated with the values held in high esteem by the regime, namely loyalty to the Party, Soviet state, and Stalin.

The government encouraged Soviet youth to emulate the lives of revolutionary heroes—real and fictional—and used the life of Pavlik Morozov to inspire the younger generation. Morozov was a boy from a village in the Ural Mountains who, in 1932, denounced his father to the secret police for hiding grain. According to Soviet authorities, after the father had been sentenced to prison for "*kulak* tendencies," Morozov's grandfather and uncle killed the boy for his treacherous behavior. The Kremlin seized upon this incident to elevate Pavlik Morozov into a martyr, and future generations of Soviet schoolchildren were force-fed an embellished story of how Morozov had been sacrificed in the name of building socialism. Mikhail Doroshin's 1933 poem "A Poem about Hate," contributed to the emergence of a Morozov cult.

The swamp's all around—
He's scared to take a step.
Then someone blocks
The Pioneer's path,
Like a fog,
Or shadow,
And whispers
Like a deaf-mute:
"Get down
On your knees!"
Maybe it's the wind,
Or maybe—No,
Pashka sees
His granddad.
Kulikanov stands
Right behind his back,
And the men surround
Pavlik like a wall.
"Listen to your elders!
Chuck the Pioneers!"
And they point their fists
At Pavlik
And just like they're singing:

"Pavlik! Pashka! Pash!
No matter what, you will be
Ours! Ours! Ours!"
They wave their fists at him
Like a big oak club.
"If you don't become ours,
Then we'll kill you."
Let them roar
Like thunder.
Pavlik Morozov
Can't be scared off
By his enemies' threats. . . .
Muter and muter
Stand the woods round the boys.
Pavlusha won't be going
To the Pioneers anymore.
Joyful and curly,
He won't come to school.
But his great glory
Will outlive everything.
"Pavlik is with us,
Pashka the Communist!"
Out in front, like a banner,
Friendly and merry.
(That's how
Everyone should live).
How much
Every schoolchild
Resembles him
Somehow.
All of their shirts
Are abloom with red ties:
"Pashka! Pashka! Pashka!
Here! There! Everywhere!"

Pavlik Morozov was fourteen years old when relatives supposedly murdered him for denouncing his father to the secret police.

CHAPTER **8**

The Great Terror

No aspect of Stalin's rule is known better and understood less than the political witch-hunt known as the purges. Beginning in the mid-1930s Stalin and the secret police (NKVD, Russian initials for the People's Commissariat of Internal Affairs) launched a bloody campaign to arrest, incarcerate, exile, and execute suspected opponents of the regime. People from all walks of life, from party members to run-of-the-mill workers and peasants, were caught up in the tragic events that led to the proliferation of the prison camp system (known in Russian as the Gulag, or the Main Directorate for Camps). Reminiscent of the Reign of Terror during the French Revolution, the purges of the 1930s, which reached their crescendo in 1937 and 1938, saw the Kremlin devour many devoted and loyal children of the revolution. It resulted in a political system where Stalin's power and authority went unchallenged and the populace, fearful of arrest and deportation, became passive subjects of the regime. The Gulag remained a chief feature of the Soviet Union until Stalin's death (and even after, though in much diminished scope) as the ongoing purges kept the prisons brimming with hapless victims.

Stalin used the purges to solidify his position as supreme leader of the Soviet Union by lashing out at imagined and potential opponents. Not only was there a dramatic drop in the population as a result of the purges, but the terror destroyed countless talented members of society who could have led fruitful and productive lives in the service of the Soviet Union. The purges also secured Stalin's position as dictator and put an end to other party leaders' readiness to stand up to him or at least express their honest opinions about policies. Stalin surrounded

Political prisoners pose for a group photograph at a camp in Dagestan, a region in southern Russia bordering the Caspian Sea, in 1923.

185

himself by "yes men" too afraid to assert themselves out of fear of falling victim to the secret police.

The purges affected all levels of society, but members of the Party bore the brunt of them. No one was safe from the tentacles of the secret police, who were under tremendous pressure to arrest "enemies of the people," individuals accused of having ties to foreign intelligence agencies, the Whites, and outlawed political parties such as the Mensheviks and Socialist Revolutionaries. The NKVD relied on denunciations and manufactured evidence, and used torture to secure confessions. Fear of the midnight knock on the door sent shivers of dread and apprehension down the spines of millions of citizens. Neighbors, co-workers, and even friends and family members reported on each other. One risked arrest and deportation for telling a joke about Stalin. Indeed, it was dangerous not to denounce the teller of an anti-Stalin joke upon hearing it. In one instance, a teenage boy denounced his father for wiping his razor blade on a scrap of newspaper that bore a picture of Stalin. The father ended up in the Gulag. Hours of interrogation without sleep or food, threats against family members, and beatings generally led to confessions of non-existent crimes.

It is clear that Stalin could not have supervised every aspect of the purges throughout the vast expanses of the Soviet Union, but no doubt exists that he and the secret police set the process in motion, established the tone, and encouraged overzealous and eager party and police officials to arrest and extract confessions from as many suspects as possible. Moreover, Stalin reviewed many lists of individuals arrested and personally signed the death warrants of tens of thousands of victims. He actively oversaw the purges and even helped establish quotas for the number of executions in each administrative region of the Soviet Union.

The roots of the Great Terror can be found in the early history of the communist regime. The Bolsheviks did not shy away from shedding the blood of those they accused of standing in the way of the revolution during the civil war. Agents of the Cheka scoured the towns and villages in their effort to "eliminate the bourgeoisie as a class," and Lenin authorized the establishment of prison camps where the "class enemies" of the regime could be incarcerated. In the 1920s the government praised the supposed benefits of corrective labor and argued that incarceration in the Gulag would help to re-educate criminals. This interest in rehabilitation fell to the wayside by the 1930s, when the government recognized the economic benefits of forced labor and the camp system. Stalin's use of terror and violence was no aberration, but his willingness to turn on other party members and accuse them of being "enemies of the people" was a new twist in the regime's effort to defend itself from real and imagined opponents.

The Party periodically cleansed itself (the Russian word for "cleansing" or "purge" is chistka) of unreliable members, particularly those who were accused of corruption and careerism and who came from unreliable class backgrounds such as the nobility and well-to-do peasantry. During the 1920s the Party conducted a series of such cleansing actions designed to get rid of the dead weight in its midst, but punishment was limited to expulsion from the Party, not imprisonment, deportation, and execution as in the 1930s. The Party readmitted many of those excluded in the 1920s, particularly after the disgraced members recanted their shortcomings and promised to avoid the political mistakes of their past. The regime also held show trials prior to those of the 1930s. For example, during the First Five-Year Plan the Soviet government put on trial dozens of factory managers and engineers, accusing them of sabotaging the industrialization drive.

The hallmark event of the purges was the series of public trials of leading party officials who were accused of a variety of preposterous crimes, from a conspiracy to assassinate Lenin to an effort to restore capitalism with the help of Nazi Germany and Japan. They began in 1936 and were orchestrated by Stalin and the secret police. At these trials some of the most prominent members of the Party, such as Trotsky, Kamenev, Bukharin, and Zinoviev, were accused of plotting to overthrow the Soviet Union and collaborating with the enemies of the Soviet Union. The trials lasted until 1938 and relied on trumped-up accusations, bogus evidence, and confessions extracted through torture. The spectacle of heroes of the revolution confessing to the most heinous crimes justified to the public the existence of a vast secret police network to scrutinize the daily activities of all Soviet citizens and ferret out alleged traitors, counter-revolutionaries, and saboteurs. Zinoviev, Kamenev, and Bukharin were found guilty and executed, along with dozens of other prominent political figures, including most of the military's general staff and the entire regional leadership of the Party. Given the existence of press censorship and inability of foreign diplomats and journalists to travel freely and collect news and information independently, it is not surprising that non-Soviet accounts accepted at face value the government's wild accusations. Besides, governments in the 1930s still commanded the trust of people who assumed they were being told the truth. The truth about the purges and the existence of the Gulag was hard to come by and became well known only after World War II.

Several nagging questions that defy easy resolution are how Soviet citizens understood the purges and why so many individuals became part of the purge machinery. The enormous scope of the purges *cannot be explained by fear and terror alone. To be sure, many millions of people kept quiet and did not register their protest because they were afraid of running afoul of the secret police. Yet the purges and immense prison camp system would have foundered without the active participation of hundreds of thousands, perhaps millions, of individuals. There is no doubt that sadists found a welcome home in the prison cellars of the secret police, where suspects were subjected to insidious forms of torture and beatings. Many of those involved in the huge bureaucracy that ran the purges were merely following orders, doing a job that they believed was necessary because they accepted the regime's pronouncements about traitors and enemies in their midst. Many of the guards were politically unsophisticated peasant recruits fresh from the countryside and therefore unlikely to question the logic and veracity of the accusations mouthed by party officials and repeated in the press. Moreover, many individuals stood to gain professionally and materially by denouncing others to the secret police: they could settle personal scores, get a promotion, and even perhaps move into the apartment of the person they denounced. The press characterized "enemies of the people" as pigs, vultures, rats, and spiders, depictions that dehumanized purge victims and made the purge process all that much easier. For many citizens, the Party did not make mistakes.*

The costs of the purges were enormous and long lasting in psychological, social, political, and economic terms. The exact total of purge victims may never be known. Stalin and the secret police sowed the seeds of mistrust, fear, and insecurity among all Soviet citizens. Virtually all families were touched in some manner by the purges: no one could be sure that friends, neighbors, relatives, and co-workers were not denouncing them to the authorities. Perhaps this was the most tragic of all the consequences of the purges, since it left a lasting legacy on the very fabric of interpersonal relations for decades.

The Gulag

The Soviet government set up the Gulag soon after 1917 in order to deal with people accused of a range of crimes, ranging from theft to political opposition. By the late 1920s a countrywide system of forced labor camps had emerged. In 1926 several camp prisoners (apparently sentenced for theft, not political crimes) described the abominable conditions in which they lived in a letter addressed to party leaders in the Kremlin. Unlike later prisoners of the Gulag, however, the writers of this appeal were released for reasons of ill health.

We appeal to you, asking you to pay a minimum of attention to our request.

We are prisoners who are returning from the Solovetskii concentration camp because of our poor health. We went there full of energy and good health, and now we are returning as invalids, broken and crippled emotionally and physically. We are asking you to draw your attention to the arbitrary use of power and the violence that reigns at the Solovetskii concentration camp.... It is difficult for a human being even to imagine such terror, tyranny, violence, and lawlessness. When we went there, we could not conceive of such a horror, and now we, crippled ourselves, together with several thousands who are still there, appeal to the ruling center of the Soviet state to curb the terror that reigns there.... the former tsarist penal servitude system in comparison to Solovki had 99% more humanity, fairness, and legality.... The beating and humiliation have reached such nightmarish levels, there aren't words to describe it. People die like flies, i.e., they die a slow and painful death. We repeat that all this torment and suffering are placed only on the shoulders of the penniless proletariat, i.e., on workers who, we repeat, were unfortunate to find themselves in the period of hunger and destruction accompanying the events of the October Revolution, and who committed crimes only to save themselves and their families from death by destruction....

If you complain or write anything ("Heaven forbid"), they will frame you for an attempted escape or for something else, and they will shoot you like a dog. They line us up naked and barefoot at 22 degrees below zero and keep us outside for up to an hour. It is difficult to describe all the chaos and terror that are going on in ... Solovki.... All annual inspections uncover a lot of abuses. But what they discover in comparison to what actually exists is only a part of the horror and abuse of power which the inspection accidentally uncovers. One example is the following fact—one of a thousand—which is registered ... and for which the guilty have been punished: THEY FORCED THE INMATES TO EAT THEIR OWN FECES.... It is no exaggeration to say that this is the "Spanish inquisition.".... And if 50% come back from there, then in most cases (except for the people who have money, because they get along with their money) they are living corpses. But everywhere people say and write that Soviet authority does not punish but corrects. We are such living corpses.... It is possible that you think that this is our imagination, but we swear to you all by everything that is sacred to us that this is only one small part of the nightmarish truth, because it makes no sense to make this up....

In a prison cell:
>   "How many years did you get?"
>   "Twenty-five."
>   "For what?"
>   "Nothing."
>   "Liar! You only get ten years for doing nothing."

Poetry is respected only in this country. There's no place where more people are killed for it.

—Poet Osip Mandelstam In Nadezhda Mandelstam, *Hope Against Hope* (1976)

Lubianka
Lubianka was headquarters of the secret police and had its own prison.

The secret police employed both physical and psychological methods to wear down their prisoners and extract confessions. A particularly effective way to break the resistance of prisoners so they would admit to political crimes they did not commit was to threaten violence against beloved family members. Stalin ensured the loyalty of some of his closest advisors by having their wives thrown into prison. The use of informers, including close friends and family members, was also widespread. The Gulag was filled with criminals of all sorts, from common thieves, rapists, and murderers to dekulakized peasants, Orthodox priests, intellectuals, and those condemned for counter-revolutionary activities. Such a mix of prisoners made for a volatile situation, and the non-political prisoners, along with prison guards, frequently felt justified in picking on and abusing the political prisoners. The inhabitants of the Gulag did not always accept their fate passively or with equanimity. Prisoners sometimes went on hunger strikes to protest conditions in a particular camp.

Russian writers, poets in particular, commanded the awed respect of educated Russians. They were viewed as the moral compass of society, witnesses of the truth in the face of an oppressive government. In a memoir Nadezhda Mandelstam describes her husband Osip's arrest and interrogation in 1933 for reciting a poem that describes Stalin's fingers as wormlike and his moustache like a cockroach. "M." in the excerpt refers to Osip Mandelstam, who died in the camps in 1938.

At the very first interrogation M. had admitted to being the author of the poem on Stalin, so the stool pigeon's task could not have been merely to find out something that M. was hiding. Part of the function of these people was to unnerve and wear down prisoners under interrogation, to make their lives a misery. Until 1937 our secret police made much of their psychological methods, but afterward these gave way to physical torture, with beatings of the most primitive kind. After 1937 I never again heard of anyone being held in solitary confinement cells, with or without stool pigeons. Perhaps people picked out for such treatment after 1937 did not leave the Lubianka alive. M. was put through the physical ordeal which had always been applied. It consisted mainly of not being allowed to sleep. He was called out every night and kept for hours on end. Most of the time was spent not in actual questioning, but in waiting under guard outside the interrogator's door. Once, when there was no interrogation, he was wakened all the same and taken to see a woman who kept him waiting at the door of her office for many hours, only to ask him at the end of it whether he had any complaints. Everybody knew how meaningless it was to make complaints to the prosecutor, and M. did not avail himself of this right. He had probably been called to her office simply as a formality, and also to keep him awake even on a night when the interrogator was catching up on his own sleep. These night birds lived a preposterous life, but all the same they managed to get some sleep, although not at the times when ordinary mortals did. The ordeal by deprivation of sleep and a bright light shining right in the eyes are known to everybody who had gone through such interrogations. . . .

The work of undermining a person's sanity was carried on quite systematically in the Lubianka, and since our secret police is a bureaucratic institution like any other, all procedures involved were probably governed by precise instructions. Even though the personnel were specifically selected for the job, one cannot ascribe what went on to their wicked nature, since the same people could overnight have become kindness itself—if so instructed. . . .

The interrogator's arrogance was reflected not only in his manner, but also in . . . very superior remarks that smacked of the literary drawing room. The first generation of young Chekists, later to be removed and destroyed in 1937, was distinguished by its sophisticated tastes and weakness for literature—only the most fashionable, of course. In my presence Christophorovich said to M. that it was useful for a poet to experience fear . . . because it can inspire verse, and that he would "experience fear in full measure." Both M. and I noted the use of the future tense. . . .

Apart from people who were forced into cooperating, there were hosts of volunteers. Denunciations poured into every institution on a quite unmanageable scale. . . .

Because of this system. . . , people developed two kinds of phobia—some suspected that everybody they met was an informer, others that they might be taken for one. . . .

One final question: was it my fault for not getting rid of all our friends and acquaintances, as did most good wives and mothers at that time? My guilt is lessened only by the fact that M. would in any case have given me the slip and found a way of reading his outrageous poem—and in this country all real poetry is outrageous—to the first person he met. He was not one to put a gag on himself and lead a life of voluntary seclusion.

Eugenia Ginzburg, a loyal party member accused on trumped-up charges of being a Trotskyist terrorist, survived nearly 20 years in the Gulag. She chronicled her experiences in a two-volume memoir (*Journey into the Whirlwind* and *Within the Whirlwind*). Ginzburg described conditions in the infamous Butyrka prison in Moscow where she was interrogated and

W̄e thought (perhaps we wanted to think) that Stalin knew nothing about the senseless violence committed against the communists. . . ."

—Journalist and novelist Ilya Ehrenburg remembering 1938 in his memoir

Prisoners transport lumber for use in the construction industry in the mid-1930s. The Gulag served the economic goals of the regime because it facilitated the extraction of valuable resources from underdeveloped areas of the country.

languished before sentencing. She was spared the beatings and torture depicted here, though she endured 2 years of solitary confinement.

It began all at once, not by degrees or with any sort of prelude. Not one, but a multitude of screams and groans from tortured human beings burst simultaneously through the open windows of our cell. In the Butyrka prison, an entire wing on a certain floor was set aside for night interrogations, and it was doubtless equipped with the latest refinements of the torture chamber. . . .

Over and through the screams of the tortured, we could hear the shouts and curses of the torturers. Added to the cacophony was the noise of chairs being hurled about, fists banging on tables, and some other unidentifiable sound which froze one's blood.

Although these were only sounds, they conjured up such a vivid picture that I felt I could see it in every detail. . . .

How long could it go on? Till three o'clock, they had told me. But surely no one could endure this longer than a minute. Yet the noise went on and on, dying down from time to time and then bursting out again. An hour—two, three, and four hours, from eleven til three o'clock every night. I sat up in bed: "May I never experience all that it is possible to get used to." Yes, my cellmates had got used even to this. Most of them were asleep or, at all events, were lying quietly, their heads buried under blankets in spite of the stifling heat. Only a few newcomers, like me, were sitting up in their bunks. Some had stuffed their fingers into their ears, some were as if petrified. Every now and then the supervisor would stick her head through the flap-window with the command:

"Lie down. It's against the rules to sit up after lights out."

Suddenly a long-drawn-out shriek of pain was heard, not from a distance but in our cell. A young woman with a long, disheveled braid rushed to the window and, as if demented, beat against it with her head and hands.

"It's him! I know it is, it's his voice! I don't want to go on living, I don't, I can't! Please let them kill me. . . ."

Several women jumped up and surrounded her, dragging her away from the window and trying to convince her that she was mistaken, that it was not her husband's voice. But she was not to be comforted. No, she would know his voice among a thousand—it was he they were torturing and mutilating; and was she to lie here and be silent? If she screamed and made a disturbance they might kill her right away, and that was all she wanted—how could she possibly live after this? . . .

By now it was nearly three o'clock, and the sounds were dying down. Once more I heard a chair thrown to the ground, once more a man's stifled sob. Then silence.

I could see in my mind's eye the torn, bloody victims as they staggered or were carried out of the torture chamber. . . .

Ginzburg was deported to the infamous Kolyma gold mines located in the far northwest corner of Siberia.

Unhindered by the guards, we stood by the barbed-wire fence which separated our compound from the men's, and gazed spellbound at the long line of men who passed before us—silent, with bowed heads, plodding wearily in prison boots similar to ours. Their uniforms were also similar, but their trousers with the brown stripe were even more like convicts' garb than our skirts. Although one might have thought the men were stronger than we were, they seemed somehow more defenseless and we all felt a maternal pity for them. They stood up to pain so badly—this was every woman's opinion—and they would not know how to mend anything or be able to wash their clothes on the sly as we could with our light things. . . . Above all, they were our husbands and brothers, deprived of our care in this terrible place. As someone expressed it . . . "The poor dears have no one to sew their buttons on for them."

Each face seemed to me to resemble my husband's; I was so tense my head ached. All of us were straining to try to find our loved ones. Suddenly one of the men at last noticed us and cried out:

"Look, the women! Our women!"

What happened next was indescribable. It was as if some strong electric current had flashed across the barbed wire. It was clear at that moment how alike, deep down, all human beings are. All the feelings that had been suppressed during two years of prison, all that each one of us had borne solitarily in himself or herself, gushed to the surface and mingled in a flood that seemed to be both within us and around us. The men and women were shouting and reaching out to each other. Almost all were sobbing aloud.

"You poor loves, you poor darlings! Cheer up, be brave, be strong!" Such were the words that were shouted both ways across the wire. . . .

The next stage was the throwing of "presents" across the wire. The emotional tension on both sides needed an outlet in action: we each longed to give something, but we had no proper possessions to give. So one heard:

"Take my towel! It's not too badly torn!"

"Girls! Anybody want this pot? I made it from a prison mug I stole."

"Here, take this bread. You're so thin after the journey!"

There were also violent cases of love at first sight. As if by magic, these almost disembodied human beings recovered their sensibility, which had been dulled by such cruel sufferings. Tomorrow or the day after, they would be led off in different directions and never see one another again. But today they gazed feverishly into each other's eyes through the rusty barbed wire, and talked and talked. . . .

I have never in my life seen more sublimely unselfish love than that which was shown in those fleeting romances between strangers—perhaps because, in their case, love indeed was linked with death.

Every day the men would write us long letters—jointly and individually, in verse and prose, on greasy bits of paper and even on rags. They put all their insulted, long-pent-up manhood into the pure vibrant passion of these letters. For them we were a collective image of womanhood. They were numbed by pain and anguish at the thought that we, "their" women, had undergone the same bestial indignities as had been inflicted on them.

One of these letters began: "Dear ones—our wives, sisters, friends, loved ones! Tell us how we can take your pain upon ourselves."

At the 18th Party Congress in 1939, someone sneezes during Stalin's speech.

Stalin demands, "Who sneezed?"

Silence.

"Give every tenth delegate ten years in a labor camp." The delegates are counted off, and every tenth is led away.

"Who sneezed?" Silence.

A brave delegate finally stands and admits, "I did."

Stalin answers, "God bless you."

Not all prisoners in the Gulag accepted their fate without protest. In 1936 a contingent of former supporters of Trotsky found themselves in a coal-mining center known as Vorkuta in northern Siberia. They managed to hold a secret meeting in the barracks and decided to launch a hunger strike demanding more food, shorter workdays, better care for the old, infirm, and ill, and separation of political prisoners from common criminals, who tended to prey upon the former. An account of the events written by an unknown eyewitness appeared in a Trotskyist publication in 1961.

Three weeks later, October 27, 1936, the massive hunger strike of
the political prisoners began, a strike without precedent and a model
under Soviet camp conditions. In the morning, at reveille, in almost
every barrack, prisoners announced themselves on strike. The barracks occupied by the Trotskyists participated 100 percent in the
movement. . . . Close to 1,000 prisoners, of whom half worked in
the mine, participated in this tragedy, which lasted more than four
months.

Having begun at the end of October 1936, the hunger strike
lasted 132 days, ending in March 1937. It culminated with the complete victory of the strikers who received a radiogram from the headquarters of the NKVD, drawn up in these words: "Inform the hunger strikers held in the Vorkuta mines that all their demands will be
satisfied."

The Trotskyists were then taken back to the mine, received food
reserved for the sick and, after a period of time, they went back to
work, but only above ground; certain of them worked in the office of

Prisoners dig a ditch in the Gulag during the mid-
1930s. Much of the economic growth experienced
by the Soviet Union during the first three Five-
Year Plans depended on the slave labor provided
by inmates of the Gulag.

the director of the mine, in the capacity of paid workers, bookkeepers, economists, etc. Their workday did not exceed eight hours; their food ration was not based on their production norm. . . .

[A] certain number of prisoners waited with impatience for the autumn of 1937 and the twentieth anniversary of the October Revolution; they hoped, on this occasion . . . that the government would declare a large-scale amnesty, since a little while earlier the very promising "Stalinist Constitution" had been adopted. But the autumn brought bitter disillusions.

The harsh regime of the camps grew abruptly worse. The sergeants and their assistants in maintaining order—common criminals—having received new orders from the camp director, armed themselves with clubs and pitilessly beat the prisoners. The guards, the watchmen close to the barracks, tormented the prisoners. To amuse themselves during the night they fired on those who went to the toilets. Or else, giving the order *"On your bellies,"* they forced the prisoners to stretch out, naked, for hours on the snow. Soon there were massive arrests. . . .

The whole winter of 1937–38 some prisoners . . . waited for a decision regarding their fate. Finally, in March, three NKVD officers . . . arrived by plane at Vorkuta, coming from Moscow. They came . . . to interrogate the prisoners. Thirty to forty were called each day, superficially questioned five to ten minutes each, rudely insulted, forced to listen to vile name-calling and obscenities. Some were greeted with punches in the face. . . .

At the end of March, a list of twenty-five was announced. . . . To each was delivered a kilo of bread and orders to prepare himself for a new convoy. After fond farewells to their friends, they left the barracks, and the convoy departed. Fifteen or twenty minutes later, not far away, about half a kilometer, on the steep bank of the little river . . . , an abrupt volley resounded, followed by isolated and disorderly shots; then all grew quiet again. Soon, the convoy's escort passed back near the barracks. And it was clear to all in what sort of convoy the prisoners had been sent.

Two days later, there was a new call, this time of forty names. Once more there was a ration of bread. Some, out of exhaustion, could no longer move; they were promised a ride in a cart. Holding their breath, the prisoners remaining in the barracks heard the grating of snow under the feet of the departing convoy. For a long time there was no sound; but all, on the watch, still listened. Nearly an hour passed in this way. Then, again, shots resounded in the tundra; this time, they came from much further away. . . .

The executions in the tundra lasted the whole month of April and part of May. Usually one day out of two, or one day out of three, thirty to forty prisoners were called. . . .

At the beginning of May, a group of women was shot. . . . One of these women had to walk on crutches. At the time of execution of a male prisoner, his imprisoned wife was automatically liable to capital punishment; and when it was a question of well-known members of the Opposition, this applied equally to any of his children over the age of twelve.

Three Views of the Purges

Stephen Podlubny, a medical student who had become an informer for the secret police in 1932, spent the most dangerous year of the purges—1937—fearing arrest. The authorities arrested his mother in December 1937 for concealing her background as a dekulakized peasant. Podlubny described efforts to visit his mother in prison.

December 6, 1937. No one will ever know how I made it through the year 1937. No one will know because not a single day of my life this year has been illuminated in this so-called diary. I can't even recall the details of my life in this year myself, and if everything turns out all right, and there are only 3 more weeks to go, I'll cross it out like an unnecessary page, I'll cross it out and banish it from my mind though the black spot, the massive ugly black spot like a thick blood stain on my clothes, will be with me most likely for the rest of my life.

It will remain because my life during these 341 days of 1937 has been as ugly and disgusting as the clotted blood that oozes out in a thick red mass from under the corpse of a man dead from the plague. The feeling a man has who's not used to the sight of blood, and sees a scene like that or recalls it, that [is] what I experience when I go through my memories of this past year.

A painful and disgusting year. Or rather, my life this year has been painful and disgusting. Maybe it always seems that way, that the unpleasant experience you're going through at the moment is worse than anything you've been through before, but it really does seem to me that this year was if not the very worst of all the years I've ever been through at least it was one of the most painful ones. It leaves a miserable impression. It seems to me that the noose around my neck keeps getting pulled tighter and tighter every year. It feels like it's tightening more and more rapidly, at a regularly increasing

Stalin's pipe is missing. He calls the NKVD and orders them to find it. In two hours, he finds it himself in his own boot. He calls the NKVD back: "Don't bother, I found it."

"Forgive us, Comrade Stalin, but we've already arrested ten people for stealing your pipe."

"Let them go."

"We can't, they've all confessed."

rate and that it keeps getting proportionately tighter and tighter at the same time, for example I can't remember a time this year when the noose around my throat was loosened and I was given even a day to breathe freely, filling my chest with air.

Maybe I won't be able to express the intensity of the grief that I experienced this year, but I have to say that I expect the noose to tighten even more in the near future, maybe I won't be able to express it all or I won't have the patience to write it all down, for it's all too disgusting, but if I wondered whether it was worth going on living, I'd have to say there wasn't much pleasant or sweet in my life. Right now I am calm and that's why I can just move the pen across the paper, tracing the curving letters of these not altogether pleasant words. Naming the things I've been through. . . .

Barracks at a prison camp in the Ural Mountains, 1919–1920. The high rates of illness and death among prisoners testify to the harsh living and working conditions in the Gulag.

I lost all my good friends and my friends from the institute and was left all alone. Solitude is no fun. . . .

That's all just the general scheme of things, it doesn't say anything about my feelings, but what I went through each time something happened in the overall scheme of things and my situation in general drove me to despair. . . .

12/19/1937. Exactly 10 days have passed since Mama was invited to go down "for a minute" to the 4-th Section of the MUR (Moscow Criminal Investigation Department) and that was the last I saw of her. Not only did I not see her, I didn't even manage to find out where she was.

In spite of the fact that the information office at 38 Petrovka Street opens at 10:30 when I arrived this morning at 7:00 to sign up I was already 71st in line. This is where you get information about people under arrest, who is where, that is, whether he's still at Petrovka or whether he's already been sent off to the camps. A small cramped and dirty hall smelling of fresh human sweat. . . .

Naturally the question arises as to why people are being put in prison.

There are various reasons. For robbery, drunkenness, drunken brawling, for previous convictions, for a word spoken at the wrong time and place, but many people just don't know the reason. He was arrested and there he is in prison and I don't know why. Maybe he knows, but if he doesn't well then the person in charge of his case or the one who signed his arrest order ought to. A man is not always in control of his fate.

There used to be a saying, "We are all under the will of god." Now this saying goes "We are all under the will of the NKVD." Oh, what a life! Nothing but trials and tribulations and there's no end in sight. . . .

1/11/1938. . . . I got to see her today in "Moscow Prison No. 3," as they call it officially. Tears streamed down from her aged, wrinkled eyes, she had trouble getting the words out. "The NKVD . . . has sentenced me to eight years." How horrible, 8 years. It's so easy to pronounce, but so hard to live through. And for what?! The official category is "for concealing social origins," but how can you call it concealing when all the official powers knew about her social origin all the way back in 1934. And they say that there is justice in this world. There is no justice in the world anymore, justice died together with the good people, and the devil will leave in peace the scoundrels. The law. I'm not an anarchist by nature and I respect the law, but how can such injustice be done in the name of the law. They consider her a danger to society. You'd think they'd caught a bandit, but even bandits get lighter sentences than that. Well, so what, you can't break down a stone wall with just your head. Can this be the end of justice on earth. No there will be justice. Many people have perished in the name of justice, and as long as society exists, people will be struggling for justice. Justice will come. The truth will come.

Leonid Potyomkin, an engineering student the same age as Podlubny, was someone who genuinely believed that a conspiracy existed to sabotage the Soviet Union's efforts to build socialism. He was not disaffected from life in Stalin's Russia and takes pride in the accomplishments of the Soviet Union. His diary entries from 1935 and 1936 included thoughts on a film about Sergei Kirov, the popular party leader of Leningrad who was assassinated in late 1934.

1/26/35. The film *Kirov* makes an extraordinarily valuable and strong impression. The enormous thirst of our leaders to study, live, and work is reflected in the enormous interest with which everyone in the auditorium holds their breath as they follow every action

The principles and aims of mass terror have nothing in common with ordinary police work or with security. The only purpose of terror is intimidation. To plunge the whole country into a state of chronic fear, the number of victims must be raised to astronomical levels, and on every floor of every building there must be several apartments from which the tenants have suddenly been taken away. The remaining inhabitants will be model citizens for the rest of their lives.

—Nadezhda Mandelshtam in *Hope Against Hope* (1976)

Mironych

Mironych is a term of endearment for Kirov, whose middle name was Miron.

Stalin helps to carry the urn containing the ashes of Sergei Kirov to its final resting place. Kirov was head of the party in Leningrad when a disgruntled party member shot him in December 1934. Historians dispute the reasons for the assassination; some claim that Stalin ordered the murder because he resented Kirov's popularity.

and movement of their beloved leaders. I want to study as comprehensively as possible the turbulent, multifaceted life of S. M. Kirov, who was so selflessly devoted to the cause of the world communist revolution. The documentaries did not encompass all of his colossal activity in its entirety, but in each individual incident, insignificant though it may be in size, the seething energy of Mironych blazes forth. It is a graphic, living example of the work, leadership, and managerial concern of the Bolsheviks.

And the joyful, fervent speech of Sergei Mironovich is an example of genuinely revolutionary, emotionally enrapturing speech, whose profound sincerity and precision, which enrich the meaning of the words and reveal the enormous significance of the sentences, captivate the listener. It convinces you that the oratorical art of the school of Lenin and Stalin is the most paramount, mighty, and delightful of all the arts. In this film, together with our dear, beloved government, you reexperience the enormous loss that inflames the columns of intrepid workers, millions strong, and their unquenchable hatred toward class enemies.

You leave the auditorium wrapped in an irrepressible, impetuous headlong drive to work with Kirov's managerial solicitude, initiative, and energy. . . .

August 1936. . . . Youth is happy in that it has a future. And this youth must be spent in such a way that the future should bloom forth like wonderful greenhouses in the present. How beautiful is the life I have lived up to now, but so far I have achieved very little. And I'm sorry that I have experienced so little of the happiness of youth, that at times I have not noticed it. Youth you filled me with an impulse and you, o life lived impetuously and brightly, you did not recognize any difficulties, you pushed me on up the steep peaks of life. You demanded from me everything of which a man can only dream, you gave me great resplendent plans. . . . The mighty joy of mankind in bloom. I rush forth to achieve the unachievable even more forcefully without sparing my energy to turn dream into reality. Life, you must reward me with the flowers of an unexperienced joy. Let my life ascend as a beautiful firework, be it only a momentary flash, at mankind's celebration of its triumph.

Some victims of the purges engaged in no small amount of self-deception when they argued that they had been arrested and incarcerated by mistake. Such a mentality was buttressed by the fact that Stalin did not play a public role in the purges, preferring to remain behind the scenes and to allow his henchmen to be visible. For the vast majority of Soviet citizens, Stalin was the country's infallible leader who was leading them to the bright future of socialism. Surely, they thought, Stalin would not allow innocent people to be tortured and deported. Thus, the only reasonable explanation of the purges must be that Stalin did not know.

Stalin at work at his country estate. His daughter Svetlana sits on the lap of Lavrenty Beria, who would become head of the secret police in 1938.

Eugenia Ginzburg illustrates the tenacity with which many of her fellow prisoners clung desperately to their faith in the ultimate correctness of the Party and Stalin's policies. The conversation took place on a closed freight train that was transporting Ginzburg and others to Kolyma. To conceal the fact that the train's cargo consisted of human beings, the NKVD had the phrase "Special Equipment" written on the train's side.

Even now—we asked ourselves—after all that has happened to us, would we vote for any other than the Soviet system, which seemed as much a part of us as our hearts and as natural to us as breathing? Everything I had in the world—the thousands of books I had read, memories of my youth, and the very endurance which was now keeping me from going under—all this had been given me by the Soviet system, and the revolution which had transformed my world while I was still a child. How exciting life had been and how gloriously everything had begun! What in God's name had happened to us all? . . .

This set off a terrible argument. In spite of all the evidence, at least twenty members of our company asserted with lunatic insistence that Stalin knew nothing of the illegalities that were going on.

"It's those hellhounds of the secret police," said Nadya Korolyova, "and Ezhov, whom he trusted so much. But now Beria will put things right, you'll see. He'll prove to Stalin that we're all innocent, and we'll soon be let out, you mark my words. We must all of us write to Stalin so that he knows the truth, and when he does, how can he let such things happen to the people? . . ."

The Trial of Bukharin

At Bukharin's trial in 1938, Andrei Vyshinsky, the chief prosecutor, summarized the case against Bukharin. As in the 1936 trial of Zinoviev and Kamenev, Vyshinsky highlighted the connection between both the Right and Left Oppositions with Trotsky.

The state relied on public confessions to convince both Soviet citizens and foreigners that the defendants were guilty of treason. The American ambassador to the Soviet Union, Joseph Davies, commented to foreign journalists covering the 1937 trial of military leaders, "They're guilty. I've been a district attorney, and I can tell."

The Trotskyites and Bukharinites, that is to say, the "bloc of Rights and Trotskyites," the leading lights of which are now in the prisoners' dock, is not a political party, a political tendency, but a band of felonious criminals, and not simply felonious criminals, but of criminals who have sold themselves to enemy intelligence services, criminals whom even ordinary felons treat as the basest, the lowest, the most contemptible, the most depraved of the depraved.

The so-called "bloc of Rights and Trotskyites" is an organization engaged in espionage, acts of diversion and wrecking, political murder and in selling their country to the enemy. . . .

The "bloc of Rights and Trotskyites" now in the dock—as the trial has shown with the utmost clarity—is only an advance attachment of international fascism, is a pack of hangmen and surreptitious murderers, with whose aid fascism is operating in various countries, . . .

Bukharin and the other conspirators, as can be seen from the materials of the investigation, aimed at frustrating the Brest-Litovsk Peace, overthrowing the Soviet government, arresting and killing Lenin, Stalin . . . and forming a new government made up of Bukharinites, . . .

All the accused stand convicted of having, according to the indictment, in 1932–33 organized, on the instruction of intelligence services of foreign states, a conspiratorial group called the "bloc of Rights and Trotskyites," which set itself the aim of committing the crimes which have been fully proved here.

It has been proved that this bloc consisted of agents of the intelligence services of several foreign states, it has been proved that the "bloc of Rights and Trotskyites" maintained regular illegitimate relations with certain foreign states with the object of obtaining their help for putting into effect its criminal designs, for the overthrow of the Soviet government and for establishing the power of the landlords and capitalists in the U.S.S.R.

It has been proved that the "bloc of Rights and Trotskyites" regularly engaged in espionage on behalf of these states and supplied their intelligence services with most important state secret material.

It has been proved that in pursuance of the same aims the "bloc of Rights and Trotskyites" systematically perpetrated wrecking and diversionist acts in various branches of our national economy—in the sphere of industry, agriculture, finance, municipal economy, railways, etc.

It has been proved that the "bloc of Rights and Trotskyites" organized a number of terrorist acts against leaders of the Communist Party of the Soviet Union . . . and of the Soviet government, ...

It has been proved that the bloc had organized, but fortunately for us had not succeeded in effecting, a number of terrorist acts against the leaders of our Party and government.

Such are the circumstances of the present case. Such is the part taken in this case by each of the accused who are now awaiting your verdict, Comrades Judges.

There exist no words with which one could depict the monstrousness of the crimes committed by the accused. But, I ask, do we need any more words for that? No. Comrades Judges, these words are not needed. All the words have already been spoken. Everything has been analyzed to the minutest details. The entire people now see what these monsters are.

Our people and all honest people throughout the world are waiting for your just verdict. May this verdict of yours resound through the whole of our great country like a bell calling to new feats of heroism and to new victories! May your verdict resound as the refreshing and purifying thunderstorm of just Soviet punishment!

Our whole country, from young to old, is awaiting and demanding one thing: the traitors and spies who were selling our country to the enemy must be shot like dirty dogs!

Our people are demanding one thing: crush the accursed reptile!

Time will pass. The graves of the hateful traitors will grow over with weeds and thistle, they will be covered with eternal contempt of honest Soviet citizens, of the entire Soviet people. But over us, over our happy country, our sun will shine with its luminous rays as

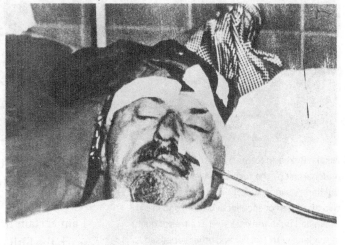

Trotsky lies on the verge of death in 1940. Trotsky, who was living in exile in Mexico City, survived several assassination attempts before a Soviet agent succeeded in plunging an ice pick into his forehead.

bright and as joyous as before. Over the road cleared of the last scum and filth of the past, we, our people, with our beloved leader and teacher, the great Stalin, at our head, will march as before onwards and onwards, towards communism!

Nikolai Bukharin (center) and two other prisoners under arrest by the secret police in 1937. Despite Bukharin's support of Stalin in the 1920s, the two disagreed over collectivization, and in 1938 Stalin had Bukharin executed as a traitor guilty of working with Trotsky and other supposed enemies of the Soviet Union.

Shortly before his execution, Bukharin dictated his final testament to his wife, Anna Larina, who committed it to memory and made it public many years later.

I am leaving life. I bow my head, but not before the proletarian scythe, which is properly merciless but also chaste. I am helpless, instead, before an infernal machine that seems to use medieval methods, yet possesses gigantic power, fabricates organized slander, acts boldly and confidently. . . . Since the age of eighteen, I have been in the Party, and always the goal of my life has been the struggle for the interests of the working class, for the victory of socialism. These days the newspaper with the hallowed name *Pravda* [Truth] prints the most contemptible lie that I, Nikolai Bukharin, wanted to destroy the achievement of October and restore capitalism. This is an unheard-of obscenity. . . . In what may be the final days of my life, I am certain that sooner or later the filter of history will inevitably wash the filth from my head. I was never a traitor: I would have unhesitatingly traded my own life for Lenin's. I loved Kirov and never undertook anything against Stalin. . . . Know, comrades, that the banner you bear in a triumphant march toward communism contains a drop of my blood, too!

Literature and the Purges

The government relied on the efforts of poets, novelists, and playwrights to defend the purges in a concerted public campaign. One such writer was Demian Bedny (pseudonym for Efim Pridvorov), a poet whose simple verse "We Dealt the Enemy a Cruel Counterblow" bitterly attacked enemies of the revolution in 1937.

Monstrous! I can hardly put in words
That thing my head can find no place for,

For which no name would do, such an awful evil
That it's hard to find a word to fit its horror.
How despicable is the hissing voice of spies!
How disgraceful the sight of enemies among us!
  Shame to the mothers that gave birth
    To these dogs of unprecedented foulness!
    These vicious dogs, whose fury is before us,
    Whose abominable names
Will join the ranks—for ever and all time—
  With the vilest names on earth.
What dogs! Mad dogs leave home
    And flee the pen
    Where they were born—But these! . . .
The poison oozes from their fascist gut.
When they stuck their snouts in the fascist trough,
They meant to bring misfortune to their homeland!
    A nest of spies has been uncovered!
    The spies remanded to the court!
All those Feldmans, Yakirs, Primakovs,
Putnas and Tukhachevskys—common rabble!
They tried to put the fascist fetters
On our Union, the country of their birth.
The vile spies were working with a plan:
The spies were salesmen, their homeland was their ware.
Unmasking them was fortunate for us:
What a joy to realize that we dealt
  The enemy camp a cruel counterblow!
Nary an ash will remain of these loathsome vermin!
Let the vicious fascist choir sing their requiem.
The Soviet land has grown, gained strength, and flourished
  In defiance of its evil foes.
Despite its foes, it will get even stronger,
Equally great in battle and at work.
Didn't we study in the school of Lenin?
Heading with Stalin toward our radiant destiny,
Standing together in our unconquerable will,
  Haven't we forged our power?!
Yes! Along the road our Revolution chose,
We will arrive at worldwide victory.
  And none of these damned traitors will bar the way!!

Feldman
Feldman, Yakir, and so on were military commanders put on trial in 1937.

The secret police reported that many workers and peasants, who tended to blame Party and government officials for their problems, welcomed the purges as just retribution. One peasant woman told others on her collective farm: "What kind of life is this, that we all sit around hungry? For four years they've been taking everything and don't even leave you a strand of flax, even if it means you have to go around naked. You can't buy anything; maybe now that Kirov has been killed, just as earlier they killed the tsars, perhaps life will become a little easier."

Similarly, a male worker noted, "They've killed one dog, this Kirov; maybe they will give an extra card to the worker. But probably all of the ration cards have gone to these dogs [the leaders]; I wouldn't be sorry if they'd string them all up."

The secret police evidently had quotas to meet that were established in conjunction with Moscow officials. In 1937 an NKVD directive ordered its agents to arrest 222,650 "former kulaks, criminals, and other anti-Soviet elements," with some 72,000 of them designated for summary execution. The directive left it up to local authorities to ascertain whom to arrest and kill.

The Great Terror has generated a rich body of memoirs, novels, and short stories that seeks to describe and explain the purges. We have an abundance of first-hand accounts by people who found themselves caught up in the whirlwind of the purges. The poem "Requiem" by Anna Akhmatova, one of the great poets of the 20th century in any language, remained unpublished in the Soviet Union until the 1980s. Akhmatova's son had been arrested during the height of the purges, and the poet found herself standing day after day in endless lines at prisons in the hope she could find out information about her son. In her introduction to the poem, Akhmatova wrote: "One day somebody 'identified' me. Beside me, in the queue, there was a woman with blue lips. She had, of course, never heard of me; but she suddenly came out of that trance so common to us all and whispered in my ear (everybody spoke in whispers there): 'Can you describe this?' And I said: 'Yes, I can.' And then something like the shadow of a smile crossed what had once been her face."

Requiem

Prologue
In those years only the dead smiled,
Glad to be at rest:
And Leningrad city swayed like
A needless appendix to its prisons.
It was then that the railway-years
Were asylums of the mad;
Short were the locomotives'
Farewell songs.
Stars of death stood
Above us, and innocent Russia
Writhed under bloodstained boots, and
Under the tyres of Black Marias.

1
They took you away at daybreak. Half
waking as though at a wake, I followed.
In the dark chamber children were crying,
In the image-case, candlelight guttered.
At your lips, the chill of an ikon,
A deathly sweat at your brow.
I shall go creep to our wailing wall,
Crawl to the Kremlin towers. . . .

5

For seventeen months I've called you
To come home, I've pleaded
—O my son, my terror!—grovelled
At the hangman's feet.
All is confused eternally—
So much, I can't say who's
Man, who's beast any more, nor even,
How long till execution.
Simply the flowers of dust,
Censers ringing, tracks from a far
Settlement to nowhere's ice.
And everywhere the glad
Eye of a huge star's
Still tightening vice. . . .
And if ever in this country they should want
To build me a monument

I consent to that honour,
But only on condition that they

Erect it not on the sea-shore where I was born:
My last links there were broken long ago,

Nor by the stump in the Royal Gardens,
Where an inconsolable young shade is seeking me,

But here, where I stood for three hundred hours
And where they never, never opened the doors for me.

Lest in blessed death I should forget
The grinding scream of the Black Marias,

The hideous clanging gate, the old
Woman wailing like a wounded beast.

And may the melting snow drop like tears
From my motionless bronze eyelids,

And the prison pigeons coo above me
And the ships sail slowly down the Neva.

As a teenager, Mary Leder moved with her parents from southern California to the Soviet Union in 1931. She spent the next thirty-four years living, studying, and working in Moscow.

The extent of the sweep and suffering was not apparent to me, for arrests were made public only selectively. Solid information was scarce. . . . When the arrests occurred, I was more interested than horrified, and accepted the assertions that revolutions were not made in a day and that the events represented the continuation of the class struggle. To have been able to read between the lines so as to analyze the available information without access to any other points of view, either in the press or privately, would have required more political acumen and common sense experience than I had at the time.

—Mary Leder in *My Life in Stalinist Russia* (2000)

Black Marias
"Black Marias" refer to the cars that the secret police used when they arrested people, usually in the middle of the night.

Epilogue

The turmoil of the 1930s began to subside by 1939. The 1936 constitution proclaimed the achievement of socialism, thereby implying that the revolutionary era was drawing to a close. The Stalinist system that had upended society stabilized, shaping the Soviet economic, social, political, and cultural landscape for another 50 years. The worst excesses of the purges were over and the economy of Five-Year Plans began to provide more of the basic necessities of life. Shortages of food and consumer goods persisted because of the shortcomings of the planned economy. People grumbled about food shortages, inadequate housing, and onerous labor legislation that criminalized absenteeism and lateness. Millions also mourned their loved ones, missing or dead as a result of collectivization and the purges. In addition, they resented the privileges and material comforts enjoyed by many party members and government officials. However, many of these same embittered people still retained faith in the promises of 1917, even if they felt that the promises had been squandered and even if they wondered about the price of building socialism as dictated by Stalin.

The dream of building a socialist utopia in Russia failed and a "workers' paradise" never materialized. The Party's emphasis on the centralization of power and its zeal to employ the secret police and political repression spelled a quick end to the democratic tendencies of 1917. Civil war underscored just how fragile the fledgling regime's grip on power was and led to increased bureaucratization

Soldiers and mourners pay their respects to Stalin on the day of his funeral in March 1953. The Politburo placed Stalin's body next to that of Lenin in the mausoleum on Red Square.

as the party-state came to rely on itself to maintain political control. The result was an authoritarian behemoth that ruled over society and did not tolerate dissent. Moreover, the communists' fervent belief that they alone possessed a true understanding of how to guide Russia into the radiant future of socialism reinforced their sense that a non-communist path of development had to be ruthlessly suppressed. The challenge of building an industrialized society out of an overwhelmingly agrarian one prompted the communist state to employ violence and coercion to modernize the Soviet Union, even when these policies went against the wishes and interests of the majority of its inhabitants. Finally, the personality of Stalin cannot be ignored; his insatiable desire for personal power combined with the regime's ruthlessness to create conditions ripe for the kinds of policies and abuses that characterized the 1930s.

Economic stagnation, the political bankruptcy of communist ideology, and rising nationalism among some of the national minorities making up the Soviet Union eventually caused the dissolution of the Kremlin's power. Yet the fact that the communists held the reins of power for nearly 75 years is remarkable. No regime can hold onto power that long simply through the secret police and political repression. Soviet communism, notwithstanding its undeniable viciousness, shortcomings, and failings, provided the basis for the Soviet Union's victory in World War II and its emergence as one of the world's two atomic and industrial superpowers after 1945.

The fundamental features of the Soviet Union's political, economic, cultural, and social life that had emerged between 1917 and 1939 would characterize life under communism until 1991. Soviet citizens took tremendous pride in the fact that Stalin's policies put the Soviet Union on the path towards a modern industrialized society. It offered, over time, an improved standard of living, rising educational levels, and some of the benefits of 20th-century technology. For several generations of Soviet citizens, communist rule was not an unmitigated disaster because Soviet power tended to translate into a better life for themselves and their children and grandchildren. The Soviet state provided free medical care and education for all citizens, it subsidized housing, food, and transportation, and it guaranteed work for all adults. For those who could remember life in the two decades after the revolution, such developments could be viewed as the partial fulfillment of the promises of 1917 to create a more just and equitable society. Tragically, however, the free society imagined by many Russians was never to be. And the Soviet state crushed anyone who dared remind the communist leaders of their broken promises.

Assessments of Stalinism

Many Soviet and non-Soviet observers believed that the policies of Stalin in the 1930s enabled the Soviet Union to play a decisive role in defeating Germany after its invasion on June 22, 1941, which triggered the Soviet Union's involvement in World War II. While the costs of economic development in terms of wasted resources, human and non-human, were tremendous, some observers have argued that the price was worth paying. After all, the rapid industrial growth of the 1930s provided the infrastructure needed to produce the weapons that ultimately pushed back the German army to Berlin. At the end of his account of life in Magnitogorsk, written during World War II when he again living in the United States, John Scott offered his assessment of the Soviet path of industrialization. Acknowledging the costs of stressing industrial output and harboring no illusions about the vicious nature of Stalin's rule, Scott still harbored belief in the ideals of socialism and concluded that the policies pursued by the regime in the 1930s would provide the means to defeat Germany.

When I left Magnitogorsk I was profoundly shocked by the fact that so many people I had known had been arrested. The whole thing seemed stupid, unreasonable, preposterous. The Stalinist constitution of 1936 had promised a democratic and free society. Instead the NKVD seemed to have run away with the show, the purge appeared to be consuming everything that had been created. . . .

The millions of expropriated kulaks, the political exiles in Siberia were a lost tribe. They had been sacrificed on the altar of Revolution and Progress. They would die off in twenty or thirty years, and by that time, perhaps, Soviet society would be able to function without scrapping blocks of its population every decade. It was a cruel concept, but there it was, one item in a long list of expenditures for Magnitogorsk, . . . for survival.

One conclusion reached before I left Magnitogorsk I still believe to be sound. Westerners have no place in Russia. It is the Russians' country, and it is their Revolution. Men and women from Western Europe may occasionally succeed in understanding it, but it is almost impossible for them to fit into it.

I survived black bread, rotten salt fish, the cold, and hard work, which was unusual. I did not survive the purge. I think I understood it, its causes, its inevitability in . . . Russia, but I could not live with it. I probably could not have stuck it out, even had it tolerated me. . . .

I left Magnitogorsk with the conviction that I had been a very minor actor in a world premiere. I had participated in an enterprise carried out for the first time, and from which the rest of the world would learn much, both positively and negatively. Not only had I helped to build an industrial base which would prove of vital importance in the forthcoming war against Germany, I had participated in the collective effort of one hundred and seventy-odd million people building a society along collective lines, coordinated and synchronized by a general plan.

It was an historic landmark. . . .

Scott wanted his comments in *Behind the Urals* to lend credence to Stalin's comment made in 1931 that Russia had to industrialize or risk annihilation by enemies.

Even if Moscow is lost, the Red armies will be able to go on fighting for months, even years, basing themselves on the stronghold of the Urals supplemented by factories and skilled workers evacuated from the western parts of the Soviet Union. All this sums up one basic reason why the Soviet Union has not suffered decisively as a result of Hitler's attack. . . .

Here, then, lies the answer to the question so many people in America have been asking themselves since June 22, 1941: "How are the Russians able to do so well? What makes Russia click?"

Russia has always had masses of men and incalculable natural resources. During the last ten years the Russian people shed blood, sweat, and tears to create something else, a modern industrial base outside the reach of an invader—Stalin's Ural Stronghold—and a modern mechanized army. In the process million of Russians and Ukrainians, Tartars and Jews, became competent technicians and efficient soldiers.

At the same time the population was taught by a painful and expensive process to work efficiently, to obey orders, to mind their own business, and to take it on the chin when necessary with a minimum of complaint.

These are the things that it takes to fight a modern war.

The death of Stalin in 1953 did not alter the basic contours of the system that matured under his direction and impetus. Stalin's successors saw no need to reform this system of Five-Year Plans and collectivized agriculture, but they did desire to dissociate themselves from the bloodshed of the Stalin era. In 1956 Nikita Khrushchev, who was making a bid to solidify his power as General Secretary of the Communist

Nikita Khrushchev addresses the Twentieth Party Congress in 1956. He forcefully denounced the crimes of Stalin, saying that Stalin "did not tolerate collegiality in leadership and work, . . . and practiced brutal violence, not only toward everything that opposed him, but also toward that which seemed to his capricious and despotic character, contrary to his concepts."

Party, delivered a speech to the delegates at the Twentieth Party Congress. The speech ushered in a period of de-Stalinization by attributing the purges to Stalin's "cult of personality," or Stalin's need for personal glorification.

At the present we are concerned with a question which has immense importance for the party now and for the future—we are concerned with how the cult of the person of Stalin has been gradually growing, the cult which became at a certain specific stage the source of a whole series of exceedingly serious and grave perversions of party principles, of party democracy, of revolutionary legality. . . .

We have to consider seriously and analyze correctly this matter in order that we may preclude any possibility of a repetition in any form whatever of what took place during the life of Stalin, who absolutely did not tolerate collegiality in leadership and in work, and who practiced brutal violence, not only toward everything which opposed him, but also toward that which seemed to his capricious and despotic character, contrary to his concepts.

Stalin acted not through persuasion, explanation, and patient cooperation with people, but by imposing his concepts and demanding absolute submission to his opinion. Whoever opposed this concept or tried to prove his viewpoint, and the correctness of his position, was doomed to removal from the leading collective and to subsequent moral and physical annihilation. . . .

Stalin originated the concept "enemy of the people." This term automatically rendered it unnecessary that the ideological errors of a man or men engaged in a controversy be proven; this term made possible the usage of the most cruel repression, . . . against anyone who in any way disagreed with Stalin, against those who were only suspected of hostile intent, against those who had bad reputations. . . . In the main, and in actuality, the only proof of guilt used, against all norms of current legal science, was the "confession" of the accused himself; and, as subsequent probing proved, "confessions" were acquired through physical pressures against the accused. . . .

. . . The formula, "enemy of the people," was specifically introduced for the purpose of physically annihilating such individuals. . . .

You see to what Stalin's mania for greatness led. He had completely lost consciousness of reality; he demonstrated his suspicion and haughtiness not only in relation to individuals in the USSR, . . .

Comrades: We must abolish the cult of the individual decisively, once and for all; . . .

Despite this attack on Stalin, Khrushchev and others did not try to remove Stalin's corpse from the mausoleum, which he shared with Lenin. It was not until 1961 that Khrushchev had accumulated sufficient power to unceremoniously remove Stalin's body from the mausoleum without fear of provoking a backlash among those in the party who still worshipped Stalin. At the Twenty-Second Party Congress, held in October 1961, Khrushchev extended his accusations of criminal behavior beyond Stalin to include other prominent party officials, both living and dead. He also hinted at the impact the purges had on society as a whole. Khrushchev depended on other party members to support his policy of de-Stalinization. Dora Lazurkina, a party member since 1902, spoke to the assembled delegates at the Congress in order to prepare them for the removal of Stalin's body. Her use of Lenin's middle name, Ilyich, indicates that she and Lenin were on close, personal terms. Stalin was eventually buried with other prominent communists along the wall of the Kremlin behind the mausoleum.

Comrades, when we get to our localities we will have to tell the truth honestly, as Lenin taught us to, tell the truth to the workers and the people, about what happened at the Congress and what was talked about. And it would be incomprehensible, after what has been said and revealed at the Congress, if Stalin were left side by side with Ilyich. I always carry Ilyich in my heart, always, comrades, and at the most difficult moments the only thing that carried me through was

that I had Ilyich in my heart, and could consult with him as to what I must do. . . . I consulted with Ilyich yesterday, it was as if he were alive and standing in front of me, and he said, "It is unpleasant for me to be side by side with Stalin, who brought so many troubles upon the party."

The poet Yevgenii Yevtushenko described the removal of Stalin from the mausoleum in the 1962 poem "The Heirs of Stalin." Yevtushenko expressed a sentiment that many others in Soviet society held, namely that Stalin's death did not mean the death of Stalinist methods. The emergence of another Stalin was not a far-fetched idea given the large numbers of individuals who continued to support the dead leader. After 1961 Stalin dropped out of sight as mention of his name in the media became taboo. By the end of the decade, however, discussion of Stalin's crimes in the halls of power had stopped because the Kremlin leadership feared that further denunciations of Stalin could undermine the legitimacy of the communist system.

The Heirs of Stalin

Mute was the marble,
    Mutely glimmered the glass.
Mute stood the sentries,
        bronzed by the breeze.
Thin wisps of smoke curled over the coffin.
        And breath seeped through the chinks
as they bore him out the mausoleum doors.
Slowly the coffin floated,
        grazing the fixed bayonets.
He also was mute—
        he also!—
            mute and dead.
Grimly clenching
        his embalmed fists,
just pretending to be dead,
            he watched from inside.
He wished to fix each pallbearer
            In his memory:
young recruits
        from Ryazan and Kursk,
so that later he might
            collect enough strength for a sortie,
rise from the grave,
            and reach these unreflecting youths.
He was scheming.
        Had merely dozed off.
And I, appealing to our government,
                petition them
to double,
    and treble,
            the sentries guarding this slab,
and stop Stalin from ever rising again
                and, with Stalin,
                    the past.
I refer not to the past,
        so holy and glorious,
of Turksib,
    and Magnitka,

and the flag raised over Berlin.
By the past, in this case,
            I mean the neglect
of the people's good,
            false charges,
                        the jailing of innocent men.
We sowed our crops honestly,
Honestly we smelted metal,
and honestly we marched,
            joining the ranks.
But he feared us.
            Believing in the great goal,
he judged
      all means justified
                  to that great end.
He was far-sighted.
            Adept in the art of political warfare,
he left many heirs
            behind on this globe.
I fancy
   there's a telephone in that coffin:
Stalin instructs
      Enver Hozha.
From that coffin where else does the cable go!
No, Stalin has not given up.
                  He thinks he can
                              cheat death.

We carried
      him
            from the mausoleum.
But how to remove Stalin's heirs
                  from Stalin!
Some of his heirs tend roses in retirement,
thinking in secret
            their enforced leisure will not last.
Others,
      From platforms, even heap abuse on Stalin
but,
   at night,
         yearn for the good old days.

No wonder Stalin's heirs seem to suffer
these days from heart trouble.
                    They, the former henchmen,
hate this era
        of emptied prison camps
and auditoriums full of people listening
                            to poets.
The Party
        discourages me
                from being smug.
"Why care?"
        some say, but I can't remain
                        inactive.
While Stalin's heirs walk this earth,
Stalin,
    I fancy, still lurks in the mausoleum.

Reflection on the Soviet Experience

In the mid-1980s Mikhail Gorbachev assumed the post of First Secretary of the Communist Party and initiated a drive to reform the economic and political systems through the twin policies of *glasnost'* (openness) and *perestroika* (restructuring). When Gorbachev addressed the country on the 70th anniversary of the 1917 Revolution, he tempered his criticism of Stalin with an acknowledgment of how Stalin's policies led to the social and economic development of the country.

How complex and contradictory our affairs and fates have sometimes been. There has been everything—the heroic, great victories and bitter failures. We reflect on 70 years of intense creative activity from the position of a people ready to mobilize all its strength and the entire enormous potential of socialism for the revolutionary transformation of life. . . .

About the 1920s and 1930s after Lenin. Despite the fact that the Party and society had armed themselves with the Leninist concept of building socialism with Vladimir Ilyich's works of the post-October period, the search for a path proceeded in a very complex way, in a sharp ideological struggle and in an atmosphere of political debates. At the center of these debates were fundamental problems of the development of society, first of all the

question of the possibility of the construction of socialism in one country. . . .

In short, sorting things out and finding the only correct course in such a complex and stormy atmosphere was of the utmost difficulty. The nature of the ideological struggle was also complicated to a significant degree by personal rivalries in the Party leadership. . . .

This applies above all to L. D. Trotsky, who after Lenin's death displayed inordinate claims to leadership in the Party, fully confirming Lenin's assessment of him as an excessively self-assured and always equivocating and dishonest politician. Trotsky and the Trotskyists denied the possibility of building socialism in conditions of capitalist encirclement. In foreign policy, they put their stakes on exporting the Revolution, and in domestic policy on "tightening the screws" on the peasantry, on the exploitation of

A red kerchief bearing the image of Lenin at age 4 was worn by schoolchildren and Pioneers. Children were also required to wear on their school uniforms red star-shaped pins with the same image. Soviet youths were encouraged to be as perfect as Lenin supposedly had been as a young boy.

the countryside by the city. . . . Trotskyism was a political trend whose ideologists, using leftist, pseudorevolutionary phrases as a cover, in effect took a defeatist position. . . . In practical terms, what was involved was the fate of socialism in our country, the fate of the Revolution.

In these conditions, it was necessary to publicly debunk Trotskyism and to lay bare its antisocialist essence. . . .

The Party proposed a hitherto unknown path of industrialization—without relying on external sources of financing and without waiting for many years of accumulations . . . to move heavy industry forward at once. This was the only possible path in those conditions, even though it was inconceivably difficult for the country and the people. It was an innovative step, one in which the masses' revolutionary enthusiasm was considered to be a component of economic growth. Industrialization raised the country to a qualitatively new level in a single spurt. . . .

At the same time, the period we are talking about also brought losses. They had a certain connection with the very successes about which I have spoken. People at that time came to believe in the universal effectiveness of rigid centralization, in the proposition that command methods were the shortest and best way to accomplish any task. This had an effect on the attitude toward people and toward their living conditions. . . .

Today it is clear that, in an enormous undertaking that affected the fate of most of the country's population, there was a deviation from Leninist policy with respect to the peasantry. . . . The conviction had arisen that all problems could be solved in a single stroke, in an extremely brief time. Whole provinces and regions of the country began competing to see who could achieve full collectivization the fastest. Arbitrary percentage schedules were issued from above. Flagrant violations of the principles of collectivization occurred everywhere. Nor were excesses avoided in conducting the struggle against the kulaks. The line aimed at combating the kulaks, correct in itself, was often interpreted so broadly that it encompassed a large part of the middle peasantry as well. . . .

There is a great deal of debate now about Stalin's role in our history. His was an extremely contradictory personality. Keeping to positions of historical truth, we must see both Stalin's indisputable contribution to the struggle for socialism and the defense of its gains and the flagrant political mistakes and arbitrary actions committed by him and his entourage, for which our people paid a great price and which had grave consequences for the life of our society. It is sometimes claimed that Stalin did not know about instances of lawlessness. The documents that we have at our disposal indicate this is not so. The guilt of Stalin and his immediate entourage before the Party and the people for the mass repressions and lawlessness they committed is enormous and unforgivable. This is a lesson for all generations. . . .

An honest understanding both of our enormous achievements and of past misfortunes, a complete and accurate assessment of them, will provide real moral guidelines for the future.

Timeline

August 1914
Russia enters World War I on the side of the Allies

December 1916
Assassination of Rasputin

February 1917
Abdication of Tsar Nicholas II; formation of Provisional Government and Petrograd Soviet of Workers' and Soldiers' Deputies; establishment of "dual power"

April 1917
Lenin returns to Russia from exile in Switzerland; Lenin's "April Theses" call for "All Power to the Soviets"; Public release of Milyukov memo to the Allies; the Bolshevik party adopts a more radical stance

May 1917
Socialists enter cabinet of Provisional Government

July 1917
"July Days" mass demonstrations by workers in Petrograd; Alexander Kerensky appointed prime minister

August 1917
General Lavr Kornilov, commander of the Russian army, attempts military coup

September 1917
Bolsheviks gain majority in Petrograd and Moscow soviets

October 1917
Bolsheviks overthrow the Provisional Government in the name of Soviet power and issue decrees on land, workers' control, and peace

November 1917
Elections to Constituent Assembly

December 1917
Cheka established; Ukraine declares independence from Russia

January 1918
Bolsheviks disperse Constituent Assembly; Gregorian calendar adopted

February 1918
Capital moved from Petrograd to Moscow

March 1918
Treaty of Brest-Litovsk signed with Germany; Bolsheviks adopt name "Communist Party"

June 1918
Outbreak of civil war; beginning of War Communism

July 1918
Tsar and his family executed in Ekaterinburg

August 1918
Assassination attempt on Lenin; Bolsheviks begin to requisition food from peasants to feed soldiers and workers

November 1918
Armistice ends World War I

Summer 1920
Peasant revolts break out

November 1920
Defeat of White armies

February–March 1921
Red Army brutally represses sailors' revolt at Kronstadt

March 1921
Ban on factionalism at the Tenth Party Congress; Lenin introduces New Economic Policy

1921–1922
Famine in Volga region results in deaths of millions; Herbert Hoover leads relief efforts

April 1922
Stalin appointed General Secretary of Communist Party

December 1922
The Bolsheviks establish the Union of Soviet Socialist Republics

December 1922– January 1923
Lenin dictates his "testament" advising the party leadership to dismiss Stalin as General Secretary

January 1924
Death of Lenin sparks succession struggle; Petrograd renamed Leningrad in his honor; Stalin expounds on idea of "Socialism in One Country"; Bukharin tells peasants to "enrich themselves"

December 1927
Stalin and Bukharin defeat "Left Opposition" comprising Trotsky, Zinoviev, and Kamenev; Trotsky expelled from Communist Party

Late 1928
First Five-Year Plan launched to promote industrialization; beginning of cultural revolution; Bukharin and Stalin debate about collectivization and the future of New Economic Policy; Stalin defeats the "Right Opposition" and starts "revolution from above"

January 1929
Trotsky expelled from Soviet Union

November–December 1929
Beginning of mass collectivization and dekulakization; Stalin calls for the liquidation of the *kulaks* as a class"; Stalin turns 50 and the cult of Stalin begins

December 1932
Kremlin declares the First Five-Year Plan a success after four years; internal passports instituted to hinder the exodus of peasants seeking to escape collectivization and maintain law and order in cities

1932–1933
Several million peasants die in a famine caused by collectivization

August 1934
Socialist Realism adopted as cultural policy

December 1934
Sergei Kirov assassinated in Leningrad

August 1935
Beginning of Stakhnovism, a movement that encouraged workers to increase labor productivity through hard work, teamwork, and initiative

December 1936
Stalin Constitution enfranchises all Soviet citizens and enshrines the principles of Soviet socialism as a beacon of freedom

1936–1938
The Party under Stalin's direction purges the Party, government, and military of suspected "enemies of the people"; public show trials of leading Bolsheviks take place and result in executions; people from all walks of life face arrest by secret police

December 1938
Great Terror winds down

August 1939
Non-aggression pact signed between Germany and Soviet Union

June 1940
Soviet Union annexes part of Poland and Estonia, Latvia, and Lithuania

June 1941
Germany invades Soviet Union

March 1953
Stalin dies

February 1956
Nikita Khrushchev gives speech at the Twentieth Party Congress in which he blames Stalin and his "cult of personality" for the purges

Further Reading

General Sources

Carr, E. H. *The Bolshevik Revolution, 1917–1923*. 3 volumes. London: Macmillan, 1950–1953.

———. *The Russian Revolution: From Lenin to Stalin*. New York: Palgrave Macmillan, 2004.

Cohen, Stephen. *Rethinking the Soviet Experience: Politics and History Since 1917*. New York: Oxford University Press, 1985.

Deutcher, Isaac. *The Unfinished Revolution*. New York: Oxford University Press, 1967.

Figes, Orlando. *People's Tragedy: A History of the Russian Revolution*. New York: Viking, 1996.

Fitzpatrick, Sheila. *The Russian Revolution, 1917–1932*. New York: Oxford University Press, 1987.

Freeze, Gregory, ed. *Russia: A History*. 2nd edition. New York: Oxford University Press, 2002.

Hosking, Geoffrey. *The First Socialist Society: A History of the Soviet Union from Within*. Cambridge, Mass.: Harvard University Press, 1990.

Lewin, Moshe. *The Making of the Soviet System: Essays in the Social History of Interwar Russia*. New York: Pantheon, 1985.

Lincoln, W. Bruce. *Passage Through Armageddon: The Russians in War and Revolution, 1914–1918*. New York: Simon and Schuster, 1986.

———. *Red Victory: A History of the Russian Civil War*. New York: Simon and Schuster, 1989.

Malia, Martin. *The Soviet Tragedy: A History of Socialism in Russia, 1917–1991*. New York: Free Press, 1994.

Service, Robert. *A History of Twentieth-Century Russia*. Cambridge, Mass.: Harvard University Press, 1997.

Suny, Ronald. *The Soviet Experiment: Russia, the USSR, and the Successor States*. New York: Oxford University Press, 1998.

Thompson, John. *A Vision Unfulfilled: Russia and the Soviet Union in the Twentieth Century*. Lexington, Mass.: D. C. Heath, 1996.

Von Laue, Theodore. *Why Lenin? Why Stalin?* 2nd edition. New York: Lippincott, 1971.

Russia in War and Revolution, 1917–1921

Avrich, Paul. *Kronstadt 1921*. Princeton, NJ: Princeton University Press, 1991.

Brovkin, Vladimir, ed. and trans. *Dear Comrades: Menshevik Reports on the Bolshevik Revolution and the Civil War*. Stanford, Calif.: Hoover Institution Press, 1991.

———. *The Mensheviks after October: Socialist Opposition and the Rise of the Bolshevik Dictatorship*. Ithaca, N.Y.: Cornell University Press, 1986.

Burbank, Jane. *Intelligentsia and Revolution: Russian Views of Socialism, 1917–1922*. New York: Oxford University Press, 1986.

Chamberlin, William. *The Russian Revolution, 1917–1921*. Originally published in 1935. Reprint, Princeton, N.J.: Princeton University Press, 1987.

Ferro, Marc. *October 1917: A Social History of the Russian Revolution*. London: Routledge and Kegan Paul, 1980.

———. *The Russian Revolution of February 1917*. Englewood Cliffs, NJ: Prentice-Hall, 1972.

Figes, Orlando. *Peasant Russia, Civil War: The Volga Countryside in Revolution, 1917–1921*. New York: Oxford University Press, 1989.

Holquist, Peter. *Making War, Forging Revolution: Russia's Continuum of Crisis, 1914–1921*. Cambridge, Mass.: Harvard University Press, 2002.

Koenker, Diane. *Moscow Workers and the 1917 Revolution*. Princeton, N.J.: Princeton University Press, 1981.

Koenker, Diane, William Rosenberg, and Ronald Suny, eds. *Party, State, and Society in the Russian Civil War: Explorations in Social History*. Bloomington, Ind.: Indiana University Press, 1989.

Pipes, Richard. *The Russian Revolution*. New York: Vintage, 1990.

———. *Russia under the Bolshevik Regime*. New York: Knopf, 1993.

Rabinowitch, Alexander. *The Bolsheviks Come to Power: The Revolution of 1917 in Petrograd*. New York: Norton, 1976.

Raleigh, Donald. *Revolution on the Volga*. Ithaca, N.Y.: Cornell University Press, 1986.

Rosenberg, William. *Liberals in the Russian Revolution*. Princeton, NJ: Princeton University Press, 1974.

Smith, Steve. *Red Petrograd: Revolution in the Factories*. Cambridge, U.K.: Cambridge University Press, 1983.

Steinberg, Mark D., ed. *Voices of Revolution, 1917*. New Haven, Conn.: Yale University Press, 2001.

Steinberg, Mark D., and Vladimir M. Khrustalev, eds. *The Fall of the Romanovs: Political Dreams and Personal Struggles in a Time of Revolution*. New Haven, Conn.: Yale University Press, 1995.

Thompson, John. *Revolutionary Russia, 1917*. 2nd edition. New York: Macmillan, 1989.

Trotsky, Leon. *The History of the Russian Revolution*. New York: Simon and Schuster, 1932.

Wade, Rex. *The Russian Revolution, 1917.* New York: Cambridge University Press, 2005.

New Economic Policy: The 1920s

Ball, Alan. *And Now My Soul is Hardened: Abandoned Children in Soviet Russia, 1918–1930.* Berkeley: University of California Press, 1994.

———. *Russia's Last Capitalists: The Nepmen, 1921–1929.* Berkeley: University of California Press, 1987.

Corley, Felix. *Religion in the Soviet Union: An Archival Reader.* New York: New York University Press, 1996.

Fitzpatrick, Sheila, Alexander Rabinowitch, and Richard Stites, eds. *Russia in the Era of NEP.* Bloomington: Indiana University Press, 1991.

Gorsuch, Anne. *Youth in Revolutionary Russia: Enthusiasts, Bohemians, Delinquents.* Bloomington, Ind.: Indiana University Press, 2000.

Graham, Loren. *The Ghost of the Executed Engineer: Technology and the Fall of the Soviet Union.* Cambridge, Mass.: Harvard University Press, 1993.

Kirschenbaum, Lisa. *Small Comrades: Revolutionary Childhood in Soviet Russia, 1917–1932.* New York: RoutledgeFalmer, 2000.

Lewin, Moshe. *Lenin's Last Struggle.* New York: Random House, 1968.

Mally, Lynn. *Culture of the Future: The Proletkult Movement in Revolutionary Russia.* Berkeley, Calif.: University of California Press, 1990.

Siegelbaum, Lewis. *Soviet State and Society between Revolutions, 1918–1929.* Cambridge, U.K.: Cambridge University Press, 1992.

Von Hagen, Mark. *Soldiers in the Proletarian Dictatorship: The Red Army and the Soviet Socialist State, 1917–1930.* Ithaca, N.Y.: Cornell University Press, 1990.

The Stalin Revolution: Industrialization and Collectivization

Conquest, Robert. *The Harvest of Sorrow: Soviet Collectivization and the Terror-Famine.* New York: Oxford University Press, 1986.

Fitzpatrick, Sheila. *Stalin's Peasants: Resistance and Survival in the Russian Village After Collectivization.* New York: Oxford University Press, 1994.

Kotkin, Stephen. *Magnetic Mountain: Stalinism as a Civilization.* Berkeley, Calif.: University of California Press, 1995.

Lewin, Moshe. *Russian Peasants and Soviet Power: A Study of Collectivization.* New York: Norton, 1968.

Rosenberg, William, and Lewis Siegelbaum, eds. *Social Dimensions of Soviet Industrialization.* Bloomington, Ind.: Indiana University Press, 1993.

Rossman, Jeffrey. *Worker Resistance Under Stalin: Class and Revolution on the Shop Floor.* Cambridge, Mass.: Harvard University Press, 2005.

Shearer, David. *Industry, State, and Society in Stalin's Russia, 1926–1934.* Ithaca, N.Y.: Cornell University Press, 1996.

Siegelbaum, Lewis. *Stakhanovism and the Politics of Productivity in the USSR.* Cambridge, U.K.: Cambridge University Press, 1986.

Viola, Lynne. *The Best Sons of the Fatherland: Workers in the Vanguard of Soviet Collectivization.* New York: Oxford University Press, 1987.

———. *Peasant Rebels under Stalin: Collectivization and the Culture of Resistance.* New York: Oxford University Press, 1996.

Viola, Lynne, ed. *The War Against the Peasantry, 1927–1930: The Tragedy of the Soviet Countryside.* New Haven, Conn.: Yale University Press, 2005.

The Purges and Life in Stalin's Russia

Conquest, Robert. *The Great Terror: Stalin's Purge of the Thirties.* New York: Macmillan, 1973.

Davies, Sarah. *Popular Opinion in Stalin's Russia: Terror, Propaganda and Dissent, 1934–1941.* Cambridge, U.K.: Cambridge University Press, 1997.

Figes, Orlando. *The Whisperers: Private Life in Stalin's Russia.* New York: Metropolitan Books, 2007.

Fitzpatrick, Sheila. *Everyday Stalinism: Ordinary Life in Extraordinary Times: Soviet Russia in the 1930s.* New York: Oxford University Press, 1999.

Garros, Veronique, Natalia Korenevskaya, and Thomas Lahusen, eds. *Intimacy and Terror: Soviet Diaries in the 1930s.* New York: New Press, 1995.

Getty, J. Arch. *Origins of the Great Purges: The Soviet Communist Party Reconsidered, 1933–1938.* Cambridge, U.K.: Cambridge University Press, 1985.

Getty, J. Arch, and Roberta Manning, eds. *Stalinist Terror: New Perspectives.* Cambridge, U.K.: Cambridge University Press, 1993.

Getty, J. Arch, and Oleg Naumov, eds. *The Road to Terror: Stalin and the Self-Destruction of the Bolsheviks, 1932–1939.* New Haven, Conn.: Yale University Press, 1999.

Getty, J. Arch, and Oleg Naumov, eds. *Yezhov: The Rise of Stalin's "Iron Fist".* New Haven, Conn.: Yale University Press, 2008.

Gill, Graeme. *Stalinism.* London: Macmillan Press, 1990.

Goldman, Wendy. *Terror and Democracy in the Age of Stalin.* New York: Cambridge University Press, 2007.

Hochschild, Adam. *The Unquiet Ghost: Russians Remember Stalin.* New York: Viking Penquin, 1994.

Khlevniuk, Oleg, ed. *The History of the Gulag: From Collectivization to the Great Terror.* New Haven, Conn.: Yale University Press, 2004.

King, David. *The Commissar Vanishes: The Falsification of Photographs and Art in Stalin's Russia.* New York: Metropolitan, 1997.

Knight, Amy. *Beria, Stalin's First Lieutenant.* Princeton, N.J.: Princeton University Press, 1993.

———. *Who Killed Kirov? The Kremlin's Greatest Mystery.* New York: Hill and Wang, 1999.

Medvedev, Roy. *Let History Judge: The Origins and Consequences of Stalinism.* New York: Knopf, 1971.

Petrone, Karen. *Life has Become More Joyous, Comrades: Celebrations in the Time of Stalin.* Bloomington, Ind.: Indiana University Press, 2000.

Rigby, T.H., ed. *Stalin.* Englewood Cliffs, NJ: Prentice-Hall, Inc., 1966.

Siegelbaum, Lewis and Andrei Sokolov, eds. *Stalinism as a Way of Life: A Narrative in Documents.* New Haven, Conn.: Yale University Press, 2000.

Solzhenitsyn, Alexander. *The Gulag Archipelago, 1918–1956: An Experiment in Literary Investigation.* Translated by Thomas P. Whitney. New York: Harper & Row, 1974.

Tucker, Robert, ed. *Stalinism: Essays in Historical Interpretation.* New York: Norton, 1977.

Ward, Chris. *Stalin's Russia.* London: Edward Arnold, 1993.

Ward, Chris, ed. *The Stalinist Dictatorship.* London: Edward Arnold, 1998.

Werth, Nicholas. *Cannibal Island: Death in a Siberian Gulag.* Princeton, N.J.: Princeton University Press, 2007.

Art and Culture in the Soviet Union

Bowlt, John, ed. *Russian Art of the Avant-Garde: Theory and Criticism, 1902–1934.* New York: The Viking Press, Inc., 1976.

Brandenberger, David. *National Bolshevism: Stalinist Mass Culture and the Formation of Modern Russian National Identity.* Cambridge, Mass.: Harvard University Press, 2002.

Carter, Huntly. *The New Theatre and Cinema of Soviet Russia.* New York: International Publishers, 1925.

Gleason, Abbott, Peter Kenez, and Richard Stites, eds. *Bolshevik Culture: Experiment and Order in the Russian Revolution.* Bloomington, Ind.: Indiana University Press, 1985. *The Great Utopia: The Russian and Soviet Avant-Garde, 1915–1932.* New York: Solomon Guggenheim Museum, 1992.

Groys, Boris. *The Total Art of Stalinism.* Princeton, N.J.: Princeton University Press, 1992.

Hoffmann, David. *Stalinist Values: The Cultural Norms of Soviet Modernity, 1917–1941.* Ithaca, N.Y.: Cornell University Press, 2004.

Kenez, Peter. *The Birth of the Propaganda State: Soviet Methods of Mass Mobilization, 1917–1929.* Cambridge, U.K.: Cambridge University Press, 1985.

Rosenberg, William, ed. *Bolshevik Visions.* 2 volumes. Ann Arbor: University of Michigan Press, 1990.

Schwarz, Boris. *Music and Musical Life in Soviet Russia, 1917–1981.* Enlarged edition. Bloomington, Ind.: Indiana University Press, 1983.

Stites, Richard. *Revolutionary Dreams: Utopian Vision and Experimental Life in the Russian Revolution.* New York: Oxford University Press, 1989.

———. *Russian Popular Culture: Entertainment and Society Since 1900.* Cambridge, U.K.: Cambridge University Press, 1992.

Stites, Richard, and James von Geldern, eds. *Mass Culture in Soviet Russia: Tales, Poems, Songs, Movies, Plays, and Folklore, 1917–1953.* Bloomington, Ind.: Indiana University Press, 1995.

Taylor, Richard, ed. *The Film Factory: Russian and Soviet Cinema in Documents.* Cambridge, Mass.: Harvard University Press, 1988.

Von Geldern, James. *Bolshevik Festivals, 1917–1920.* Berkeley, Calif.: University of California Press, 1993.

White, Stephen. *The Bolshevik Poster.* New Haven, Conn.: Yale University Press, 1988.

Youngblood, Denise. *Movies for the Masses.* Cambridge, U.K.: Cambridge University Press, 1992.

Women

Farnsworth, Beatrice. *Alexandra Kollontai: Socialism, Feminism, and the Bolshevik Revolution.* Stanford, Calif.: Stanford University Press, 1980.

Goldman, Wendy. *Women at the Gates: Gender and Identity in Stalin's Russia.* Cambridge, U.K.: Cambridge University Press, 2002.

———. *Women, the State and Revolution: Soviet Family Policy and Social Life, 1917–1936.* Cambridge, U.K.: Cambridge University Press, 1993.

Stites, Richard. *The Women's Liberation Movement in Russia: Feminism, Nihilism, and Bolshevism, 1860–1930.* Princeton, N.J.: Princeton University Press, 1978.

Document Collections

Bunyan, James. *Intervention, Civil War, and Communism in Russia, April–December 1918: Documents and Materials.* Baltimore, Md.: The Johns Hopkins Press, 1936.

Bunyan, James, and H. H. Fisher. *The Bolshevik Revolution, 1917–1918: Documents and Materials.* Stanford, Calif.: Stanford University Press, 1934.

Daniels, Robert, ed. *A Documentary History of Communism: From Lenin to Gorbachev.* Hanover, N.H., and London: University Press of New England, 1993.

Golder, Frank, *Documents of Russian History, 1914–1917.* New York: The Century Co., 1927.

Koenker, Diane, and Ronald Bachman, eds. *Revelations from the Russian Archives: Documents in English Translation.* Washington, D. C.: Library of Congress, 1997.

Suny, Ronald, ed. *The Structure of Soviet History: Essays and Documents.* New York: Oxford University Press, 2003.

Wade, Rex, ed. *Documents of Soviet History.* 6 volumes. Gulf Breeze, Fla.: Academic International Press, 1991–2004.

Memoirs

Andreev-Khomiakov, Gennady. *Bitter Waters: Life and Work in Stalin's Russia. A Memoir.* Boulder: Westview Press, 1997.

Dolot, Miron. *Execution by Hunger.* New York: W. W. Norton and Company, 1985.

Engel, Barbara, and Anastasiia Posadskaya-Vanderbeck, eds. *A Revolution of Their Own: Voices of Women in Soviet History.* Boulder, Col.: Westview Press, 1998.

Ginzburg, Evgenia. *Journey into the Whirlwind.* New York: Harcourt Brace Jovanovich, 1967.

Goldman, Emma. *My Disillusionment in Russia.* London: The C. W. Daniel Company, 1925.

Hindus, Maurice. *Red Bread: Collectivization in a Russian Village.* Bloomington, Ind.: Indiana University Press, 1988.

Kopelev, Lev. *Education of a True Believer.* New York: Harper and Row, 1980.

Leder, Mary. *My Life in Stalinist Russia: An American Woman Looks Back.* Bloomington, Ind.: Indiana University Press, 2001.

Mandelshtam, Nadezhda. *Hope Against Hope: A Memoir.* New York: Atheneum Publishers, 1970.

Scott, John. *Behind the Urals: An American Worker in Russia's City of Steel,* enlarged edition. Bloomington, Ind.: Indiana University Press, 1989.

Slezkine, Yuri, and Sheila Fitzpatrick, eds. *In the Shadow of Revolution: Life Stories of Russian Women from 1917 to the Second World War.* Princeton, N.J.: Princeton University Press, 2000.

Vilensky, Simeon, ed. *Till My Tale is Told: Women's Memoirs of the Gulag.* Bloomington, Ind.: Indiana University Press, 1999.

Biography

Cohen, Stephen. *Bukharin and the Russian Revolution: A Political Biography, 1888–1938.* New York: Oxford University Press, 1980.

Deutscher, Isaac. *Stalin: A Political Biography,* 2nd edition. New York: Oxford University Press, 1966.

Service, Robert. *Lenin: A Biography.* Cambridge, Mass.: Harvard University Press, 2000.

———. *Stalin: A Biography.* Cambridge, Mass.: Belknap Press of Harvard University Press, 2005.

Tucker, Robert. *Stalin as Revolutionary, 1879–1929: A Study in History and Personality.* New York: Norton, 1973.

———. *Stalin in Power: The Revolution from Above, 1928–1941.* New York: Norton, 1990.

Volkogonov, Dmitrii. *Lenin: A New Biography.* New York: Free Press, 1994.

———. *Stalin: Triumph and Tragedy.* New York: Grove Weidenfeld, 1991.

———. *Trotsky: The Eternal Revolutionary.* New York: Free Press, 1996.

Literature

Chukovskaya, Lydia. *Sofia Petrovna.* Evanston, Ill.: Northwestern University Press, 1994.

Gladkov, Fyodor. *Cement.* Evanston, Ill.: Northwestern University Press, 1994.

Grossman, Vasily. *Forever Flowing.* New York: Harper and Row, 1972.

Kataev, Valentin. *Time, Forward!* Bloomington, Ind.: Indiana University Press, 1976.

Koestler, Arthur. *Darkness at Noon.* New York: Modern Library, 1941.

Olesha, Iurii. *Envy.* New York: W. W. Norton and Company, 1981.

Shalamov, Varlam. *Kolyma Tales.* New York: W. W. Norton and Company, 1980.

Sholokhov, Mikhail. *And Quiet Flows the Don.* New York: A. A. Knopf, 1934.

Solzhenitsyn, Aleksandr. *One Day in the Life of Ivan Denisovich.* New York: Bantam Books, 1990.

Zamiatin, Yevgeny. *We.* New York: Penguin Books, 1993.

Websites

The Alexander Palace Time Machine
http://www.alexanderpalace.org/palace/mainpage.html

A virtual tour of palaces via photos and articles, with diaries and memorabilia of the royal family.

Communal Living in Russia: A Virtual Museum of Soviet Everyday Life
www.kommunalka.spb.ru/

Video tours of communal apartments, audio clips of apartment residents, historical documents, and essays that provide insight into apartment living in the Soviet Union.

Forced Labor Camps
http://www.osaarchivum.org/gulag/

Gulag-related holdings of the Open Society Institute, an archive of historical documents relating to human rights. Provides photos and papers with English translations.

Gulag: Many Days, Many Lives
http://gulaghistory.org/

Life in the Gulag presented through archival documents, photographs, art, film, and a bibliography.

Kennan Institute-National Public Radio Russian History Audio Archive
http://www.wilsoncenter.org/index.cfm?topic_id=1424&fuseaction=topics.media

Audio archive of speeches and voices of key political figures from the Soviet Union such as Lenin and Stalin.

Lenin Mausoleum: A History in Photos
http://www.aha.ru/~mausoleu

The history of Lenin and his mausoleum, with articles, audio clips of Lenin's speeches, and photographs, including those of Lenin and Stalin on display. Links to other sites devoted to Lenin and Stalin.

Revelations from the Soviet Archives: Documents in English Translation
http://www.loc.gov/exhibits/archives/

A collection of documents and photographs from the archives of the Soviet Union exhibited at the Library of Congress in 1992.

Seventeen Moments in Soviet History
http://www.soviethistory.org/index.php

A narrative history of the Soviet Union. Presents documents, music, audio clips, images, and videos associated with 17 major events, framed by short essays. Browse by year or by subject.

Soviet Music
http://www.sovmusic.ru/english/index.php

A collection of Soviet songs about war, the military, patriotism, and leaders. Lyrics and MP3 files available. Also contains speeches and posters.

Soviet Poster Collection
http://hoohila.stanford.edu/poster/

The Hoover Institution at Stanford University owns more than 3,000 posters produced in the Soviet Union. Search by date, artist, poster text, and keywords.

Stalinka: Digital Library of Staliniana
http://images.library.pitt.edu/s/stalinka

A digital library about the Stalin phenomenon, comprising visual materials and artifacts relating to Stalin: photographs, posters, paintings, banners, sculptures, and ephemera.

The Whisperers: Private Life in Stalin's Russia
http://www.orlandofiges.com/

Letters, diaries, memoirs, interviews, and photographs of 300 families. Selected material available in English translation.

Text Credits

ix: James Bunyan, ed., *Intervention, Civil War, and Communism in Russia, April–December 1918: Documents and Materials* (Baltimore: The Johns Hopkins Press, 1936), 246–250.

Chapter 1:

11–13: Gleb Uspenskii, "From a Village Diary," in Thomas Riha, ed. *Readings in Russian Civilization*, vol. 2, *Imperial Russia* (Chicago: University of Chicago Press, 1959), 359–362.

13–14: Lev Tolstoy, *Anna Karenina*, vol. 1 (New York: Charles Scribner's Sons, 1900), 43–44.

15–16: Konstantin Pobedonostsev, *Reflections of a Russian Statesman*, (London: Grant Richards, 1898), 26–28, 32.

17–18: "Industrial Workers in the 1880s," in Thomas Riha, ed. *Readings in Russian Civilization*, vol. 2, *Imperial Russia* (Chicago: University of Chicago Press, 1959), 410–415.

18: "Public Health in Russian Cities," in Martin McCauley, ed., *Octobrists to Bolsheviks* (London: Edward Arnold Publishers, 1984), 178.

19: Reginald E. Zelnik, ed. and trans., *A Radical Worker in Tsarist Russia: The Autobiography of Semen Ivanovich Kanatchikov* (Stanford: Stanford University Press, 1986), 165–166.

20–22: Vladimir Lenin, "What is to be Done?" in *V. I. Lenin: Collected Works*, vol. 5 (London: Lawrence and Wishart, 1961), 375–376, 451–453, and 464–467.

22–23: "Platform of Union of the Russian People," in Martin McCauley, ed., *Octobrists to Bolsheviks* (London: Edward Arnold Publishers, 1984), 37–38.

23–27: "Petition Prepared for Presentation to Nicholas II on 'Bloody Sunday,'" January 9, 1905; http://artsci .shu.edu/reesp/documents/bloodysunday.htm. Translation by Daniel Field.

27–28: "A Declaration of June 9, 1905," in Stanley Page, ed., *Russia in Revolution: Selected Readings in Russian Domestic History* (Princeton: D. Van Nostrand Company, 1965), 73.

28–29: "Police Department Report," Stanley Page, ed. *Russia in Revolution: Selected Readings in Russian Domestic History*. (Princeton: D. Van Nostrand Company, 1965), 71.

29–31: *Polnoe sobranie zakonov Rossiiskoi Imperii*, 3rd series, vol. XXV, no. 26803. Translation by Robert Weinberg.

31–32: "Resolution of the Executive Committee of the St. Petersburg Soviet of Workers' Deputies," in *V. I. Lenin: Collected Works*, vol. 10 (Lodon: Lawrence and Wishart, 1962), 50–51.

32–33: "Vyborg Manifesto," in George Vernadsky, ed., *A Source Book for Russian History from Early Times to 1917*, vol. 3 (New Haven: Yale University Press, 1972), 779–780.

33–34: "Speech by Guchkov in 1913," *Russian Review*, vol. 3, no. 1 (1914), 151–152 and 157.

34–35: "Tsar Nicholas II Takes Command of His Armies," in Charles Horne and Walter Austin, eds., *Source Records of the Great War*, vol. 3, (N.P.: National Alumni, 1923), 320–321.

Chapter 2

40–41: V. I. Lenin, "On the Tasks of the Proletariat in the Present Revolution," *Selected Works in Two Volumes*, vol. 2 (Moscow: Foreign Languages Publishing House, 1951), 13–19.

42–43: "Order Number 1," in Martin McCauley, ed., *The Russian Revolution and the Soviet State* (New York: The MacMillan Press, 1975), 23–24.

43–44: N. N. Sukhanov, *The Russian Revolution, 1917*, vol. 2 (New York: Harper Torchbooks, 1962), 449–450.

45–46: "Manifesto of the Ukrainian Rada," in Frank Golder, ed., *Documents of Russian History, 1914–1917* (New York: The Century Co., 1927), 436–437.

46–47: James Bunyan and H.H. Fisher, eds. *The Bolshevik Revolution, 1917–1918: Documents and Materials* (Stanford: Stanford University Press, 1934), 32–33.

47: "Dividing the Land," in Frank Golder, ed., *Documents of Russian History, 1914–1917* (New York: The Century Co., 1927), 382.

48: "Man and the Land," in Mark Steinberg, ed. *Voices of Revolution, 1917* (New Haven: Yale University Press, 2001) 242–243.

49: "Declaration of the Provisional Government," in Mark Steinberg, ed., *Voices of Revolution, 1917* (New Haven: Yale University Press, 2001), 240–241.

49–50: "Conditions of the Troops at the Front," in James Bunyan and H.H. Fisher, eds., *The Bolshevik Revolution, 1917–1918: Documents and Materials* (Stanford: Stanford University Press, 1934), 24–26.

51: Maxim Gorky, "One Must Not be Silent" in *Untimely Thoughts* (New Haven: Yale University Press, 1995), 83–84.

52–53: "An Incendiary Speech by Trotsky," in John Curtiss, ed., *The Russian Revolutions of 1917* (D. Van Nostrand Company, 1957), 158–159.

53–55: "Lenin's Speech," in Frank Golder, ed., *Documents of Russian History, 1914–1917* (New York: The Century Co., 1927), 618–619.

55–56: Zinaida Shakhovskoi, "The Russian Revolution as Seen by a Child," in Dimitrii von Mohrenschildt, ed., *The Russian Revolution of 1917: Contemporary Acounts* (New York: Oxford University Press, 1971), 100–104.

57–59: Maxim Gorky, "For the Attention of the Workers" in *Untimely Thoughts* (New Haven: Yale University Press, 1995), 85–86 and 99–101.

Chapter 3:

64–65: "Interrogation of Pavel Medvedev," in Mark Steinberg and Vladimir Khrustalev, eds., *The Fall of the Romanovs: Political Dreams and Personal Struggles in a Time of Revolution* (New Haven: Yale University Press, 1995), 348–349.

65–67: "Note on Execution by Yurii Yurovsky," in Mark Steinberg and Vladimir Khrustalev, eds., *The Fall of the Romanovs: Political Dreams and Personal Struggles in a Time of Revolution* (New Haven: Yale University Press, 1995), 352–353.

67–68: "Struggle against the Counter-Revolution and Sabotage," in James Bunyan and H. H. Fisher, eds., *The Bolshevik Revolution, 1917–1918: Documents and Materials* (Stanford: Stanford University Press, 1934), 297.

68–69: "Destruction of Gentry Estates," in James Bunyan and H.H. Fisher, eds., *The Bolshevik Revolution, 1917–1918: Documents and Materials* (Stanford: Stanford University Press, 1934), 670–672.

69–71: *The Time of Troubles: The Diary of Iurii Got'e* (Princeton: Princeton University Press, 1988), 113, 116, 157, 228, 229, 244–245, 404.

71–73: *A Russian Civil War Diary: Alexis Babine in Saratov* (Durham: Duke University press, 1988), 38–40, 56, 77, 128, and 163.

73–74: "American Descriptions of the Volga Famine: Goodrich Letter," in Rex Wade, ed., *Documents of Soviet History*, vol. 2: *Triumph and Retreat, 1920–1922* (Gulf Breeze: Academic International Press, 1993), 295 and 298.

74–75: "Dissatisfaction among Industrial Workers," in James Bunyan, ed., *Intervention, Civil War, and Communism in Russia, April–December 1918: Documents and Materials* (Baltimore: The Johns Hopkins Press, 1936), 161 and 164–165.

75–76: "Disbanding the Tambov Soviet," in Vladimir Brovkin, ed. and trans., *Dear Comrades: Menshevik Reports on the Bolshevik Revolution and the Civil War* (Stanford: Hoover Institution Press, 1991), 84–87.

76–77: Alexandra Kollontai, *The Workers Opposition in Russia* (Chicago: Industrial Workers of the World, 1921), 22, 37, 38, and 40.

77–78: "On Party Unity," in William Chamberlin, ed., *The Russian Revolution*, vol. 2 (New York: Grosset and Dunlap, 1965), 497–498.

79–80: Emma Goldman, *My Disillusionment in Russia* (London: The C. W. Daniel Company, 1925), xi, 257, and 259.

80–82: Isaac Babel, "Crossing the River Zbrucza," in *The Complete Works of Isaac Babel* (New York: W. W. Norton and Company, 2002), 203–204.

83: V. I. Lenin, "We Loot the Looters," in James Bunyan and H. H. Fisher, eds., *The Bolshevik Revolution, 1917–1918: Documents and Materials* (Stanford: Stanford University Press, 1934), 543.

84–87: "The Programme of the Union of Toiling Peasants," www.korolev perevody.co.uk.

88–89: Paul Avrich, "What We Are Fighting For," in *Kronstadt, 1921* (Princeton: Princeton University Press, 1970), 241–243.

Chapter 4:

94–95: "Stalin's Eulogy of Lenin," in E. H. Carr, *A History of Soviet Russia: The Interregnum, 1923–1924*

(New York: The Macmillan Company, 1954), 347–348.

95–96: Nadezhda Krupskaya, "What a Communist Ought to be Like," in William Rosenberg, ed., *Bolshevik Visions*, pt. 1, 2nd ed. (Ann Arbor: The University of Michigan Press, 1990), 26–28.

97–98: Leon Trotsky, "'Thou' and 'You' in the Red Army," in *Problems of Everyday Life* (New York: Monad Press, 1973), 77–78.

98–99: "Resolution on Anti-Religious Agitation and Propaganda," in Rex Wade, ed., *Documents of Soviet History*, vol. 3, *Lenin's Heirs, 1923–1925* (Gulf Breeze: Academic International Press, 1995), 29.

99: "Memorandum," in Diane P. Koenker and Ronald D. Bachman, eds., *Revelations from the Russian Archives: Documents in English Translation* (Washington, D. C.: Library of Congress, 1997), 441–442.

100–101: "Art in Soviet Russia," in *Soviet Russia*, vol. 4, no. 12 (New York: Russian Soviet Government Bureau, March 19, 1921): 288–290.

101–102: Anatoli Lunacharsky, "The Tasks of the State Cinema in the RSFSR," in Richard Taylor and Ian Taylor, eds., *The Film Factory: Russian and Soviet Cinema in Documents* (Cambridge: Harvard University Press, 1988), 47–49.

102–104: Jacob Okuney, "A New Way for Culture Propaganda," in *Soviet Russia*, vol. 2, no. 7 (New York: Russian Soviet Government Bureau, February 14, 1920): 154. 104–105: N. Bryusova, "Proletarian Music," in William Rosenberg, ed., *Bolshevik Visions*, pt. 2, 2nd ed. (Ann Arbor: The University of Michigan Press, 1990), 253–254.

105–106: Huntly Carter, *The New Theatre and Cinema of Soviet Russia* (New York: International Publishers, 1925), 94–96 and 100.

106–107: "Electrification," in James von Geldern and Richard Stites, eds., *Mass Culture in Soviet Russia* (Bloomington: Indiana University Press, 1995), 85–86.

107–108: "AKhRR Resolution," in John Bowlt, ed., *Russian Art of the Avant-Garde: Theory and Criticism, 1902–1934* (New York: The Viking Press, 1976), 266–267.

108–110: Huntly Carter, *The New Theatre and Cinema of Soviet Russia* (New York: International Publishers, 1925), 106–109.

111–112: "Heard in Moscow," in James von Geldern and Richard Stites, eds., *Mass Culture in Soviet Russia* (Bloomington: Indiana University Press, 1995), 114–116.

112–113: Leon Trotsky, "Theses on Industry," *The Labour Monthly*, vol. 5, no. 1 (July 1923).

114: "Bukharin on the Opposition," in Robert Daniels, ed., *A Documentary History of Communism in Russia: From Lenin to Gorbachev* (Hanover: University Press of New England, 1993), 151–153.

115–116: Joseph Stalin, "October Revolution and the Tactics of Russian Communists," in *Problems of Leninism* (Moscow: Foreign Languages Publishing House, 1947), 100–101, 105, and 119–120.

116–117: "The United Opposition," in Robert Daniels, ed., *A Documentary History of Communism in Russia:*

From Lenin to Gorbachev (Hanover: University Press of New England, 1993), 147–151.

118–119: Joseph Stalin, *Political Report of the Central Committee to the Fifteenth Congress of the C.P.S.U. (B.)* (Moscow: Foreign Languages Publishing House, 1950), 105–106 and 110–111.

Chapter 5:

124: "Bukharin on Peasant Policy," in Robert Daniels, ed., *A Documentary History of Communism in Russia*, 3rd ed. (Hanover: University Press of New England, 1993), 162–163.

124–126: Joseph Stalin, "The Tasks of Business Executives," in *Problems of Leninism* (Moscow: Foreign Languages Publishing House, 1947), 355–356.

126–127: Joseph Stalin, "Problems of Agrarian Policy in the U.S.S.R.," *Problems of Leninism* (Moscow: Foreign Languages Publishing House, 1947), 303–304 and 319.

128–129: "Memorandum on Resistance in the Countryside," in Diane P. Koenker and Ronald D. Bachman, eds., *Revelations from the Russian Archives: Documents in English Translation* (Washington, D.C.: Library of Congress, 1997), 376–377.

129: "Document 45: Decree," in Felix Corley, *Religion in the Soviet Union: An Archival Reader* (New York: New York University Press, 1996), 84–85.

132–134: Lev Kopelev, *Education of a True Believer* (New York: Harper and Row, Publishers, Inc., 1980), 226, 229–230, and 232–235.

134–135: "Letter of M. D. Mikhailin," in Lynne Viola, V. P. Danilov, N.A. Ivnitskii, and Denis Kozlov, eds., *The War Against the Peasantry, 1927–1930: The Tragedy of the Soviet Countryside* (New Haven: Yale University Press, 2005), 136–137.

136: Sarah Davies, *Popular Opinion in Stalin's Russia* (Cambridge: Cambridge University Press, 1997), 52.

136–139: Vasily Grossman, *Forever Flowing* (New York: Harper and Row, 1972), 155–158 and 160.

139–144: John Scott, *Behind the Urals* (Bloomington: Indiana University Press, 1989), 19–21, 96–98, and 118–119.

144–146: M. Ilin, *Moscow Has a Plan: A Soviet Primer* (London: Jonathan Cape, 1931), 214–218.

147: Maurice Hindus, *Red Bread: Collectivization in a Russian Village* (Bloomington: Indiana University Press, 1988), 77–78.

147–148: "Report on Anti-Regime Political Attitudes," in Diane P. Koenker and Ronald D. Bachman, eds., *Revelations from the Russian Archives: Documents in English Translation* (Washington, D. C.: Library of Congress, 1997), 51–53.

149–150: "Riutin Platform," in Alex Cummings, ed., *Documents of Soviet History*, vol. 6, *Restoration of Order, 1932–1934* (Gulf Breeze: Academic International Press, 2004), 11–13.

1501–151: Maxim Gorky, et al., *Belomor: An Account of the Construction of the New Canal between the White Sea and the Baltic Sea* (New York: Harrison Smith and Robert Hass, 1935), 20–21 and 23.

Chapter 7:

166–167: "Speech by Avdienko," in T. H. Rigby, ed., *Stalin: Great Lives Observed* (Englewood Cliffs: Prentice-Hall, 1966), 111–112.

167–168: "Official Biography of Stalin," in T. H. Rigby, ed., *Stalin: Great Lives Observed* (Englewood Cliffs: Prentice-Hall, 1966), 115–118.

168–169: Walter Kolarz, *The Peoples of the Soviet Far East* (New York: Praeger, 1954), 80. Reproduced with permission of ABC-CLIO, LLC, Santa Barbara, CA.

169–170: "Glory to Stalin," in Frank Miller, *Folklore to Stalin* (Armonk: M. E. Sharpe, Inc., 1990), 161–163

170: Nadezhda Mandelstam, *Hope against Hope* (New York: Atheneum Publishers, 1970), 13.

171–172: Joseph Stalin, "Report to the Seventeenth Congress of the C.P.S.U. (B.)," *Problems of Leninism* (Moscow: Foreign Languages Publishing House, 1947), 499–500 and 502–503.

172–173: "For the Fatherland," in *The Communist Conspiracy: Strategy and Tactics of World Communism* (Washington, D.C.: U. S. House of Representatives, 1956), 287–288.

174–175: "Public Discussion on the Law on the Abolition of Abortion," in Rudolf Schlesinger, *The Family in the U.S.S.R.* (London: Routledge and Kegan Paul Limited, 1949), 251–254.

176: "Abortions Cannot be Categorically Forbidden," in Rudolf Schlesinger, *The Family in the U.S.S.R.* (London: Routledge and Kegan Paul Limited, 1949), 257–258.

176–177: "Father," in Rudolf Schlesinger, *The Family in the U.S.S.R.* (London: Routledge and Kegan Paul Limited, 1949), 268–269.

177–178: "Speech by Andrei Zhdanov," in John Bowlt, ed. and trans., *Russian Art of the Avant-Garde: Theory and Criticism, 1920–1934* (New York: The Viking Press, 1976), 293–294.

178–179: Boris Shumyatsky, "A Cinema for the Millions," in Richard Taylor and Ian Christie, eds., *The Film Factory: Russian and Soviet Cinema in Documents* (Cambridge: Harvard University Press, 1988), 358–359.

180–181: Henry Sigerist, *Socialized Medicine in the Soviet Union* (New York: W. W. Norton and Company, 1937), 170–172.

182–183: James von Geldern and Richard Stites, eds., *Mass Culture in Soviet Russia* (Bloomington: Indiana University Press, 1995), 154–156.

Chapter 8:

188–189: "Report by G. Zheleznov," in Diane P. Koenker and Ronald D. Bachman, eds., *Revelations from the Russian Archives: Documents in English Translation* (Washington, D.C.: U. S. Government Printing Office, 1996), 146–147.

190–191: Nadezhda Mandelstam, *Hope Against Hope: A Memoir* (New York: Atheneum Publishers, 1970), 75–77, 79, 88, and 92.

192–194: Eugenia Ginzburg, *Journey into the Whirlwind* (New York: Harcourt Brace Jovanovich, Inc., 1967), 159–161 and 344–346.

195–197: "Trotskyites at Vorkuta," *International Socialist Review*, vol. 24, no. 3 (Summer 1963): 94–97.

197–199: "Diary of Stefan Podlubny," in Veronique Garros, Natalia Korenevskaya, and Thomas Lahusen, eds., *Intimacy and Terror: Soviet Diaries of the 1930s* (New York: The New Press, 1995), 302–303, 305–307, 330.

199–200: "Diary of Leonid Potyomkin," in Veronique Garros, Natalia Korenevskaya, and Thomas Lahusen, eds., *Intimacy and Terror: Soviet Diaries of the 1930s* (New York: The New Press, 1995), 260 and 288–289.

201: Eugenia Ginzburg, *Journey into the Whirlwind* (New York: Harcourt Brace Jovanovich, Inc., 1967), 227 and 283.

202–204: *Report of Court Proceedings in the Case of the Anti-Soviet "Bloc of Rights and Trotskyites,"* (Moscow: People's Commissariat of Justice of the U.S.S.R., 1938), 626–627, 629, 648, 696–697.

204: Anna Larina, *This I Cannot Forget: The Memoirs of Nikolai Bukharin's Widow* (New York: W. W. Norton and Company, 1993), 343–345.

204–205: Demyan Bedny, "We Dealt the Enemy a Cruel Counterblow," in James von Geldern and Richard Stites, eds., *Mass Culture in the Soviet Union* (Bloomington: Indiana University Press, 1995), 301–302.

206–207: Anna Akhmatova, "Requiem" in D. M. Thomas, trans., *Anna Akhmatova* (Athens, Ohio: Ohio University Press, 1976), 22–32.

Epilogue

211–212: John Scott, *Behind the Urals* (Bloomington: Indiana University Press, 1987), 247–249 and 263–266.

213–214: *The Anti-Stalin Campaign and International Communism* (New York: Columbia University Press, 1956), 3, 10, 12, 13, 63, and 87.

214–215: D. A. Lazurkina, "Please Take Him Away," in T. H. Rigby, *Stalin: Great Lives Observed* (Englewood Cliffs: Prentice-Hall, 1966), 127–128.

216–218: Yevgenii Yevtushenko, "The Heirs of Stalin" in George Reavey, trans., *The Poetry of Yevgeny Yevtushenko*, rev. ed. (London: Calder and Boyars, 1967), 161–165.

218–221: M.S. Gorbachev, "October and Restructuring: The Revolution of 1917," in *Current Digest of the Soviet Press*, vol. 39, no. 44 (December 2, 1987): 1–10. Copyright East View Information Services. All rights reserved. Reproduced by permission.

Sidebars:

20: Karl Marx, *Critique of the Gotha Program*, (London: The Electric Book Company, 2001), 20.

21: http://www.spartacus.schoolnet.co.uk/LRUSlenin.htm.

38: Allan K. Wildman, *The End of the Russian Imperial Army: The Old Army and the Soldiers' Revolt, March–April 1917* (Princeton: Princeton University Press, 1980), 244.

45: "Killing of Officers," in Frank Golder, ed., *Documents of Russian History, 1914–1917.* (New York: The Century Co., 1927), 400.

53: November 16, 1917, *The Time of Troubles: The Diary of Iurii Got'e* (Princeton: Princeton University Press, 1988), 80–81.

57: James von Geldern and Richard Stites, eds., *Mass Culture in Soviet Russia* (Bloomington: Indiana University Press, 1995), 119.

64: Alan Ball, *And Now My Soul is Hardened* (Berkeley: University of California Press, 1994), 77.

67: James Bunyan, *Intervention, Civil War, and Communism in Russia, April–December 1918: Documents and Materials* (Baltimore: The Johns Hopkins Press, 1936), 227.

71: Armand Hammer, *The Quest of the Romanoff Treasure* (New York: William Farquhar Payson, 1932), 44.

73: *A Russian Civil War Diary: Alexis Babine in Saratov* (Durham: Duke University press, 1988), 208 and 210.

74: "Red Army Oath," in James von Geldern and Richard Stites, eds., *Mass Culture in Soviet Russia* (Bloomington: Indiana University Press, 1995), 15.

76: Daniel Brower, "The City in Danger" in Diane Koenker, William Rosenberg, and Ronald Suny, eds., *Party, State, and Society in the Russian Civil War: Explorations in Social History* (Bloomington: Indiana University Press, 1989), 76.

80: "Conditions in Petrograd," in Martin McCauley, ed., *The Russian Revolution and the Soviet State, 1917–1921* (London: The Macmillan Press, 1975), 276–277.

81: *The Time of Troubles: The Diary of Iurii Got'e* (Princeton: Princeton University Press, 1988), 112.

83: Diane P. Koenker and Ronald D. Bachman, eds., *Revelations from the Russian Archives: Documents in English Translation* (Washington, D. C.: Library of Congress, 1997), 12.

92: Alan Ball, "Private Trade and Traders during NEP," in Sheila Fitzpatrick, Alexander Rabinowitch, and Richard Stites, eds., *Russia in the Era of NEP: Explorations in Soviet Society and Culture* (Bloomington: Indiana University Press, 1991), 89.

96: Rex Wade, ed., *Documents of Soviet History*, vol. 3 (Gulf Breeze: Academic International Press, 1995), 305.

99: Song, Isabel Tirado, "The Village Voice," in *The Carl Beck Papers in Russian and East European Studies*, no. 1008: 51.

104: Boris Schwartz, *Music and Musical Life in Soviet Russia*, enlarged edition (Bloomington: Indiana University Press, 1983), 47.

116: Isaac Deutscher, *Stalin: A Political Biography* (New York and Oxford: Oxford University Press, 1949), 290.

124: Joseph Stalin, *Problems of Leninism* (Moscow: Foreign Languages Publishing House, 1947), 288.

128: Yulius Telesin, *Tysiacha i Odin anekdot* (Tenafly: Hermitage, 1986), 60. Translation by Robert Weinberg.

132: Fedor Belov, *The History of a Soviet Collective Farm* (New York: Praeger, 1955), 12–13.

136: Author's Collection.

139: James von Geldern and Richard Stites, eds. *Mass Culture in Soviet Russia* (Bloomington: Indiana University Press, 1995), 212.

140: James von Geldern and Richard Stites, eds., *Mass Culture in Soviet Russia.* (Bloomington: Indiana University Press, 1995), 213.

145: Jeffrey Rossman, *Worker Resistance Under Stalin: Class and Revolution on the Shop Floor* (Cambridge: Harvard University Press, 2005), 66–67.

147: James von Geldern and Richard Stites, eds., *Mass Culture in Soviet Russia* (Bloomington: Indiana University Press, 1995), 213.

148: Yulius Telesin, *Tysiacha i Odin anekdot* (Tenafly: Hermitage, 1986), 60. Translation by Robert Weinberg.

149: James von Geldern and Richard Stites, eds., *Mass Culture in Soviet Russia* (Bloomington: Indiana University Press, 1995), 284.

169: Sarah Davies, *Popular Opinion in Stalin's Russia* (Cambridge: Cambridge University Press, 1997), 156.

172: Sarah Davies, *Popular Opinion in Stalin's Russia* (Cambridge: Cambridge University Press, 1997), 40.

178: James von Geldern and Richard Stites, eds., *Mass Culture in Soviet Russia.* (Bloomington: Indiana University Press, 1995), 487.

181: Boris Shumyatsky, "Battle for New Genres," in Richard Taylor and Ian Christie, eds., *The Film Factory: Russian and Soviet Cinema in Documents* (Cambridge: Harvard University Press, 1988), 368–369.

182: James von Geldern and Richard Stites, eds., *Mass Culture in Soviet Russia.* (Bloomington: Indiana University Press, 1995), 329 and 284.

189: Yulius Telesin, *Tysiacha i Odin anekdot* (Tenafly: Hermitage, 1986), 100. Translation by Robert Weinberg.

190: Nadezhda Mandelstam, *Hope Against Hope: Memoir* (New York: Atheneum Publishers, 1970), 159.

192: Ilya Ehrenburg, *Memoirs, 1921–1941* (Cleveland and New York: The World Publishing Company, 1963), 426.

194: James von Geldern and Richard Stites, eds., *Mass Culture in the Soviet Union* (Bloomington: Indiana University Press, 1995), 330.

197: James von Geldern and Richard Stites, eds., *Mass Culture in the Soviet Union* (Bloomington: Indiana University Press, 1995), 329.

199: Nadezhda Mandelstam, *Hope Against Hope: Memoir* (New York: Atheneum Publishers, 1970), 316–317.

202: Robert Tucker, *Stalin in Power* (New York: W. W. Norton and Company, 1990), 408.

206: Lesley A. Rimmel, "Another Kind of Fear," in *Slavic Review*, vol. 56, no. 3 (Fall 1997): 489–490, reprinted with the permission of the publisher, American Association for the Advancement of Slavic Studies; Document 170 in J. Arch Getty and Oleg Naumov, eds., *The Road to Terror: Stalin and the Self-Destruction of the Bolsheviks, 1932–1939* (New Haven: Yale University Press, 1999), 473–480.

207: Mary Leder, *My Life in Stalinist Russia* (Bloomington: Indiana University Press, 2001), 112.

Picture Credits

Acknowledgments

The authors want to thank each other for their mutual support, devotion, and encouragement during the long gestation of this project. We also want to express gratitude to our son Perry, who has put up with our scholarly preoccupations.

Index

About the Authors

Robert Weinberg is a professor of history at Swarthmore College. He is the author of *The Revolution of 1905 in Odessa: Blood on the Steps* (1993) and *Stalin's Forgotten Zion: Birobidzhan and the Making of a Soviet Jewish Homeland* (1998). His research focuses on Jews in 19th- and 20th-century Russia and the Soviet Union.

Laurie Bernstein is associate professor of history and director of women's studies at Rutgers University, Camden. She is the author of *Sonia's Daughters: Prostitutes and Their Regulation in Imperial Russia* (1995) and editor of Mary Leder, *My Life in Stalinist Russia: An American Woman Looks Back* (2001). Her latest research centers on dependent children in the Soviet Union.

CPSIA information can be obtained at www.ICGtesting.com
Printed in the USA
LVOW03s1214300715

448231LV00003B/13/P